THE ECONOMICS OF HOPE

Creating a Just and Sustainable Local Economy in the Shadow of a Globalized World

DAVID A. BEATON AND
C. RUSSELL BEATON

LUMINARE PRESS

WWW.LUMINAREPRESS.COM

THE ECONOMICS OF HOPE:
Creating a Just and Sustainable Local Economy in the Shadow of a Globalized World
Copyright © 2019 C. Russell Beaton and David A. Beaton

Printed in the United States of America

Cover Design by Claire Flint Last

Luminare Press
442 Charnelton St.
Eugene, OR 97401
www.luminarepress.com

LCCN: 2019911939
ISBN: 978-1-64388-158-4

We dedicate this work, long in progress, to our loyal wives Delana and Anita. We promise them that conversations at all future family dinners will be free to go in many directions other than inequality and climate change...

TABLE OF CONTENTS

PART ONE:
The Economic Crisis

PART TWO:
The Ecological Crisis

PART THREE:
Localism—Taking Matters into Our Own Hands

Our Basic Premise

The overriding purpose of economics as a discipline is really quite simple: To address the question of how human beings meet their material needs. However esoteric or philosophical our instincts and behaviors, we all have material needs. During earlier times of "Cave Man Economics," the challenge was straightforward: survive.

Alas, things have gotten more complicated. Cave folks didn't worry about getting rich, buying political control, servicing the yacht, or choosing just the right hedge fund manager. There was little or no surplus above subsistence. And if some "surplus" arose, it was probably simply in the form of leisure time. In fact, (eat your heart out) evidence exists that early humans may have had much more leisure time than we enjoy today. Hunt for a couple of hours, gather for a couple and then doodle a bit on the wall of the cave.

Indeed, tied inextricably as earliest homo sapiens were to the random whims of nature, it almost certainly had to be that way. If meeting material needs had been a constant all-consuming battle, a particular vicissitude of nature—an extreme weather event, volcanic activity, etc.,—would probably have ended the human experiment. There had to be some slack in the system.

But even the most imaginative cave person could never have foreseen the slack in the form of surplus above basic needs that modern post-industrial mankind has managed to build into our world...! To be sure, apologists of our current system can argue that economics has done its job admirably—and then some. Our problem with modern economics, and the driving premise behind this entire work, is not that we have learned to produce too much, it's that we have done such a miserable job of distributing it.

On second thought, we **do** have a problem with producing too much, or more specifically with the **way** it's produced. Additionally, our increasingly unequal society creates problems with **what** is produced as well as for **whom.** And, there are serious resulting negative impacts on the global environment and resource base. For simplicity, this leads to our two overriding topics for the book: inequality and climate change—and to a degree, their interaction.

But, you say, "Isn't that two basic premises, and not just one?" This perceptive observation leads to the identification of one overriding culprit in creating a situation which, as we will demonstrate, threatens crisis proportions. That culprit is *globalized corporate capitalism*. Much has been written about each of the three terms buried in that phrase: globalization, corporations and capitalism, our chosen dominant economic ethos. Although we will eagerly share our own critical perspectives, we do not seek to re-invent the wheel or add materially to the volumes that already exist in diagnosing the problem. Just be clear: Our view is that globalization and the dominant behavior of transnational corporations are at the root causes of both our rapidly deteriorating income and wealth distribution as well as the climate change problems facing our entire world.

MEA CULPA TIME

Most books don't start with an apology. The purpose of this book is to develop practical guidelines for common citizens to create healthier, more resilient and sustainable local economies in their chosen community. Clearly, we must start with the identification of the problem as we see it, but we are resolute in our determination not to end there—as many other insightful and perceptive works in effect do. We view the practical action guidelines as the most important part of the book.

Enter, stage left, the "apology." As stated, we fully realize that the central root problem of our times is the dominance of globalized corporate capitalism. It threatens in many ways to rupture both our economic and environmental health. Indeed, it has already ruptured all but token remnants of our democratic polity. But after clearly identifying that as the culprit, we do not choose to take it on, at least from the top down. We would support any reasonable "national movement" efforts to do so, but we fear that ability to make a real difference is beyond our pay grade—as we imagine it is for you as well. Clearly, this decision not to engage the corporate capitalist enemy with yet another frontal assault at the national/international level flies in the face of conventional wisdom. We constantly hear from the left that the ills of corporate capitalism—e.g., inequality, loss of good jobs, resource depletion and climate control—are global in nature and demand global solutions. We are not quarreling with that logic; rather it's simply that trying to effect top-down change by winning political battles in Washington, D.C., is a proven failed strategy. The fundamental economic and ecological crises that corporate capitalism has caused have risen to such emergency proportions—as their political power has risen to virtually unassailable level—that the clock has run out. There is no longer time to assume a democratically-based challenge to top-level corporate structures can be successfully mounted in time to avert severe economic and ecological crises.

Therefore, we feel compelled to admit that the topic of this book may be accused of "nibbling around the edges" of the real problem. Thus we acknowledge that upfront in response to a strong desire not to be accused of being naïve or simplistic. So, in the absence of the sweeping ability to overthrow global corporations and return economic power to the people, nibble we will.

Meanwhile, we invite you to begin work in your community to **go around** corporate control in addition to anything you might be involved in to **topple** it. At the very least, a satisfying sense of community may emerge. And who knows what could happen in the bigger picture when others hear of and admire your efforts? To shamelessly invoke some tired old metaphors, remember: The tortoise really **did** win... Rome wasn't built in a day... David did finally catch Goliath between the eyes with a rock... Put your community thinking cap on and carefully consider what follows here.

PART ONE:

THE ECONOMIC CRISIS

Understanding the Origins of America's Economic Crisis

The dominant premise driving this book is that America, and indeed the world, faces two transcendent crises: economic and environmental. No less important to our coverage here is the assumption that they are intrinsically related, both as to cause and potential solutions. As social critics, we long to underscore this inextricable holistic relationship by analyzing and explaining everything at once...! But alas, books necessarily require sequential linearity. Accordingly, this first section outlines the nature of the man-made *economic* challenges, and Part Two explores the problems facing the *environment* and the natural world. Each section concludes with its own specific take on the all-important issue of growth, and the central role it plays in creating and enabling both foreboding challenges to the modern world.

Featured is a dominant characteristic for each crisis. In the economic sphere, we focus on the disturbing increase in income and wealth inequality. In the ecological realm, climate change is addressed as the penultimate result of decades of kicking environmental problems "upstairs." We have few reservations about convincing a random reader that climate change offers a substantial threat to life as we know it (despite the unexamined skepticism of current leadership), but to that average reader the current status of our economy may not seem to offer as much cause for concern. After all, the stock market is up and unemployment is down, so what's the problem?

Economic crises are certainly nothing new in any Industrial Age economy, with many economic variables regularly coming into play. America was rocked by many other economic emergencies before the Great Depression of the 1930s and the recent Great Recession of 2007–2010. Early economic theorists were hyper-concerned with the mysterious origins of the business cycle. (Who can forget the intriguing sunspot theory...?) Even if not so "Great," the panics of the late 19th century gave notice that economic turmoil was to be a standard recurring feature of capitalistic economies. Why focus on inequality?

As we write this, the economic elites of the world are meeting in Davos, Switzerland, for their annual celebration of inequality. One could scarcely imagine a venue less likely to involve concern for the economic storm clouds threatening the poor of the world. Yet, even amidst the caviar and shrimp cocktails, here is a verbatim portion of a published comment from one economic expert describing the information presented to the attendees of the conference:

> "Typically each annual meeting has a theme. This year there are several: the slowing global economy, the fracturing of the international trade system, the growing levels of unsustainable debt everywhere, volatile financial asset markets with asset bubbles beginning to deflate, rising political instability and autocratic drift in both the advanced and emerging economies, accelerating income inequality worldwide–to mention just a short list."

Or:

> "Ray Dalio, the billionaire who found and manages the world's biggest hedge fund, Bridgewater Associates, warned that he and other investors had squeezed financial markets to such "levels where it is difficult to see where you can squeeze" further. He publicly admitted in

a Bloomberg News interview that, in the future profits will be low "for a very very long time". The era of central banks providing free money, low rates, and excess liquidity have run their course, according to Dalio. He added the global economy is mired in dangerously high levels of debt, comparing it to the 1930s."

Thus, even the global corporate and public sector elites recognize that all is not well in the economic sector. However, their concerns focus on macro global financial issues as opposed to the difficulty of common workers in having enough to eat or pay the rent at the end of the month. We have difficulty feeling empathy for their worries about the health of their hedge fund as they wing home from Davos in their private jets. (There were reportedly some 1500 such vehicles that descended on that opulent Swiss village...) Our point, however, is that the previously mentioned economic storm clouds promise ultimately to rain on everyone's party. Some will get wetter than others....

It remains that for here, we focus on inequality. Our overriding purpose is to energize citizens in communities to assert more control of their own local economy. You and your neighbors can neither enjoy the caviar nor do anything about leveraged buyouts and international currency manipulation. We write this book precisely for the purpose of insulating you and your friends, neighbors and relatives from the vagaries of the breathless oscillations in the variables commanding the attention of the Davos regulars. Inequality remains as the economic variable that most affects your daily life.

ELEMENTS OF PART ONE

Part One addresses key terms and ideas recurrent throughout the book, in addition to focusing on the economic as opposed to the environmental challenges that we face. Chapter I identifies our approach to economic analysis and to the business firm itself that will frame much of our analysis. Chapters 2 and 3 cull some sacred cows out of the herd, and admit to being the only chapters clearly written by only one of the two co-authors. The others are all purely collaborative. Those two chapters have the dual purpose of giving the reader an insight into our individual professional backgrounds while underscoring the fact that an element of radicalism colors both perspectives.

Much of the blame for our economic malaise rests with the evolution of our system into its current form of globalized monopoly capitalism. This is hardly an unaddressed topic; and we urge interested readers to access elements of our brief bibliography for several excellent and insightful coverages. But, with complete appreciation for these other well-researched works, we take our conclusions in different directions. Chapters 4, 5, and 6 offer in-depth definitions that we deem necessary to support our ultimate recommendations. Presented more specifically are the pertinent characteristics of the institution of the corporation (Chapter 4), what we mean by corporatism (Chapter 5) and finally our intended ideal final system of Localism (Chapter 6).

Inequality is a complex phenomenon. We believe it is no less than fatal if not dealt with effectively by a democratic society, and at the very least exacerbates solutions to all other economic challenges. Chapter 7 digs more deeply into current inequality between and within sectors of our economic systems and indeed our culture at large. Here we also flesh out additional elements of our approach to currently accepted economic theory and practice, and thus expand the approach of Chapter 2, which specifically discussed trade. Included is a critique of the role of capitalism itself. (*Don't miss this one...!*)

IT ALWAYS COMES BACK TO GROWTH

Part One wraps up with an examination of the special conundrum of economic growth, which remains the Holy Grail of public policy. (*Whatever the economic question, the answer is growth...*) Conservatives may favor supply-side, trickle-down approaches while liberals prefer Keynesian bottom-up stimulation. But one thing can be agreed upon: *desirability of more growth*. The current crisis is no exception; Republicans on the right and Democrats on the left argue mostly only about how to best maximize new growth.

Three directions are common for discussing and critiquing growth. These mirror the widely discussed three legs of the sustainability stool. First, one can focus on its role as the kingpin of economic theory. Second are the sociocultural perspectives, and third, growth is widely discussed from the viewpoint of its environmental and resource availability impacts.

Chapter 8 sheds light on the supposed panacea of perpetual growth from the first of these: an institutional and economic theory point of view. Is growth the desirable epitome of economic analysis, or simply a fall-back answer to a flawed illogical system? Although we allow both chapters to foray into the second—the sociocultural aspects—growth from the third perspective of environment and resources is the topic of Chapter 13 at the end of Part Two, which deals with our growing ecological and energy crises. One un-debatable conclusion will emerge: The sustainability notion that lends us this analytical framework is difficult if not impossible to reconcile with a notion of perpetual growth. Sustainability and resilience in some form must define any acceptable permanent solution.

And from there we will need to proceed to Part Three and see what we can do about it.

CHAPTER 1

Core Economic Philosophy

We are in an economic crisis. Some believe this and some don't. *(But how can that be? The Dow is hitting new heights...!)* It is necessary to know where best to search for evidence, but if you look carefully beneath the headlines all the economic news is far from comforting. Let us be clear: In our view, the critical indicator is the growing number who are left out. We hear short term good news that the economy is finally bouncing back from the collapse of the housing bubble and the subsequent 2008 meltdown.

This does not sugar coat the relentless growth of wealth and income inequality along with recent increases in epidemic homelessness. Something is still pathologically wrong. The successful Wall Street bond trader does not offset the homeless veteran on the streets of Baltimore. A rising Dow Jones Average doesn't mitigate hunger and unemployment in Detroit or Los Angeles. (The U.S. stock market has approximately tripled since the end of the Great Recession. Do you really feel three times better off?)

Thoughtful analysis suggests that something must change. The mission of this book is to propose, support and accelerate that change. Thus, we can clearly and emphatically state the problem that leads to the assertion that we have an economic crisis: Pure and simple, it is ***inequality***. Despite several intermittently healthy economic periods over the last 45 years, the ongoing and mounting empirical evidence since the late 1970's has underscored continually worsening income and wealth distribution; and as we speak it isn't getting any better. Our central question: ***Why is this the case, and what can we do about it?*** Now, the plot thickens.

In our view, the appropriate place to start is by focusing attention on the business firm itself—the primary mechanism used by our culture to produce the private sector goods and services that we all want and need. In the broadest cultural sense, the job of a business firm is simply to meet our material needs. As such, the temptation is to view it simply as a neutral servant of society, and not in any way a cultural force. It merely produces some product or service for our use, and that's the superficial way it is normally viewed.

However, we introduce the premise here, and make the case more fully in Chapter 7, that the business firm *as it has recently evolved* is an immensely powerful cultural determinant. Indeed, our central thesis revolves around that premise. Nonetheless, understanding its fundamental role in a culture, as well as in an economy, requires a different perspective. Specifically, we must understand the corporate role as a distributor, or more accurately a REdistributor—and not of the goods it sells, but of the income streams that it impacts. In standard economic terminology, the problem is not aggregate *production*—we produce plenty of stuff—it is *distribution*, or who gets to consume the fruits of that production. Every producing entity buys valuable resources, produces and sells something, and then re-distributes the proceeds of those sales back to the productive inputs—including workers and owners.

The deeper analysis of Chapter 7 will focus on the two main productive factors that become the primary concern for all economic inquiry relating to income distribution: labor and management. You might recognize these economic actors with other terms that have historically evolved (workers and owners; Capital and Labor; Proletariat and Bourgeoisie; more recently perhaps, the 1% and the 99%, and—well, you get the idea...) In short, these are historically the two competitors that have vied for their share of the fruits of production since the advent of capitalism in the wake of the Industrial Revolution. Given that the business entity takes money from its customers and then creates a new distribution pattern by paying its workers, management and owners, it unavoidably plays a vital role as a societal redistributor.

For the record, although we do not address this issue here, government is the other major institutional redistributor. (But it is a deep irony that corporate redistribution, bad as it might be, is the major cause of socially disruptive inequality and yet is tacitly accepted or even celebrated, while government redistribution—to rectify inequality, distribute benefits more broadly and stabilize society—is roundly criticized by those same corporate interests.) Did you ever notice that a top level government worker earning a high salary can be castigated in public, (other than a top level college football coach earning ten times what the university president earns. Of course—that's OK...) while a corporate CEO earning 50 times that is lionized as an American hero in Fortune or Money Magazine? So much for the mantra: "We don't have class warfare..."

But, back to work. Of primary interest to our analysis here is the pattern of the expenditures as the firm covers its costs (and distributes profits) in the normal course of doing business. Again, we attempt to demonstrate (prove?) this more fully in Chapter 7, which focuses on the inequality implications. To understand clearly the important role of the firm in determining the income distribution in a market-based society, we will imagine the entire size gamut of business firms, ranging from a one person single proprietorship up to a large multinational firm. You will want to take careful note of where that leads us.

WHAT ABOUT ECONOMIC DEVELOPMENT?

Communities throughout the nation have bought into a fruitless "race for the top." Most have vigorous and often well-funded economic development efforts that are frequently coordinated with surrounding counties, regions and the state at large. They seek export-based firms providing "family wage" jobs. These efforts are angled toward responding to this question: Couldn't every community just seek a corporation or two—a branch plant perhaps—or encourage existing smaller companies to aggressively grow? Then our increasing average incomes and rising standard of living would create general prosperity and allow us the wealth to deal with any problems that might emerge. (Amazon is breaking ground in our home city of Salem, Oregon, as we speak—a new "fulfillment center...")

Some pertinent facts suggest that such a strategy is simply not possible. A few years ago, the top Fortune 200 firms produced about 26% of the world's output. That's an eye-opening figure, but we could live with that, and hope for something close to full employment, as long as in creating that output they employ something close to a quarter of the world's labor force. Want to guess what percentage of the world's workforce they *did* employ? The answer: **One third of one percent**. If this economic structure is accepted as a desirable state of affairs, the logical ultimate end game apparently would be to produce all the world's production with none of the world's workers. And where is the purchasing power for your intended market...? Doesn't sound like the Capitalism we all know and love...

Corporations will argue, in response to critics of obscenely high CEO and executive compensation, they still pay run-of-the mill workers very well. That may be true, but the figures above indicate that is not the problem—the overall problem is that this entire paradigm impoverishes those who do **not** work for corporations—and (in our relative opulence here in the U.S.) we tend to forget: *That is going to be most of us*. The other argument that CEOs are so highly paid because they make such monumentally important decisions is so self-serving that it doesn't deserve a response. Plus, they essentially set their own salaries, including multi-million-dollar golden parachute clauses should they be deemed to have "failed." (Job security for the 1%, don't you know: "You've really screwed up and you're fired, but here's $20 million to tide you over into retirement...")

Local officials routinely cite the well trained and hard-working workforce, the quality environment and lifestyle, excellent schools, and a cooperative mayor with an abundance of zoned shovel-ready sites in their city, waiting to welcome your corporate presence to our fine community. Seemingly, every candidate for office has an agenda of "improving the economy." Chambers of Commerce and organized economic development efforts echo the call.

An actual conversation with an executive seeking to locate a new branch plant a few years ago yielded this comment: "You don't understand, we have 5,000 cities making this same case to us. And we're thinking of going to Mexico." For every successful industrial attraction effort across the nation, there are probably over 100 failures. There simply are not enough corporate jobs to go around to make this overall strategy at all viable for everyone. Corporations are more in the business of destroying jobs than creating them—often even after they *do* happen to locate in a given city. The fact of a corporation leaving a community a few years after its ballyhooed initial entrance is a particularly controversial and wrenching occurrence for that local economy.

Just for sport, we advise you to consider the wild lottery scramble currently being played out as Amazon seeks to bless some lucky American city with its "Second Headquarters" presence. (Too bad. We in Salem are only getting a branch plant...) Just prior to this writing, it was announced that the contest that was earlier narrowed to 20 candidate cities is over, and two localities have won! (New York City and somewhere in North Carolina—Amazon couldn't choose, so is going with a dual—or a third—headquarters configuration.) The money that was spent (and subsidies proposed) in municipal fawning may almost match the sales of Amazon itself! And 18 expenditure packages of the other finalists will be wasted—not counting costs already borne by the more than 200 cities that were initially in the running, and were earlier eliminated. And already, thoughtful elements in the two communities are worrying about the disruptive effects of all those new jobs on transportation, urban infrastructure, local political decision-making, housing availability and prices, and so on.

Without further comment here, this economic development process is discussed and critiqued in Chapter 19, since criticism of an existing system or practice is much more effective and understandable when accompanied by concrete suggestions for a positive alternative that can do something about it. That is where Localism comes in.

LATE FLASH! New York citizens have registered enough objections that Amazon has decided to pull out of the decision to locate there. Maybe somebody is finally catching on...

We digress; but allow us to prematurely present the final summary conclusion that will be developed and addressed much more specifically in Chapter 7, which is devoted to focusing in more depth on the causes of inequality:

Economic Growth has become a blueprint for Inequality, Monopoly and Unemployment

THE ALL-IMPORTANT ROLE OF GROWTH

What do we find if we follow that lead and turn our attention solely to the role of economic growth in this problematic model? First, we note the common mandate that every firm, once started, should seek to grow. National leaders and every state, city and municipality propose growth as the Holy Grail common objective. Seeking growth has virtually become our public religion. Significantly, it is observably the firms that grow that succeed, and in so doing push out smaller potential competitors that failed to grow.

You have probably heard some version of the rhetoric: "If we can just increase the economic growth in our area, we could better afford to treat the inequality and plight of the homeless and poor—as well as clean up the environment." The relationships among these issues are sorted out in more detail in Chapter 7, immediately before Chapter 8 concludes Part 1 by devoting itself to the issue of growth from an economic theory point of view. In Part 2 we turn to the role of energy and climate change, concluding with a return to examination of the growth ethic—this time from the perspective of resource availability and the environment. And finally, in Part 3 we get to the important question: *What can we do about it?*

VALUE ADDED: THE BOTTOM LINE

The stark fact is that prosperity and resilience have been siphoned out of many communities due to structural economic changes over the last several decades since World War II. The groundwork for this actually began with the Industrial Revolution, but that is a much more expansive story. Straightforward and creative employment of residents using the natural resources available in that locality ought to be the path to keeping a local economy healthy. The wealth that is there should support the people who are there. Instead, this ability has become more and more limited, as the value added that should have been created and enjoyed by local citizens has been expropriated by other outside wealthy and powerful interests. Economic imperialism and colonialism on a world-wide international scale is merely the same phenomenon writ large. Indeed, capturing that wealth source has become the tacit goal of virtually all major corporations.

Thus, the key notion characterizing what is central to any effort to reverse this—and indeed to fuel any successful Localism movement—is seeking to increase **value added**. It is not an exciting or "sexy" concept, but no term captures more succinctly what is necessary for success in the process of returning jobs, multiplied purchasing power and general economic health to local areas. Be alert for this to re-emerge as one of two unifying themes in the final section addressing action suggestions. The term "value added" is one that we often hear in common usage, but it will be defined and discussed more specifically at that time—where it is needed in order to prescribe actually *doing something* about the state of inequality.

Finally, we note that the discouraging economic situation for many local economies occurs because corporations are *successful*. It has nothing to do with business failure. Clearly, in the last few decades, the capitalistic model has visibly ramped up and evolved into the phenomenon of *globalization*, which underscores and accelerates the above observations as well as the conclusions reached in Chapter 7. Inequality, monopoly and unemployment are now widely acknowledged factors among nations, and not just within regions, cities and neighborhoods. Globalization has put Capitalism on steroids....

Interestingly, it may be due to this increasingly apparent fact that national capitalism has evolved to global capitalism that is finally leading people, some simply in (an often ill-considered) response to old-fashioned nationalism, to organize and plan movements to fight or mitigate the trends. It isn't happening a moment too soon, even if some of the efforts appear almost futile or smack of being right for the wrong reasons. Value added needs somehow to be recaptured by local communities everywhere. This book is about the "why" and the "how." The "who" and the "for whom" should ideally be you.

CHAPTER 2

Why Free Trade Isn't Your Friend

Debunking Conventional
Economic Wisdom

A major methodological principle of this book is that there are important conventional economic assumptions about the way the world works that are no longer correct. Further, if we choose to rely on this "conventional wisdom," we will be led astray—and not just by degree, but in tragic ways that offer strong potential for threatening our entire way of life.

These are strong words, and merit careful elaboration. This brief chapter merely begins that elaboration of some unconventional radicalism through an important example—the issue of trade. Additional exemplification of this premise occurs throughout the book, especially surrounding the issue of economic growth, but will become more apparent in the final section suggesting potential action items. Although this chapter is strikingly incomplete in identifying all the ways economic conventional wisdom can lead us astray these days, addressing the ubiquitous issue of trade is absolutely central in understanding the failings of conventional economic theory and practice.

Any effort to radically alter the way something important is done or thought about is guaranteed to encounter vigorous resistance. This resistance will come in two forms. The first, and perhaps less important, is a simple self-interest-based argument. It will come from individuals and institutions that perceive that the proposed changes will go against their vested economic interests. If the initial sense is that it will affect them financially, people will simply disagree with some new and untested "radical" proposal almost as an involuntary reaction.

The second and more fundamental reason for opposition falls back on the "conventional wisdom" that normally supports the traditional practice. Invariably, there will be a semi-forgotten philosophical justification, probably rooted in some academic discipline, which supports the practice. This justification is probably incompletely understood, but is nonetheless predictably trotted out as needed in times of crisis and threat to the practice or belief.

This book questions the current workings of our corporatized global economy, and proposes for any given community a preferred alternative, which we call Localism. Since the issue at hand is the long-term economic health and stability of virtually all of our communities, it can hardly be called insignificant. The strength of the resistance to any new paradigm is normally proportional to the importance of the affected issues. In this case, the opposition to change is firmly rooted not only in the economy, but the culture, and can be expected to be formidable.

Such is the case for the belief that a corporate-driven global economy is both inevitable and, if we play our cards right, desirable for American citizens. Oh, to be sure, there currently are large and growing pockets of resistance—more along the "desirable or not" than along the more problematic "inevitable or not" lines. Oppositional groups find more agreement that it's hurting us than agreement that it can somehow be stopped.

And here is where the second issue, that of underlying philosophical justification, comes in. As an economist I am sensitive to this issue. I find myself deeply critical of the serious problems cropping up in our rapidly globalizing world—in particular the rampantly increasing inequality—yet deeply dismayed at the complicit enabling offered by my own discipline.

After considerable introspection, I have become convinced that the appropriate entry point for addressing the malaise of inappropriate conceptual backing is through an example. This will not, of course, provide a full comprehensive "general theory" of the problem, but let's look at this example and generalize from there.

The following economic adage is held with near-religious fervor among my fellow colleagues:

TRADE HELPS EVERYONE

This simple three-word mantra is an unquestioned principle, both for professional economists and for the powerful corporate interests that seek to justify and benefit from their globalizing behavior. Please forgive a few moments of wonkish retreat into the arcane history of economic thought. (I can hear you now: "Oh dear, an economics lesson—just what I've always tried to avoid...") No, indeed. Hang on—keep your seatbelt fastened, and we'll help you negotiate a soft landing in the real world in no time at all.

This adage has its roots in the (original) *Principles* book by the Classical economist David Ricardo, published in 1799. Specifically, he proposed the Theory of Comparative Advantage, which in its simplest form advocates that the surest path to wealth and prosperity was for nations to specialize in producing what they do best, and then trade with other nations who are doing the same—presumably with other products. As a result, workers in "producing" nations would enjoy higher wages, and consumers in the "importing" countries would enjoy lower prices—a win/ win situation if there ever was one. In short, a "surplus" is created due to specialization and trade, as contrasted with self-sufficiency, and that surplus is shared by both producers and consumers. I'll spare you the graphical and mathematical proof of this happy proposition, but let's just say that the profession of economics has enjoyed a more than two century love affair with the concept.

And what's not to like? Well, there are many people, domestically and internationally, who don't care much for how the international trade scene has been working out for them in these last few globalizing decades. Let's examine those complaints in more depth, with an eye toward uncovering the economic theory implications. Much criticism is heaped upon the transnational corporation, which has inarguably become the pre-eminent institution on the entire global scene. Their reach, augmented by international trade agreements such as GATT, NAFTA, and the WTO, and lubricated by the IMF and World Bank, extends well beyond the power of most sovereign nations. Indeed, it is their sway over the internal politics of their various host nations that originally crafted such agreements—which as it has turned out have largely had the bottom line effect of insuring and protecting corporate profits.

But that's another story—and we'll get to that. The important question here is how this all affects, or is affected by, a current globalized version of the Theory of Comparative Advantage. Another sometimes ignored Ricardian stipulation that becomes critical is the following: In order that these "gains from trade"—as the discipline of economics self-servingly refers to them—can be realized, **the ownership of the goods being traded must change hands at the border**. This important assumption means that an independent business entity that produced the goods *sells* those goods to another entity as the import/export process transpires. And each entity gets to keep the gains and pass them on to their workers or consumers, respectively.

This point provides the entrée for one of two powerful critiques of the current features of the world of trade. Given the ubiquitous presence of multinational corporations world-wide, and the obvious fact of branch plants being established in many "low wage" countries, (can you say: *outsourcing* or *off-shoring*) it is often the case that the goods do **not** change ownership at the border. What is happening is that the corporation, taking advantage of its control of technology (As Dave will elaborate) and superior resource mobility, is merely producing in countries with the lowest wages and selling in countries with the highest prices. Ricardo would instantly recognize (*more quickly than some of his modern disciples*) that this isn't fair at all: The corporation is expropriating the surplus that would have gone to workers in the form of higher wages, and also keeping the gains that should have accrued to consumers in the form of lower prices. This is not the rhetoric we hear, however, and indeed there is more to be said later in this book as we dig into the contention that the Walmarts of this world (beneficially) result in lower prices for all of us.

There is another curious irony that deserves mention in passing. Flash back to when the international agreements were being debated and passed—for instance when China was admitted to the WTO. Big business interests were effusing: "Look at that massive market of 1.3 billion people—American workers can produce products *here* and sell our stuff to **China**...!" Our recent and continuing trade deficits with China of up to ten dollars of imports for every one dollar of exports indicates that things have worked out exactly the opposite of that: We produce stuff in *China* and sell it back *here*. Was the real target in the minds of the transnational corporations promoting the WTO China's consumer purchasing power or was it merely their cheap labor? *Make the world safe for outsourcing...*

In order to address the second powerful critique of globalized trade, it is useful to revisit Ricardo's main example. He imagined trade between England and Portugal, whereby England produced and exported textiles to Portugal, and in return imported Portuguese wine. The obvious assets which led to this mutually beneficial arrangement were the superior climate and wine-making skills of Portugal, and less benign climate (but good for woolens) and superior industrial development of England in its early Industrial Revolution stages.

Note that these qualities are inherent to primary natural resource characteristics. It is the same reason that Oregon and Washington have historically exported lumber and wood products, and Kansas and Nebraska export wheat. Indeed, virtually all communities over the years have realized and acted on this principle in doing what they do best and developing industries that rely on their innate natural resource endowments. We have regionally and even locally embraced comparative advantage, in addition to its obvious international ramifications. Interestingly, note that the tourism industry even today responds to this comparative advantage principle as localities rely on scenery, weather, fishing, hunting, winter and/or water sports, etc., in order to thrive. And salaries and incomes in those areas have increased, just as Ricardo predicted. The central fact is that, within limits, the resources in question are fixed and cannot be re-located or competed away.

Think about what has happened as a result of free trade policies within the current globalized world. Businesses seek out the lowest wage countries for their production, and the lowering of labor costs immediately results in higher profits. This loss of jobs to the low-wage havens drives wages down in the richer "importing" counties. Since the profits accrue to the owners and managers of corporations, the result is a distinct transfer of wealth from the poorer to the richer. This "Reverse Robin Hood Effect" has devastating results for income inequality, and is a completely predictable result of free trade within a globalization model.

There is a secondary effect over time that will even disrupt the short-term profit euphoria of the wealthy elite. To wit, the purchasing power of average citizens whose jobs have been exported is stagnant or declining, and this financial wealth should, in a less globalized world, be the primary source of sales for the corporate output. As this pool of wealth shrinks, investment opportunities decline, since there simply aren't good sales prospects. And in the U.S. we lament a disappearing middle class.

The corporate sector has turned to increased financial activities and speculation to substitute for stodgy productive sector sales. They promote, through credit cards and the like, the spending of next year's income when this year's income proves inadequate. They can artificially hold down interest rates and encourage refinancing of homes to hold up current consumption—people in effect spending their home equity in addition to next year's income on current con-sumption. But these are short term fingers in the dike, and stimulate behaviors that dangerously support speculative "bubbles." Housing prices, perhaps... Sound familiar?

How to reconcile and conclude this with our old friend David Ricardo? As noted, his Theory of Comparative Advantage was innately angled toward natural resource-based primary inputs. *It was **not** talking about labor.* Particular skills were assumed to be connected with the resource. (Winemakers could not be re-trained to be textile workers, and vice-versa.) The current globalized model has changed all that. *Labor* has become the key resource for coun-tries to offer in order to attract the otherwise footloose global corporations. Implementing comparative advantage has morphed into a wage rate race to the bottom.

This has fundamentally important implications both for Ricardo and our current world economy. To the credit of my profession of economics, comparative advantage is still applicable in those (dimin-ishing numbers of) areas where semi-unique endowments of natural resources exist; and development of those sectors can predictably increase incomes for workers. However, for the massive portion of the productive world economy, where labor itself has become the key resource, it is a mathematically predictable certainty that this leads to downward pressure on working wages and enhancement of returns to the already well-to-do: i.e., crushing inequality. Sadly, that has become the primary product of corporate globalism.

The inevitable implication is that this most venerated principle of economic theory no longer holds. I feel concern for my fellow economists—having to retrain at this point in one's career (as dis-placed manufacturing workers have also painfully learned) can be uncomfortable indeed. As I indicated at the beginning of this chapter, and as we will contend throughout the book, there are other central principles of economics that no longer serve us well in this world of globalizing inequality—either because the common application of it is distorted in practice or because the economic principle itself is flawed—*for these times*. Thankfully, there are also many that can and should be strongly relied upon. Choosing carefully between the two will be a major task of our unfolding story.

To sum up this important symbolic example, the realities of the modern world suggest that an accurate and up-to-date version of our old adage should read more like the following:

TRADE IMPOVERISHES (almost) EVERYONE

—C. RUSSELL BEATON, PH.D.
Emeritus Professor of Economics
Willamette University, Salem, Oregon

CHAPTER 3

Why Technology Isn't Your Friend Either

Debunking Conventional
Technology Wisdom

Technology has become one of the untouchable mantras of modern American society. Leaders of all sorts, along with the general public, look to advanced technology for solution to all manners of problems: economic decline in a competitive global economy, food to feed an exploding population, climate change, energy and resource depletion, and protection from hostile forces in a violent world. But, while we endlessly extol technological benefits, few criticize the unintended—but often painfully real—liabilities.

Simply put, the message of this chapter is that one of the unacknowledged byproducts of technology is the enabling of globalization. It has done so, as Russ has just suggested, under cover of another untouchable mantra: free trade. By giving mobility to large financial and productive transnational corporations, these interests have been able to find the global "sweet spots" of lowest cost, least regulation and highest revenues. This allows transnational corporations to capture lucrative rents on both ends of the globalization spectrum, and leaves David Ricardo's classic theory of Comparative Advantage in tatters. The theory was never meant to target labor, which today remains the highest single cost of productive corporations.

So how have these huge peripatetic corporations been able to pull off this scam on an ostensibly democratic and watchful society? After all, the main result of free trade in America and other advanced industrialized nations has been to inflict ruinous rising levels of inequality—inequality that threatens economic, political and social stability in countries supposedly the most stable on the globe. In the jumble of colliding influences currently roiling American affairs, there are plenty of causes from which to pick; but one that stands out is *technology.*

ADVANCED TECHNOLOGY: THE GIFT THAT KEEPS ON GIVING (WELL, AT LEAST TO CORPORATIONS)

In the minds of the American public few things have the glitzy patina of technology. And, of course, because high-tech is better than low-tech (perfectly in keeping with the Enlightenment legacy notion of perpetual progress), advanced electronic technologies such as computers and communications systems are among the most awe-inspiring. Many of our ideas about technology come from—or at least are reinforced by—the vast array of technological devices currently flooding the marketplace for all consumers to see and enjoy. As you are probably aware from personal experience, it is not difficult to convey to ordinary citizens (and kids and grandkids...!) that they have a form of life-enhancing magic virtually at their fingertips. Therefore, if there is a common meme for technology that parallels the one for free trade, it would probably be something like this:

TECHNOLOGY HELPS EVERYONE

But, turning away from the distracting smart phones, tablets and other hand-held gadgetry that fill our daily lives, let's focus on technologies that are key tools used by corporations in the workplace where goods and services are produced. Such corporately-deployed and controlled technologies have become the major blunt weapons by which productive corporations, aided and abetted by big corporate banks and business-friendly governments, have defined the arrangements of the present globalized economy—arrangements that have marginalized working people and created runaway inequality. While advanced technology may indeed be the shiny quarter laid under the corporate pillow, it is proving (unsurprisingly) to be the bane of working people, their communities, and even the survival of democratic institutions.

DOWNSIZING AND DE-SKILLING: THE WAY OF MODERN WORKPLACE TECHNOLOGY

The clouded mystique of technology tends to hide the two most important ways technology works: these can be called **downsizing** and **de-skilling.** In the three or four decades since electronic advancements rapidly accelerated the automation of the contemporary workplace, the American public has gradually wised up to downsizing. Simply put, substituting a machine for a human worker allows the product or service to be produced with fewer labor hours. Given the rich, concentrated energy of fossil fuels, and the resultant dramatic underpricing of oil, gas and coal during most of this period, it is no wonder so many American workers were handed their pink slips as the marvelously smart new machines were being rolled in to replace them. While many Americans have in recent years become wary of the corporate claim that technology actually creates jobs, few have a coherent notion of how "technological displacement" may be reversed.

De-skilling, on the other hand, has received far less media attention or public notice than downsizing. In simple terms, de-skilling refers to the manner in which advanced technology not only reduces the *quantity* of required workers, but also the necessary *quality* of those remaining after the downsizing. The overwhelming bulk of conventional wisdom on de-skilling runs directly contrary—180 degrees out—to the actual operation of technological de-skilling. All of us have been inundated for decades with the supposed need to upgrade our skills to be able to compete for demanding cyber-age jobs; and how, if we do not do so, we'll lose the grueling global competition to foreign workforces with superior technical skills.

This corporate-orchestrated mythmaking is a classic case of "blame the victim," ignoring as it does studies (conducted by the US Department of Labor and others) that the modern-day workplace requires no more skills on average than the American workplace of, say, a half-century ago. It also conveniently ignores studies that show perhaps 30 to 35 percent of college degree-holding American workers are holding down jobs **not** requiring their college education. Contrast this with other regular projections of the US Department of Labor estimating that only about 15 percent of the most demanded jobs in the foreseeable future will require a college degree; while fully one-third of young Americans will receive at least a bachelor's degree.

EXPROPRIATING WORKERS' SKILLS.

The process by which employer-deployed technology drives necessary worker skills downward should surprise no one. When modern, "smart" machines replace workers using older and simpler technology, two things commonly occur. First, the advanced technology, often mediated by complex software programming representing the skills and experience formerly used by the displaced human workers, takes over the job formerly done by the human workers. Keep in mind, corporations or employers own and control the technology, just as they now have first claim to all the profits. In that skills transfer, therefore, a major responsibility of the workers is being transferred to the employer/corporation. In plain terms, the employer is expropriating the property and purview of the workers...with no obvious appropriate compensation offered in return.

Conventional economic theory would dictate that the remaining workers should see higher wages, since the magnanimous act of the generous corporation—giving them the new technology with which to work—has by definition increased the productivity of the workers. Output per person-hour has unambiguously risen. Indeed, we have seen steadily increasing productivity throughout our recent history, but some 40 years ago, wage rates mysteriously stopped keeping up with the ubiquitous productivity gains. Why is this, and what do we do about it? Read on...

Second, the role of the surviving workers—those often mistakenly assumed to be unaffected—is usually changed dramatically; and, contrary to the conventional wisdom, not for the better. Instead of skilled workers experienced in any particular occupational specialty, they often become machine tenders. After all, the new machines now do the lion's share of the actual work turning out the product; but they need someone to monitor and feed them, inserting parts, paper, lubricants, software upgrades or whatever as needed. (Even the worker him or herself is often seduced into viewing this as progress: *"Isn't it nice that this new software update means I don't have to mess with that data as I did before—it's so much easier now...and what's this pink slip that just came into my inbox...?")*

It is here that the conventional wisdom governing skill upgrades is at its most blatant and contradictory extreme. The corporatist PR stresses that the automation process has weeded out the relatively unskilled, techno-phobic workers, while only those who get the education and training necessary to run the oh-so-smart machines will survive the technological transformation. Survival of the fittest—Darwin would be proud... In reality, the remaining workers not downsized immediately by the new machines are often turned into robotic button-pushers, screen-watchers and mouse-clickers. Skills necessary for the real workplace have actually *dropped*, while the conventional PR machine wisdom contends that the workforce needs more skills to keep up with modern trends. The "blame the victim" loop is effectively closed.

THE TECHNOCRATIC MINORITY: AGENTS OF CORPORATISM.

The only cohort which truly must understand the inner workings of the new workplace technologies is the small minority of technophiles who design, test, install and program them. And another important but often forgotten truth: these technocratic specialists work as instruments of the *corporation*; they are agents of management, who, like the technological weapons they wield, act to decimate the numbers, skills, power and prerogatives of the other workers—that is precisely their job description.

TECHNOLOGY AS A VEHICLE FOR GLOBAL OUTSOURCING

In addition to the downsizing and de-skilling impact of cor- porately-controlled workplace technology, technology also becomes a key enabler of geographically-dispersed globalization itself. Globalization—the economy of free trade and worldwide movements—only works by moving lots of stuff around. Even during the salad days of the Industrial Age when fossil fuels, materials and environmental absorptive capacity were seen as limitless, the resource investment and environmental impacts necessary for operating an export/import global economy were a huge extra cost. Modern transportation and electronic commu- nication technologies have not eliminated these costs—but have reduced them to levels deemed tolerable. Modern container ships, jet aircraft, fleets of diesel trucks and communications/ control technologies based on the Internet are essential to glo- balization in its present form.

Thus, a combination of the downsizing/de-skilling capabilities of workplace technology, coupled with advanced transportation/ communications technologies, is the vital grease lubricating the smooth working of the global economy by powerful corporations in their own interests. These technologies (1) allow the mountains of stuff to be moved, (2) permit essential 24/7 control of global operations from any place on earth, and (3) make the reality (or threat) of off-shoring of production and jobs possible. Together, they reduce worker power, create much slacker labor markets, lower wages and, by confiscating their skills and other bargaining chips, prevent workers from countering the already dangerous levels of income and wealth inequality. And the corporate expro- priators have the gall to contend that labor unions exert an unfair pressure on the political process.

TECHNOLOGY AS THE ENEMY OF THE ENVIRONMENT

Of course, no comprehensive consideration of the influence of technology would be complete without mentioning its environmental impacts. How modern technology often collides directly with environmental values and health is regularly obscured by the corporatist status quo and their prodigious spin machines. Modern high-tech, for example, is supposedly a case of technology continually getting greener and better. ("We're all becoming more sustainable every day in every way...") Newer machines are always more efficient and energy saving; thus constantly upgrading and updating improves overall environmental conditions.

But, with net energy of all current energy systems irreversibly declining (net energy is a fundamentally important topic we take up in Chapter 10), the immense, interwoven infrastructure required by modern high technologies like electronics means that this conventional wisdom of ever-higher energy and emissions "greenness" is false. When coupled with how intensive high-technology is typically deployed these days—that is, under the regime of *globalization*—newer technology is seldom more efficient when viewed in the proper perspective. And that perspective is *as an entire* **system.** Certainly "end-point" efficiency improvements have been made in many specific technology applications. But, when evaluated as an integrated *system,* total energy use has risen as older machinery is replaced; and total emissions that cause climate warming and many other impacts have usually also risen.

Such "compartmentalization" encouraged by fragmented thinking in disregard of holistic systems approaches is to blame for this bit of upside-down illogic. In this context, the claim that globalization is more green than older patterns of localized economies, or that nightmarishly wasteful (and polluting) systems like corn-based ethanol are combating climate warming would be falling-down laughable—if they weren't leading to such deadly serious consequences for resource depletion and the climate crisis.

OWNING TECHNOLOGY: WHY "UNDER NEW MANAGEMENT" IS ONLY A PARTIAL ANSWER

For some, the escape hatch from our corporatist-dominated tech-nology dilemma boils down to a question of ownership. To these people, wresting control of technology from the current corpo-rate owners and controllers would solve the problem. By turning controlling decisions about workplace and other technology over to some form of public or worker regime, (Worker cooperatives? Mandated corporate worker councils? Community technology panels? Government technology planning agencies?...) we could render the innately destructive characteristics of technology moot. That is, corporations would be denied the use of technology to marginalize workers in both the developed and under-developed world, thus blocking them from creating an unequal world of the 1 percent versus the 99 percent.

A FUTURE OF ECOLOGICAL SCARCITY

There is little doubt that a re-balancing of power by distributing important technology decisions is long overdue and could remedy many current problems. But by itself such a change of owner-ship—a "control democratization"—will not solve the technology dilemma America faces in the emerging world now bearing down upon us. America is rapidly confronting what can best be called a "Future of Scarcity." The nature of this future is limits—limits of energy, limits of other physical materials, and perhaps most criti-cal, limits of the biosphere to continuing to absorb the punishment industrial societies presently hand out.

If workers, or combinations of workers and the general public, were to inherit ownership and control of crucial technologies, they would still face these limits. The future of America—and the remaining world—is one of complying with the natural limits of the planet. This translates into much lower limits of almost exclusively renewable energy, spartan use of fast-diminishing minerals, metals, and other resources, and of course rigorous measures that will keep the rapidly-warming climate from spiraling catastrophically out of control. All compasses point to much more locally-centered forms of economics, politics and lifestyles. The imperative is to end the destructive, inequality-producing control of technology now exercised by transnational corporations, banks and complicit governments. A total overhaul of present technology must be in the works, and that must be preceded by a total re-think of technology by all of us. Technology will and must remain with us, but it must somehow be transformed into serving the planet as opposed to the corporate elite—posing as a proxy for the people. This is undoubtedly a multi-faceted Herculean order, and can only be approached with wise and patiently conceived long-term goals in mind. Such a mandate, among others, will permeate the proposals in Part Three of this book.

So, with these ideas and imperatives now in mind, a restate-ment of the role of technology in present-day American society might go something like this:

TECHNOLOGY IMPOVERISHES (almost) EVERYONE

Or, with priorities somewhat clarified by visions of a Future of Scarcity, perhaps this:

TECHNOLOGY IMPERILS (absolutely) EVERYONE

—DAVID A. BEATON
Coordinator, Oregon Energy Study 1973—1975
Coordinator, Information Technology Training Program, State of
Oregon 1987—1999

CHAPTER 4

What Is a Corporation?

We hear a great deal about corporations these days—most of it critical. Perhaps you have participated. Supposedly, corporations sell us shoddy products, outsource our jobs, and bombard us with unwanted and offensive advertising. Corporations pollute the environment and threaten supplies of natural resources with their mass extraction, production and distribution techniques. They are accused of attempting to own and control anything of value anywhere on the globe.

Primarily, perhaps, they supposedly dominate our politics. They have long been accused of undue political control over politicians and of dictating what our government should or should not do, whether it can raise money and how it can or cannot spend it. Taxation is demonized as pure confiscation. This control supposedly occurs through the selection and funding of candidates during any election process, and then ubiquitous lobbying and use of political threats and favors during actual governing. Either way, it's all about money. In the past, much of this has been done out of the light of day. In the opinion of many, the recent Citizens United Supreme Court decision will make such buying and selling of politicians overt and legal—and possibly even more out of the light of day.

These and many other related criticisms of corporations and corporate behavior are worthy of more detailed analysis. We will get to that, but we see a fundamental first question that must be answered, and this precedes any litany of the effects of the corporate presence. Given the importance of these issues affecting not just our economy but the very core of who and what we are as a society—we must ask: *What is a corporation?*

Any beginning economics text offers some sanitized but useful starting points. Three main characteristics stand out. First, it is a legal entity in the eyes of the law. Second, it offers limited liability to its owners. Third, and this follows from the first two, it is a convenient mechanism for raising large amounts of capital, ostensibly for undertaking large projects that might not be done otherwise. Let us address these in the reverse order.

Our founding fathers envisioned corporations as special purpose entities. When formed, it would be to undertake specific projects—projects for which there is a demonstrated collective need and which might be too large or complicated for any individual or small group of individuals. This initial concept can almost be seen as an arm of government. Building a railroad to the West might be an example. After completion of such a project, the assumption was that the corporation would cease to exist. Perpetual corporate life was not contemplated, nor was the ability, at their own discretion, to extend their influence into any other chosen corner of the lives of citizens.

Second, the meaning of limited liability as a corporate characteristic is that owners (i.e., the stockholders) of a corporation in the event of unfortunate economic circumstances may only lose as much as they have invested in purchasing the stock. In a partnership or an individually owned business, the owners are personally liable for all debts and impacts of that company, and may ultimately lose much more than the original investment, including—if things go really badly—being driven into personal bankruptcy. The lack of such personal exposure allows the directors of corporations to undertake risks and make decisions that they might not have made had their own personal fortunes been at stake.

Third, the fact that a corporation is a legal entity (in other words, a *person*) in the eyes of the law has been the subject of much debate—a debate which only promises to become more strident in this era of rampant globalization. It was far from the intentions of our founding fathers that the Constitution and the Bill of Rights should extend "personhood" to corporate entities. This interpretation only came as a result of an 1886 Supreme

Court decision—ironically, a railroad case based in California, in a decision that many legal scholars view as a mistake.

EFFECTS OF PERSONHOOD

A corporation is **not** a person. It has no feelings, no heart and soul, and has no innate wants and desires. But even as it has features that clearly distinguish it from a living breathing human being, corporations have become increasingly adept at selectively claiming the rights constitutionally conferred on such "real people," even while disavowing unwanted responsibilities because they are **not** human beings. They cannot be put in jail, given a traffic ticket, get into arguments with the next-door neighbor, join the PTA, and so on. But they certainly claim free speech under the first amendment when saturating the political process with money.

It is tempting to conclude that they have the best of both worlds: the ability to claim the right to do as they see fit when it meets their (strictly profit-driven) purposes, and at the same time the ability to escape civic and community responsibilities as "non-people" when that fits their needs.

But, finally, a fundamental question must be raised. If a corporation is not a person, and has no innate personality, desires or goals, what does it mean when we refer to the *corporate culture* or the *corporate will*? Apparently, they seek to accomplish some specific goals, and have some targeted purposes. Two points must be made.

First, the single-minded corporate purpose, notwithstanding a more varied intention at the outset of our republic, has evolved simply to **making money**. The goal of any major corporation, elevated almost to the level of religious fervor, has become to maximize the financial well-being of the stockholders. It is all about profit—which, we are constantly reminded, is **not** a dirty word.

Indeed, corporate profitability has been promoted to the status of a necessary condition without which economic progress is not even deemed possible. If business is not making money, people will have no jobs, no spending power, no economic prospects of any kind. Corporate profit must be possible or nothing of economic consequence will happen. We are brainwashed with this type of thinking at all levels, from international to national and even down to the local level. For example, we are encouraged to rejoice when the stock market is up, even though the only practical effect for most of us is to increase inequality.

DEFINING CORPORATE IDENTITY

Most importantly, we must look to the ***decision-making process*** within the corporation. Quite simply, a corporation is controlled by its board of directors and its top management, many of whom are the same people. A great deal is made of the image of the "publicly traded" firm—as if we all collectively control the company. Because the ownership shares in major corporations listed on the stock exchanges or traded in broad-based over the counter markets have literally millions of different people owning some of them—often through mutual funds or pension plans—we are encouraged to believe that we are all American Capitalists. But, where major corporations are concerned, ownership and control are two distinctly different concepts. Assuming uncritically that they are one and the same is a convenient myth that serves the interests of corporate hegemony. If you're constantly told you're empowered, you will be less likely to notice that you really have no power.

Despite the fact that the corporation's very existence and ability to operate may be allowed because they reside in a democracy, they are purposely and absolutely ***not*** democratic structures. You, as a minor shareholder, do not have a voice. Indeed, they take pride in (and often ascribe their efficiency to) the fact that they are hierarchical fiefdoms controlled from the top down. Any third world dictator would lust after the internal control of his citizens displayed by the management of a large corporation over the internal policies and operations of the company and its employees.

Further, the control is inevitably vested in a small group of people. Top management and members of the board of directors of a major (transnational or not) company may comprise no more than fifteen to twenty people. Insuring broad-based democratic participation in the major resource allocation decisions of the firm is the absolute opposite of their purpose. Those in positions of power take great pride in autocratic top-down control in the hands of as few people as possible. Effective control over major decisions may even rest effectively with just one person—an all-powerful CEO. In fact, such situations are sometimes publicly touted along with virtual canonization of the person in question. (*"Lee Iococa turns Chrysler around...! Jack Welch streamlines GE for the 21st century...!"*) Such individuals border on American heroes—or at least Wall Street heroes. But we need to dig deeper.

THE CRITICAL QUESTION

Who are these people, and what are their goals? Think about it. You would never consider blaming a car itself, as a piece of machinery, for congestion or air pollution. You would not blame the bulldozer per se for defoliating the Amazon. It would be silly to conclude that the gun fired itself in an act of armed violence. In all cases, you would go to the purposes and motivations of the owner and operator of the car, bulldozer or the gun. So it must be with the "corporation." In fact, it doesn't even have a tangible physical form, such as a car or a gun—it is merely a legal creation written on some pieces of paper. Therefore any realistic thoughts about the effects of corporations in modern society **must** (there is no other choice) focus on the **people** controlling those corporations.

Who are those people? To begin with, they are all wealthy. In order to get on the board of directors, an individual normally must own a significant block of shares. Of course "significant" may only amount to two or three percent of the outstanding shares, (5% would be a major block) but in a company with a market capitalization of, say, $10 billion, any ownership of one percent or more is valued in the hundreds of million dollars. So the board members are by definition *very* wealthy—and by virtue of just being on the board, stand to get even wealthier.

Similarly, if you are top management, your annual salary, even before performance bonuses, stock options and the like, is customarily in the millions of dollars. And the stock compensation and options, especially given the favorable tax status accorded to people in these elevated income levels, (did we mention political power…?) can amount to considerably more than the base salary. In recent years, salary and bonus incentives, often just for running up the stock price, have become intense. Public awareness, and occasional modest outrage, about this cozy situation, especially in light of the Wall Street bailout and subsequent "obscene" management bonuses, has also become intense; but there are no easy solutions. The arrangement between board (ownership) and corporate control (management), to the extent that they differ, is overtly and blatantly along the following lines: "You make us even wealthier through the company and we will make you even wealthier in return." Executive compensation has become a monument to self interest run amok, but is defended as the "American Way."

Indeed, the conclusion must be that there is virtually no one with any effective voice in the policies of a major (Fortune 500, perhaps) corporation that is not a multi-millionaire, and quite a few are no doubt billionaires. Therefore, and this is a fundamentally significant conclusion: ***Corporations and corporate decision-making are the exclusive domain of the wealthy elite***—for better or for worse for the rest of us. And they clearly would like us to think that it's for the better.

This bottom line conclusion can be stated in many ways and has fundamentally important implications. Corporations are the tool of the already wealthy and powerful to ensure that they retain their wealth and become even more wealthy and powerful. Once one reaches a certain level of wealth, (no doubt different for different multi-millionaires….) single-mindedly *increasing* that wealth is likely not as important as other things. The prime "other thing" is almost certainly *securing* that wealth. And included early on, among those "other things" inevitably we find political power. After all, once the wealth is obtained—especially for people who put much store in being wealthy—the key questions normally turn to how to protect it and how to secure and expand the effective political power afforded by that wealth.

If this whole game could be played solely on each other up in the financial stratosphere by the wealthy elite, and let us in the lower, middle and upper middle class remain unaffected and carry on life as usual, that would be one thing. We could all watch the rich, with their jet-set lifestyles, play their corporate control games on each other and jockey for position in Fortune Magazine's annual horse race of the wealthy. (We do enough of that as it is...) But even though such detachment may seem to be the case, that's not the way it really works. Innocuousness is not an option. Wealth and power need to be obtained from somewhere, and that somewhere is the rest of us—where the "rest of us," in this rampantly globalizing system, has become virtually everyone else in the world.

This control—the globalized world's modern form of imperialism—occurs in many ways: outsourcing of jobs, union demonization and opposition, automation and technological control, exploitation of foreign workers, control of vital natural resources, and countless other ways, many of which we touch on in this book.

The point is that the wealth is gleaned from most other people in the world, whether it is through higher prices, lower wages, lower quality of products (inferior health care?), environmental degradation or a myriad of other institutional results and arrangements. And make no mistake, we all support, with or without our consent, these massive accumulations of wealth. Virtually every product and service that you and I enjoy as citizen/consumers is delivered to us through a corporation. It will all be sanitized and justified through the seductive benefits of the consumer society, and protected by the threat of loss. For those of us enjoying a modicum of the "good life," we certainly don't want to risk losing it. For those who are not yet there (the poor among us or those in "lesser developed" nations) we wouldn't want to preclude the opportunity to get there. The packaging of this message comes in many forms. Don't kill the goose that lays the golden egg.

But make no mistake, whatever product they offer, or whatever processes by which they make profits and extend their influence, the main product for society as a whole is nothing less than **inequality**—past, present, and increasing into the future. The wealthy will become more wealthy and powerful and most of the rest of us will tend to have an increasingly hard time. This may seem to be a harsh indictment, even as we enjoy the latest newfangled consumer product, or as we draw our salary by working in the accounting department of XYZ Global Enterprises, but that is the economic bottom line.

Of course, the rhetoric we hear, in true Orwellian Newspeak, is exactly the opposite. Corporations supposedly employ us all, provide all the good things we like to consume, hold down prices through mass production efficiencies and competition with each other, donate to worthy charities and foundations, support all worthwhile causes in our communities, ("Our pet cause needs some *corporate support...")* and allow the affluence necessary to clean up the environment. And to counter the zero-sum game accusations contending that their wealth precludes a reasonable standard of living for the masses, there is always the Growth Ethic, combined with its errant stepson, Trickle-Down Economics. Pump money and political support to the rich, and the pie will be permanently expanding. A rising tide lifts all boats. But most boats, especially the rowboats and dinghies, increasingly appear to be anchored and in grave danger of drowning as the waters rise. The yachts are doing fine.

These sweeping allegations may seem difficult to swallow in such undocumented form, and virtually cry out for elaboration and counter-arguments. For now, however, the following is a summary of our answer to the question: **What is a corporation?**

A major corporation amounts to the following:

- **A device to glean wealth from any source in the world**

- **A device for the wealthy elite to consolidate and expand their economic fortune**

- A device to lever and multiply wealth through use of other peoples' money

- A device to translate wealth into political power

- A device to forestall populist, middle class or lower class political influence

- A device to insure monopoly and prevent effective economic competition

- The most effective device ever invented to create inequality even while producing wealth

And, above all:

- A device to preserve governmental autocracy and preclude the existence of real political democracy.

If all this is true—and honest full disclosure requires a careful and complete consideration of any counter arguments—then our description can be stated as follows:

The primary role of the large national and transnational corporation has become to serve as the chosen instrument of control for the world's wealthy elite in expanding and consolidating their control over the rest of the world.

This is a major indictment, since it implies that the corporation in its current form and mode of operation is a nothing less than the primary pathological feature of any current world malaise, both economically and environmentally. Clearly, if one accepts the seriousness of the issues identified above, this forces the conclusion that no real and lasting measures to improve, perhaps even to save, this country and indeed the world, can be achieved without dramatically limiting and reducing the role played in our economy, our environment and our culture by this omnipresent institution.

These few pages have attempted to focus on what a corporation *is,* as opposed to what it ***does***. Note that our list does not include: *A device to produce products that people need.* Indeed, it does do that, but the product or service produced has become an incidental sideline to allow the corporate owners and managers to achieve the above list. The fact, in a nutshell, is that a corporation *is* whatever its owner/managers want it to be—and they pretty much have the power to make those wishes come true.

Much more could be said along the lines of identification of the problem, but the larger goal of the rest of this work is to address the all-important issue of what we in communities anywhere in this country might do about it. First, we must necessarily turn to the related topic of **corporatism**.

CHAPTER 5

What is Corporatism?

The corporation vs. corporatism?

Although the large and powerful modern corporation must certainly rank as the *institution* that is currently the driving and organizing force in our culture, it is only the beginning aspect of the many-sided face of the socioeconomic phenomenon that we term **corporatism**. Like the pervasive reach of the institution that is the corporation, corporatism extends beyond the legal structure itself and its commerce-based mission. It has evolved into a political force, a mindset, a dominant way of viewing the world—a virtual **paradigm for modern life**. It becomes a way of organizing human activities well beyond the straightforward delivery of products and services to customers for a profit. In this section, we further explore this elusive but permeating quality, and thus flesh out our previous discussion of the corporate institution itself.

If the corporation is an entity, corporatism must qualify as a compatible mindset. And we all participate. All behavior is supported by a set of values consistent with that behavior. Our thesis, stated bluntly, is that the physical behavior and real-world ramifications, as well as the human values represented, are not only an undesirable world view as the human race faces the dangerous uncertainties ahead, they will almost certainly prove completely and disastrously incompatible with the task of creating a sustainable and fulfilling future.

A fundamentally important proviso must be injected at this point. There is a tendency to view transnational corporate behavior and/or globalization as something "out there." As we hear and read about the actions of Wall Street titans or multinational CEOs, we assume this is some other life form apart from anything we are familiar with or are involved in. To be sure, their lifestyle is far different from ours. (Please restrain your envy—that's what they want...!)

Further, we are all generally aware that the products we use, the TV we watch, transportation options we enjoy—virtually everything we have and use—imply corporate involvement in our lives. We restrain or ignore criticism because we generally enjoy much of this as instrumental to the "good life." However, the aim of this book is to stimulate *local* action, therefore we focus on how corporatism affects everyday behavior, and thus precludes effective *Localism*. How do we, patterning our thoughts and actions after Wall Street, preclude effective actions for Main Street? As we enter the door of Walmart and hail the smiling senior citizen greeter, are we thinking of Fred's Hardware or Nancy's Dress Shop that used to occupy some of the closed storefronts down on Main Street? Effective action begins with personal introspection. Let's begin the journey.

MOVING AHEAD

In defining this phenomenon, both the characteristics of corporatism as well as the implied underlying values need to be identified and discussed. Accordingly, for discussion purposes, the facets defining corporatism fall into six categories:

- **Organizational**

- **Economic**

- **Environmental**

- **Socio-cultural**

- **Political**

- **International**

For each of these categories, we briefly describe the major characteristics as we see them being manifested in these various arenas.

ORGANIZATIONAL

In beginning to grasp the essence of the modern corporation, the first place to look is internal. How does the corporation choose to organize itself? We see five characteristics:

* **Reliance on central authority**

* **Hierarchical**

* **Un-democratic**

* **Super-organized: "professionally managed" and rational**

* **Dispassionate: unemotional, practical, pragmatic**

The organizational structure within the modern corporation is decidedly **not** a democracy. They are normally run by a powerful Chief Executive Officer (CEO) who, conventional wisdom has it, essentially purports to know everything known by anyone in the bowels of the organization. Given the existing lines of control and authority (antiseptically depicted by the organizational flow chart), it is typical to assume that the CEO effectively consolidates everything that any technician or specialist in the organization knows, and is thus automatically able to make the best possible decisions for the good of the firm and its profits.

This intensely rational process is assumed to operate smoothly, according to clearly understood and agreed upon policies, with information flowing perfectly within and among "boxes" of the organizational chart. Whatever is known in one box is automatically known in the box above it, **plus** that higher box has the knowledge contained in all other lower boxes, and is thus able to put together an overall perspective that can be termed **consolidated wisdom**. The process continues to bubble upward, leading to higher and higher levels of consciousness, until it ultimately manifests itself in an all-wise and all-knowing CEO. And that's why he gets the Big Bucks, since it all results in the profit maximizing decision for the firm and its grateful stock-holders. (We're sorry. Did we say "he?" How politically incorrect is that? At least three or four of the Fortune 500 companies are now run by women...)

Of course, the information flow reality is far different. Simply drawing a line on a flow chart does nothing to ensure that real and valuable information is actually transmitted. And there is no guar-antee that it can be understood at any other (let alone "higher") level in the organization. Then there are the *people*, with their own cubby-holes, fiefdoms, personal alliances and animosities, political agendas and differing assessments of the company and its motivations. But, however this may all play out in actual orga-nizational dysfunction, the strong financial incentives for upward mobility are always in place.

The Peter Principle—that people rise to their level of incom-petence—is often hard at work here, due to the extreme spe-cialization of many of the key skills, as well as the sheer size and organizational complexity of most corporations. This virtually guarantees that many higher managers are detached from and ignorant of many key functions at lower levels. So, if/when the corporation succeeds and grows and diversifies, the natural trend can be toward evermore brain-dead, tuned-out manag-ers. They, however, will of course be paid much better than the "underlings" with the vitally needed skills...

In summary, the reality of the model looks very much like the medieval structure of Feudalism, except the currency of the Realm is not **eternal salvation**, but **money**—pure and simple. The reward is not sitting at the right hand of God, but a villa in the South of France. A spot in Heaven for repentant souls is replaced by the lure of owning a 200-foot yacht, or perhaps, to shame-lessly mix metaphors, the ability to soar up with the gods in the corporate jet. And the desire to achieve these "otherworldly" rewards will keep everyone involved happily in tune with the particular Corporate Agenda. It becomes a way of life all its own. But make no mistake—it can break down into a chaotic mess if the organizing discipline of financial gain is lost or rejected.

Of course, in the best tradition of Darwin's Theory of Natural Selection, suppose there are those who find that other goals, such as personal sense of accomplishment, self-fulfillment, enriching community relationships, service to mankind, etc., motivate them. They are likely to find the hierarchical "money-fetish" culture of the corporation unsatisfying and leave (read that: "weed themselves out of the gene pool"). Thus, over time, those who are left in the corporate "gene pool" are those whose primary goal is upward financial mobility. Others have left for their five-acre plot in rural Vermont or run-down farmstead in North Carolina where they grow their own food organically and fervently pen testimonial articles for Mother Earth News.

ECONOMIC

The economic side of corporatism should be becoming quite clear by now. It's all about money. We have just touched on the corporate feature that higher financial rewards are assumed to be the sole motivating factor for performance, pleasing one's superiors, and moving up **within** the organization. Equally important, the role of money plays a vital role for the general society **outside** the corporation. It is enlightening to examine the role played in corporatism by those not directly involved with the corporation itself.

"Outsiders" (we the people...) are urged to identify solely with our role as a *consumer* in the society. The corporation is to be seen as supplying all things of value that it is possible to desire. Further, they do so in the most efficient, least costly, highest product quality manner. In other words, corporations are seen not only to supply all our needs, they do it in the best way. Consumers should make it their business to have all information about product availability and price immediately at their fingertips, and thus to exert ultimate control over the economy by rationally choosing the products that best fit their tastes among the multitude of companies competing with each other for their favors and their dollars.

This is a page directly out of Adam Smith's **Wealth of Nations**, and it exemplifies his notion of consumer sovereignty. If the average company seeking to produce a product is very small and has no market power as it competes for the consumer dollar with many other similar companies, such an ideal of effective "consumer control" might be viable. But that is not the reality today. In a world comprised of a small number of large diversified companies, each producing a multitude of products, where the consumer is dependent on that or some similar company for not only the simple knowledge of the range of product possibilities available, but for the job that supports their potential purchase, this effectively leaves the **producer** in charge.

The essential task of the company is not primarily to produce efficiently a valuable and safe product or service, which is the barebones "textbook" version of the role of a business. Rather, it becomes to convince the consumers, through the unending welter of advertising, that they are in charge of their own economic fate. If you are somehow made to feel powerful, you are less aware that you really have no power.

This is not a new message. It has been touched upon for decades by the likes of people from Marshall McLuhan to John Kenneth Galbraith. We do not further pursue the notion of what has been termed *producer sovereignty* in this brief introductory chapter. Rather, the key notion is that the primary expected role of individuals within the system of corporatism is strictly as a consumer. As such, it becomes awkward for them to question the efficacy of the overall systemic philosophy, or even to inject their other narrower secondary economic role as contributing employees—in other words as **suppliers** of time, effort and talent into the economy. They are to be merely the **demanders** of "stuff," and as long as that role is faithfully pursued, all is supposedly well within the Realm.

Many of the primary themes of this work spin off these notions, and will occupy the central section of the book. Included, to name but a few, are increasing inequality, environmental decay, the credit crisis, the housing crisis, the role of politics in our system, outsourcing, and the notion that the serious unemployment problems of the country will be fixed with simply more and better training for people in the workforce.

ENVIRONMENTAL

We spend much time and coverage in Part Two exploring issues related to environment, energy and resources. Since our major premise is that we currently suffer from a *joint* crisis of economy and environment, any potentially helpful solutions should address them systemically. Consequently, we make two main points with respect to *corporatism* and its approach toward environment and resources.

First, *corporatism* implies and even requires production and distribution schemes on a scale that virtually guarantees negative environmental impacts—whether they be extractive, production-based, or in the transportation and distribution networks. Even the marketing facilities compatible with corporatism create urban traffic and congestion problems that stress local environmental health, let alone budgets of local government. Fundamentally, mass scale corporate production necessarily occurs in one place and consumption in another very different place. The supporting requirement, therefore, becomes extensive transportation systems and large-scale fossil fuel use.

In a well-advertised binge of globalized cost cutting, many (now transnational) manufacturing corporations have moved production facilities to low labor cost areas with lax environmental oversight and regulatory structures. Still, most consumption occurs in abandoned former production areas. An ironic—some would say *fatal*—trend develops: producers eventually lose their use for original workers as *producers,* but do not, until they're too broke to buy, lose their use for them as *consumers.* But eventually—as is on the verge of happening across the US—consumers lose their ability to *consume* at anything like the level necessary to maintain adequate system growth... thus the system commits suicide. In addition to this fundamental tragedy of globalization, consumers, therefore, have little incentive to consider environmental effects of their consumption activities. There is no effective feedback loop that works in favor of the environment. Finally, they become susceptible to the mantra that environmental protection is too expensive, and even that the environment is the "enemy" that led to their impoverishment. (*And does Trump or Bernie have it right...?*)

Second, and building on this, there is a public attitude that corporatism must promote. It is the idea that the essential public policy question revolves around the premise of the **Economy vs. the Environment**. This has several vitally important elements. Economic growth and progress must be assumed to *require* some environmental impacts, even though we are at the same time bombarded with the notion that they are manageable. Accordingly, we are strongly urged to abandon the notion of a *pristine* world. Whether "pristineness" is in truth an endangered species or not, it is nonetheless problematic to the efficacy of corporatism to have people believe in it. Such beliefs prove to be annoying distractions from the business of getting on with mainstream consumerism, and dilute the effectiveness of messages such as:

- **We can safely extract oil in the Arctic National Wildlife Reserve and simultaneously preserve all the endangered wildlife and ecosystems.**

- **We have the technology to safely offshore drill anywhere in the world with no damage to marine ecosystems.**

- **Extraction of valuable mineral resources can occur in any publicly owned lands, including national forests or national parks without any loss to wilderness or tourist values.**

The bottom line of this is that we are encouraged to believe that all environmental impacts are "manageable." The environment is something to be manipulated for human utilitarian purposes, and not to be preserved for its own innate values. Unused or un-exploited resources (read that, the *natural environment*) are assumed to be virtually wasted until converted into human use in the cash economy.

There is a sinister reality that attends this characteristic, as well as a dangerous side effect. The sinister reality is that, although all impacts are cavalierly held out as manageable, any efforts to impose regulations or regulatory structures that insure such safety precautions are vigorously opposed by corporate lobbyists in the halls of government. Corporate watchdogs are even stationed in state governments, so that fervent "enviros" attempting to protect some cherished local natural area don't give other states, or even the national government, any "wild" (pun intended) ideas. The message is apparently that any environmental impacts can be managed and mitigated, but that corporations will do so voluntarily. And we're still awaiting the arrival of the tooth fairy...

The dangerous side effect kicks in during the inevitable fluctuations in the business cycle. Given that it's the *economy vs. the environment*, all environmental improvement or mitigation is assumed to cost money. Always, the operational question is supposed to be: *Can we afford environmental protection?* Environment is billed as just one more thing on which to spend money. And when the economy turns sour, the necessary belt tightening immediately seeks out relaxed environmental regulations. Indeed, corporations await downturns as opportunities to attack and revoke existing regulations and fatally block proposed new ones. This has ominous portents for environmental progress as the current Great Recession drags on, and as calls for tax cutting and austerity grow louder.

This mindset applies in opposing environmental regulations at all levels, from the lowest local (city councils, perhaps) to the highest global (e.g., Kyoto treaty). It is in issues like this that the generalization of the corporatist mindset on the part of *everyone* will pay particular dividends. If you as a member of the general public can be induced to assume that protection of the environment or steps to avoid global climate change threaten your cherished consumption patterns, then you are more likely to believe that we cannot *afford* to enact such measures, and become willing to throw them over the side first when hard times hit. Some self-styled environmentalists may only be as green as the wad of bills in their pocket...

Two other components of corporatism and environment are addressed later, and are only mentioned at this point. First, is corporate "greenwashing," which can be defined as efforts to appear sustainable and environmentally sensitive for public relations purposes. Second is the tendency of corporate interests to manufacture their own science, so that they can "prove" that activists calling in some way for stricter regulations are really mistaken alarmists. The old "Experts don't agree" argument provides powerful incentive for the modern consumer (especially if they're in economic hard times) to oppose any proposed regulations, to proceed with "business as usual," and even to ignore the issue altogether in good conscience.

SOCIO-CULTURAL

Clearly, much of what we have already touched upon implies a certain pervasive corporate-friendly attitude within the public at large. Corporations must be seen as harmless, friendly, benign institutions that provide us with good paying jobs and furnish everything we need and want in a material sense by delivering their output back into the market place. They insure the prosperity needed for the "American Dream" and all the finer things in life that might entail.

Everything is commodified, from each new recreational experience to basic needs. For instance, the rampant expansion in recent years of the reliance on bottled water should be nothing short of frightening to thinking citizens. People are encouraged to believe that only the purchased product is safe, even though independent analyses have revealed that usually there is no further treatment of the bottled commodity beyond just packaging and selling some available natural source. Even in areas where drinking supplies are contaminated, it is usually the result of corporatist activities in the first place!

This highlights a paradox of economic commodification that has become all too common. Export-based economic activity has often created significant public costs that threaten public health, safety, and government budgets. *Corporatism's* response? Commodify the remedy: charge us even more money to clean up the mess they caused! Of course, all this counts toward an increase in GDP, so the jobs created in cleaning up the effects of other jobs are billed as part of a vibrant and growing economy.

Special attention must be afforded the phrase **Corporate Sponsorship**. From softball teams to local symphonies, corporate sponsorship is eagerly sought. Presumably, we cannot afford such enrichment opportunities without such philanthropic largesse. With an admitted generous dash of cynicism, it could be added: **"For sure, we can't afford them, since you have already looted from the community any economic surplus that would allow us to pay for such amenities on our own. Give it back...!"**

Obviously, this also occurs conspicuously at the national level. Did you all enjoy the Tostitos national football championship game, or the FedEx Orange Bowl? Did you notice at the end of the U.S. Open tennis tournament, the CEO of the sponsoring corporation got to step into the spotlight and present the trophy? And he was lavishly thanked, even by the players, for generously "making all this possible." What he may have actually done, probably because he recreationally enjoys playing the game, was get the opportunity to hob-nob with sports heroes by giving away other people's money in exchange for a bunch of well targeted advertising. In truth, the taxpayers largely funded it, of course. Shucks, he may even get to play with Chrissie Evert in a celebrity mixed doubles benefit match someday...

It will be argued in response that corporate sponsorship in local communities is normally sought from local business interests, and not from national corporations. This is certainly true, and leads to an important reminder. It is the *mindset* we are talking about, and not just the presence of some transnational institution itself. Local business people—as well they should be in many cases—are normally seen as community leaders and benefactors. This promotes a "chamber of commerce" mentality which assumes economic prosperity to be the primary value in a community, and from which springs all other features that the community might cherish. Once that assumption is met, diversity of interests and choices is encouraged, since business is enthroned as the dominant institution that provides all meaning in life. Corporate "sponsorship" has done its job as a small but highly effective down payment toward a cultural mindset. Without further prompting, locals are playing their part, and the corporatist paradigm has won out.

POLITICAL

The political ramifications of corporatism are quite straightforward: ***It's all about the money***. Very few phenomena on the American scene have attracted more attention of late than the effects of money in politics. It is widely agreed that it is polluting, corrupting and in general completely corrosive in most attempts to secure reforms that would effectively serve the poor, the working class, the environment or the general public interest.

But nothing is done about it. The reason is clear: *corporatism* controls the debate itself. The supposedly independent media are allowed to cover the debate to a point, but they are essentially wholly-owned subsidiaries of the corporate interests themselves. In a day when the last presidential election alone (not to mention all the senate, congressional, state and local races) resulted in over $2 billion spent, the money is immediately re-injected into the economy in ways that create powerful support for the status quo. Do television stations really want to give up payments for the barrage of political ads? (Hey, and if they're controversial attack ads, that will stimulate viewer interest even further...!)

Even the prevailing conventional wisdom directing effective methods of campaigning is a telling symptom. The public is supposedly too busy or unconcerned and uninvolved to get seriously interested in politics. That's for political junkies who already know how they're going to vote anyway. The only way to get to the uncommitted voter is through television (or maybe through slick and expensive last-minute mailers). It takes **money** to run an effective campaign. Money in politics? None of us like it, but that's supposedly the way it is and that's the way it has to be. *Corporatism* is again victorious—before, during, and after the campaign.

By committing modern politics to huge amounts of money, then willingly stepping in to provide the lion's share of that cash, corporatism has accomplished another key objective. It has long been a reliable funder of Republican politics. But, since the 1980s, it has also become a major funder of Democratic Party politics. Why would corporatism want to bear the preponderance of costs for *both* major parties, especially now that television has made campaigns so expensive? Simple. *Both parties are now securely in the realm of* corporatist *control.* The Democrats at least occasionally used to make rude, disgruntled noises that were anti-corporatist. Nowadays, they seldom do. The mainstream party has most eagerly traded its old role of defender of the people against anti-popular threats (chief among which was corporatism) for the economic security of reliable corporatist funding. By first helping to make sure that politics is enormously expensive, then stepping in as the major funder of **all** politics, corporations have secured virtually total control of the contemporary political process.

We leave this inviting topic at this point. As you no doubt realize, this topic has received lavish attention in many other places.

INTERNATIONAL

We cannot conclude this brief and incomplete identification of some major features of corporatism without mention of some effects that the whole pervasive mindset tends to have with regard to the rest of the world. *Corporatism* certainly does not have sole domain in the United States, but as the longstanding dominant economic world power, we are responsible for its 20th century genesis, and continue to offer it prime habitat.

European nations, for instance, are correctly seen as offering more widely available social services (e.g., public transportation, health care and education) and a much more extensive "social safety net" than is available in the U.S. People who call for implementing any similar reforms in this country—whether they mention Europe or Canada or not—are immediately chided as "European-style socialists," or worse. In any economic downturn, pressure is exerted through the corporate-dominated international forums (IMF, World Bank, GATT, WTO, OECD, G-8, etc., or simply through normal diplomatic channels) to cut back on such "unsustainable" social spending as unaffordable. Austerity programs are roundly recommended and invoked.

One apparent recent exception to this opposition is offered by the recent passage of a "national healthcare plan" in the US. Corporatism will support such measures, and even cooperate in drafting and implementing them, provided they provide for their primary objective of private profits. Any such public programs or social safety nets, in other words, must be constructed around *corporatist* institutions, and definitely not threaten their profits or overall control. If these sorts of *corporatist-friendly* conditions can be met, *corporatism* is all too willing (apparently) to join the ranks of progressive social crusaders. The exception proves the rule—the U.S. didn't get a national health care plan in Obamacare, it got a slightly different private sector health care plan.

The message here is that private markets must dominate, and that government spending is an inefficient luxury that cannot be afforded when times get tough. The alternate competing presumption that real human needs and health of communities are more important than corporate profits would be an insight dangerous to the well-being of corporatism, and cannot go unchallenged.

Of course, the world financial system has become a globalized paragon of corporatism. No sector is more corporately concentrated or integrated. As a result, the recent economic crisis of the Great Recession, and the financial breakdown that perpetrated it, has given corporatism new tools and leverage for imposing its will and securing its hold on the behavior of other "developed" nations—even though it is almost solely responsible for the collapse in the first place. The breakdowns in Greece, Iceland and Ireland offer graphic examples, and most experts predict with certainty that more are to follow.

For the lesser developed or "developing" nations, the situation is even worse. Through the mechanisms of international lending for big development projects, smaller poorer nations are led into development projects that will ostensibly help the "people" of that nation, but in reality only serve to increase the profits and the reach of global capitalism. When the wherewithal to repay loans is not available, the country can be induced to give up socially beneficial programs and/or to sell off and "privatize" control of its most valuable natural resources—all in the name of efficiency of a market system.

Internationally, the operating watchwords are the universal benefits of trade and the need to be *globally competitive,* as if we still lived by David Ricardo's straightforward theory of comparative advantage. In manners we will later elaborate, the permeating effects of transnational corporations—not even envisioned by Adam Smith or David Ricardo—have transformed the system to one where the major beneficiary is the corporation itself, and neither people in the country where production originates nor in the country where the goods are ultimately consumed.

As with all other topics in this introductory chapter, more will be said later. Certainly, the ubiquitous but elusive topic of globalization merits much attention. The extensive international operations of corporatism are of monumental importance in shaping our conclusions, and certainly any recommendations for concrete action that we choose to make. In short, we will make the case that globalization is essentially corporatism on steroids. Stay tuned.

SUMMING UP

In summary, corporatism has been so successful in extending its control over American society—and, to a lesser extent, world affairs—because it has found ways to portray itself as something it is not. Supposedly, the story goes as follows: It is democratic, not oligarchic. It empowers people broadly, rather than concentrates power in a few privileged hands. It makes the bounty of the earth widely available, rather than despoils the planet and moves us closer to resource depletion and climate disaster. It welcomes and tolerates criticism and a full exchange of diverse views, rather than ostracizing and marginalizing critics who seriously question or oppose it. Corporations are depicted as highly efficient, supremely rational, and committed to the most effective, economical delivery of goods, rather than obsessed with profits and wealth concentration that has led to extreme worldwide inequality. And, in a general cultural sense, it furnishes us the material goods that allow us to "be all that we can be," rather than locks us into a stifling consumerism that marginalizes other human alternatives and potentials.

Perhaps worst at this critical stage of history, given the ominous likelihood of a resource-short, environmentally-threatened future, corporatism pretends that it offers *sustainability*. It promises solutions through advanced technology and skilled management that will not just minimize the effects of shortages and limits, but actually allow the lavish growth binge of the Industrial Age to continue unabated.

In the extreme sense, corporatism has succeeded in establishing a milieu where many—perhaps most—Americans think no such thing as corporatism **exists**. They would be hard pressed to define fully the narrower institution of the *corporation,* let alone the general, more diffuse concept of *corporatism.* Do not forget the conclusion of the previous chapter—**the prime function of the corporate vehicle has evolved into a tool of control for the wealthy elite**.

The powerful elite making the decisions that set the tone and guide the course of corporatism recognize full well that their interests are best served by lying low: *Keep a low profile, and appear to have no more influence than the average person.* This is a big part in pretending you are something you're not; in this case pretending that corporatism is a myth, a **non-force**. (e.g., *"There is no class war; that's the tortured dream of a bunch of* *conspiracy-theorist lefties*.") A huge part of establishing a prevailing atmosphere centering around corporate commercial activity, but including themes, attitudes and other influences cutting across all economic, social and political life in America, is making those not directly connected to the institution of corporatism think it was their idea.

The indispensable allure of consumerism. Consumerism has been and remains the key to public co-option. As long as the public believes the Good Life is synonymous with continued, high-paced consumption, corporatism or any other philosophy purporting to provide the goodies, has the inside track to remaining steadfastly in the public favor. If we covet a panoply of the endless consumer goods of the American material lifestyle, we the public can be counted on by corporatist insiders to "self-regulate." Further, we are bound to think twice before joining any critical resistance movement that might well "kill the golden goose."

In the chapters ahead, we will turn from this somewhat abstract and generalized indictment of corporatism to more concrete and measurable ways it has affected—and is affecting—our economy, our politics, and our family and community lives. Understand, in no way are we suggesting that corporatism represents some insidious, regimented, sinister force; a pernicious organization with chapters, board members, a secret handshake, and that meets monthly in some five-star hotel on the outskirts of Houston or Dubai. What we are saying is that powerful corporations, working through their network of relationships to other institutions—especially government and the media—have effectively found ways to consolidate, expand and solidify their power and influence over many important aspects of American life. The wealthy are definitely in control. It is vital to understand the many permeating effects of this expansion of power if ways are to be found to devise a comfortable and viable local alternative.

A final all-important reminder: The tangible effects, pro and con, of corporations on our lives have been hashed and re-hashed, and this will no doubt continue. That is not the main point. The main point is that it has tended to give *you*, the average American, a mindset compatible with (and inadvertently supportive of) Global Corporatism—manifested even in your local actions. *Leading you through introspection to examine that mindset or world view is our main purpose in this chapter*. This is a necessary first step on the part of regular thinking citizens if we are to undertake effective local actions to make our communities more safe, sustainable, prosperous and personally satisfying. The task will be difficult, but we see it as a fundamentally optimistic endeavor: It represents the path to the best possible future we can expect.

CHAPTER 6

What Is Localism?

Localism as radical economics

nitially, it is tempting to consider a strategy of producing goods locally as just a minor addition or adjustment to what we do now—perhaps a slight throwback to earlier times. Actually, it is much more serious—our globalized economy has gone too far for that to be the case. To demonstrate this fundamentally important point, it is useful to compare the current economic operating principles of corporatism (i.e., "conventional wisdom") to principles which would apply under a strategy which we have dubbed Localism.

For ease, we will categorize these operating principles, and identify the differences, under four main headings:

1. **Marketing**

2. **Labor Force**

3. **Production Technology**

4. **Organizational Structure of the Firm**

Other categories are possible, and there are certainly possible sub-headings, but these four capture the essential differences between Localism as economic philosophy and business as usual. First, however, there are some basic realities defining any local or regional economy.

THE ESSENTIALS OF ANY ECONOMY

Under corporatism, the strategy is **produce for export**. This universally accepted principle has solid roots in economic base theory. It is patently obvious that no economy, especially a regional or local economy, is a closed system. Thus, that regional economy must import goods which it does not currently produce (automobiles, electronics, a host of demanded consumer goods—almost anything one could mention). This importing process, done in order to meet consumer demands and also to obtain intermediate goods necessary as inputs to local production activities, by definition sends money outside the local economy. Something must occur (i.e., "exports") in order to sell something outside the region and bring that money back. Otherwise, the local economy will shrivel and die.

These export-based industry sectors are known as the *basic sector*, (e.g., lumber and wood products for the Northwest economy, electronics for California's Silicon Valley, Boeing airplanes for Seattle, etc.) and are viewed as the only reliable engine for growth of a local or regional economy. Unless new dollars are brought in, no net new expansion—even of the service sector—is technically possible. As we will later address, local economic development efforts eagerly fall in line within this conceptual framework. (*So we essentially have **Globalist** thinking at the Local level as well...!*)

By contrast, the "service sector" merely distributes and recycles dollars that the basic sector brings in through exports. Hence, the service sector is assumed not to serve the fundamental robust growth of an area since it does not bring in net new dollars to the particular economy in question. It merely recycles them. Of course, the concept of spending multipliers, an important tool in identifying and quantifying aggregate economic impact of any economic change, depends totally on the structure of the economy—both basic and service sector activity.

These fundamental realities support and explain the fascination of almost any local, state or regional economic development strategy with attracting export-based new industries. Ideally, in recent years, the premium outcome is seen as the attraction of a branch facility of an existing multinational corporation. Only then, says conventional wisdom, can the local area be seen as truly "competitive in the global economy."

Localism takes giant steps in revealing that this capstone principle is somewhere between useless and disastrous. Hence, the radicalism—but how is that so, and how does it work? Let us move to the specific points organized around the four areas identified earlier.

1. MARKETING

Globalized corporate thinking leads to concentration on export-based activities. It is seen as a wise business practice to shoot for the broadest possible market for any product produced. What could possibly be wrong with this line of thinking? As it turns out, quite a bit. In recent decades, business has proven that it can locate successfully almost any place, given that it ships its products all over the world anyway. Technologies employed, including information technology, will be very similar for any firm producing similar products. Thus, the cost structure in general, including advertising, transportation, warehousing and distribution will be similar for any firm seeking to compete.

On the other hand, under localization, a firm seeks to market only in its local area. A close look at a projected income statement might indicate the advantages of Localism. For the local firm, there is no need to spend money on many items necessary to the large corporation producing essentially the same product. For instance, advertising and marketing, distribution, transportation, warehousing, many types of energy costs, etc., all can be substantially less or even missing altogether. This frees up the firm to allocate as much as possible to labor costs, our next topic. First, however, this leads to:

Radical Conclusion #1:
Don't Export—Produce for Local Markets

2. LABOR FORCE

When a firm competes in the global economy, this immediately puts the labor force in competition with any low-wage haven in the world, and exerts powerful downward pressure on wage rates. Economic development specialists in local and regional areas realize that high wage rates are a negative for major corporations, even as those specialists (paradoxically) extol the need to create "family wage jobs."

Clearly, the dictum of producing for local markets affects the choice of production technology, which is likely to be more labor intensive than would be the case for a global corporation. In response to this, the "globalist" would, with an air of superiority, mutter to himself or anyone who would listen: "inefficient," or "uncompetitive," and write that effort off as unlikely to succeed.

However, since labor is the most certain source of local value added, such a choice of technology actually expands the size of local employment multipliers and makes every dollar spent on the locally produced product much more valuable to the economy than a dollar spent on the same product produced globally. Of course, even if the capital/labor mix is the same for the locally based and owned firm as for the hypothetical major corporation, the payments for all other inputs, including profits to the owners, are to local entities. For a major corporation (branch plant, e.g.), virtually all these factor payments immediately escape the local economy. Thus, the multipliers and therefore the ultimate economic impact of the locally owned firm are dramatically higher.

What this means is that a consumer dollar expenditure simply diverted from the globally to the locally produced product (*no net new sales or dollars expended by consumers...*) has net job production benefits to the local economy. This is a powerful conclusion. Further, it means that, due to cost structure differences, the local labor force is effectively *not* in competition with cheaper workforces around the globe. This frees the local firm both to hire more workers and pay them better, and leads to:

Radical Conclusion #2:
Don't Minimize Labor Costs—Maximize Them

3.PRODUCTION TECHNOLOGY

Have you noticed, that anytime a new business startup occurs, or that an existing small business considers its future prospects, it is deemed essential to have an immediate internet presence, to set up for customer contact methods in as many ways possible and to imagine modern production technology sufficient to "become competitive in the global economy." It is not considered wise to do anything else, since growth is seen as the desirable imperative, and such moves are assumed to be the modern preconditions for growth.

The major corporation will seek the largest scale mass-production (and likely least labor-intensive) methods available. Blindly following this protocol and aspiring to global competitiveness (as conventional wisdom contends that it must) may prove the death knell for our ambitious enterprise. The technology necessary for such mass production, along with all the accompanying marketing and distribution arrangements, is very likely to make the firm *uncompetitive* for serving its own local market.

To be sure, the choice of manufacturing technologies for a firm seeking to produce only for local markets will likely be different. The goal, however, should be to choose the appropriate technology for producing as efficiently as possible on the scale necessary to serve just the local market. This leads to:

Radical Conclusion #3:
Don't choose large efficient technology,
choose small appropriate technology

4. ORGANIZATIONAL STRUCTURE OF THE FIRM

This characteristic may at first glance seem less important and technical. In truth, it may well be the crucial feature that enables the strong tendency of corporate globalism to create such devastating inequality. We give it considerable attention in Chapter 20, which is devoted to one last look at the dynamics of addressing our pre-eminent economic problem of income and wealth inequality.

The essence of the radicalism of Localism lies with the incentive and reward system which the modern corporation de facto creates. Rewards of rampant success and growth go to the owners. Thus, a wealthy capitalist class is created and unerringly enhanced. It is built into the system and reinforced into conventional understanding that a corporation's singular calling is to make profits and enhance the interests of the shareholder/owners.

Alternatively, a locally organized firm could offer the original owner/investors a fixed return and allocate to workers the additional value that is created over time through successful operation and growth. As mentioned above, this feature is important enough to be developed more fully later, but to conclude this brief section, it leads to:

Radical Conclusion #4:
Limit the returns to owners and
make growth serve the workers.

SUMMARY: BEYOND ECONOMICS; THE CRITICAL REALM OF ECOLOGICAL CRISIS

Our emphasis here is clearly on the economic attributes of Localism. How Localism may satisfy the material needs of American society in the troubling years ahead should concern us all. Yet even a cursory glance at the potentials of Localism takes us well beyond the confines of economics; questions of politics, human relationships, social and cultural matters such as where we live quickly surface. These draw immediate attention to how Localism contrasts with the corporatist oligarchic system in which we now live. Parts two and three of this book will attempt to grapple with at least some of these other influences and characteristics of Localism-based societies. To a considerable degree, our treatment will concentrate on dispelling some of the many myths of Localism, which has often been portrayed as a retrogressive step backward. If its corporatist critics sometimes stop short of branding Localism as a "return to the caves," they regularly dismiss it as a retreat to a lower standard of living and a surrender of crucial cultural values.

Finally, there is the specter of ecological or environmental crisis. Perhaps the most critical difference in Localism is what impact it might have in the ecological area. Not discounting imposing economic problems such as income and wealth inequality, the marginalization of working people, mounting debt and runaway destructive financialization, ecological collapse is the most threatening problem America and the world faces. Here, Localism offers a clear distinction with what is possible and impossible under current Corporatism. Accordingly, Localism must be carefully considered if for no other reason than its clear superiority in confronting the climate and other ecological crises over the next critical two decades.

CHAPTER 7

Getting to the Heart of Inequality

A business firm is simply a distributive mechanism. We made that point in Chapter 1, and it is time to extend the analysis. To be sure, it produces some product or service, and that's the superficial way people identify it. But understanding its fundamental *cultural* role requires that we specifically examine its function as a *RE-distributor* of the income streams, and thus the final income and wealth distribution, that it impacts. Every producing entity buys valuable resources, including hiring labor, transforms them somehow in the act of production, sells that output and then re-distributes the proceeds of those sales back to the productive inputs. In doing this, they take in money that is already distributed in some way out there in the economy according to the existing income profile of their customers, and pay out that money to all those inputs. And this inexorably changes the distribution of income. We need to pause here in order to emphasize the unvarnished meaning of this process:

The business firm, in large part, <u>creates</u> the income distribution for a market economy

Given that this is the way in which many people receive their incomes, it therefore is the basic determining factor of the income distribution. The reason for the phrase "in large part" in the above important conclusion is that there are of course many who do not work for businesses—some professionals, non-profit employees and government workers, for example. Nonetheless, the lion's share of income distribution effects emanate, directly or indirectly, from the way in which the private business sector pays its factors of production.

But even if you don't work for a business, an equally important proviso is that we *all* spend our income, however we earn it, in roughly the same way. Our expenditures inexorably run through the business sector no matter where we happen to work or however we obtain our income. That is the important point in grasping the significance of the next few pages.

As an important aside, how about the question of actually *treating* economic inequality? The process of doing something about widely agreed-upon problems necessarily invokes a controversial "R word:" Redistribution. It's a straightforward premise, in language that many are uncomfortable hearing: *If the distribution we have is socially unacceptable, then somehow we must **redistribute***. There is no other choice.

Interestingly, two areas mentioned earlier in Chapter 1, government and the non-profit sector, are the two primary "realms" that are looked to for redressing commonly perceived income distribution problems. More on that later, but practically speaking these are the only realistic options. In common parlance this amounts to administering to the less advantaged either with private charity or government action. And here, recalling rhetoric most of us can relate to, lies a seminal difference between progressives and conservatives. Progressives historically contend that the public sector must take an active role in redressing problems of unequal distribution of wealth and income. Conservatives tend more to prefer leaving the job to private charities. This preserves more of a free choice market mechanism, in that it leaves the well-to-do free to choose which causes they will support, and which they do not. (Does the phrase "Noblesse Oblige" ring a bell...?)

Further, there has historically been a vaguely specified agreement that a healthy growing economy will also assist in redressing the plight of the poor. We will have much more to say on this topic. It seems apparent that the documented problems with growing disparity and its unfortunate ramifications have gotten so severe that we will undoubtedly need both private and public efforts if we are to make significant headway.

In the final section of this book, we propose some recommendations for actions that would make the business structure itself automatically work more toward income equality, and perhaps avoid some of the inflammatory and socially disruptive political debates over the role of government that we now experience.

THE BUSINESS FIRM AS AN INCOME DISTRIBUTION DETERMINANT

Picking up from Chapter 1, the two most important factors, normally historically at odds with each other, are: labor (workers), and management (owners). Again, the telling feature is that a business enterprise, large or small, simply takes money from its customers' income distribution and pays money into the distribution of its own workers and management and owners. Whether this process is widely acknowledged or not, it is nonetheless crucial for our analysis here that this makes the business sector the major *societal redistributor*. Clearly, if we don't like what we see, achieving any other distribution than the one the private producing sector creates necessitates redistribution efforts of one kind or another—like it or not.

The existing income range variation for business customers (i.e., consumers) depends partly on the nature of the particular product, and that does not initially concern us. Rather, it is the pattern of the "payout" as the firm covers its costs (and perhaps distributes profits) that is of primary interest. The important question is how *the current business structure affects the income distribution.*

And of course, as an economic "side effect," these impacts become subversively all-important, since once they take place, the next round of business activity as money continues to circulate in a dynamic system over time begins with that new and changed income distribution. As the cycle proceeds, and we all engage in day-to-day activities of going to work, earning a salary, and spending our income for basic wants and needs, (It's called *living...*) whatever effects might result then accumulate and magnify over time. If it starts poorly, don't hold your breath, it will get worse...

To explore this more technically, let us imagine the entire size gamut of business firms from which we all buy our goods and services, beginning with the one person single proprietorship in one tail of the distribution and ranging up to a large multinational firm at the other end of the spectrum. Specifically, the focus is on returns to workers versus returns to owners. Here is the key question:

What pattern of income distributions is created among this array of firms?

With a bit of thought, answers spring out immediately. For a single proprietorship, management and labor are identical—the same person. The single proprietorship therefore by definition has no transformative effect on income distribution. "Workers" get the same as "Owners," since they are the same person. In fact, for many small but slightly larger firms employing just a few people, the range stays very small. Often, especially with new startup firms, the owner may actually earn less than some employees, especially on an hourly basis, given the large amount of time owners put in during the startup phase of the business, along with the meager profits (Can you say *initial losses...*?) that virtually always accompany the first perilous months and years of a newly started business.

As the firm size gets larger, a managerial staff that earns more than the main workforce will customarily emerge. One can imagine that small businesses employing 50 to 200 people might have a president earning in the $200,000 per year range, or perhaps more as the firm size approaches 1000 employees. For "small business" firms in this general range, the ratio of CEO salary to average salary of the workforce is reputed to be in the neighborhood of 8 to 12 times. In starker terms, the "gap" inexorably increases as the firm size increases. (And what increases the firm size? *Growth*! Stay tuned, dear reader...)

At the other end of the spectrum, for large Fortune 500 corporations, what do we find? The answer is waved before our eyes continually in the media. For the United States right now, that figure is (conservatively) in the 350 to 1 range; and has been estimated even higher. For the top 100, the figure is reportedly in the 700 to 1 range. It is tempting to focus on the critical activists' emotional railings that these levels of compensation are obscene and unfair, which they indeed are. But the overall purpose here of pointing this out is to underscore a fundamentally important technical point:

The economic impact of a large corporation is, unequivocally, to redistribute incomes badly

This allows us to extract a principle completely borne out with the data: As firm size increases, disparity between management salaries and workers' salaries increases steadily and significantly. Fine, you might say, and of what importance is this? Remember, these compensations are the payrolls of the system, and therefore, they are the income distribution. In short, the answer to your question is that it makes all the difference in the world; and we can extract another basically intuitive, but stunningly important conclusion:

Small firms tend to support equality of income and wealth, and large firms increase inequality

There are several useful ways to dig into this premise more deeply, including the predictable objections to concluding that this large salary range is a negative feature of a capitalist free market economy. (You've no doubt heard the arguments: "*A true meritocracy **should** have income differentials...*" or perhaps: "*Income differentials are necessary to preserve incentives to work harder...*")

Some of this may be true, and in no way are we recommending equal salaries for all. Rather, the point is that we presently have broad social agreement that the current situation has become unacceptable, and is continually worsening—and something must be done. It is enlightening to explore some of the other peripheral issues. For instance, a corollary implication is that a geographic area where the composition of employers is largely small businesses will tend to have a more equal income distribution; **but**, it will be pointed out, it will also have lower average salaries—i.e., be a poorer area absolutely. And isn't that undesirable?

Speaking to this requires another corollary observation. Large firms tend to cluster around cities, with the largest cities hosting the largest corporations. (You will not find Exxon headquarters in a small town out on the prairie west of Laramie, Wyoming...) If we accept that fact, the implication would be that a small poor town, in order to become richer should simply seek larger firms to come in (or, with predictably slower results, promote growth of their existing employment base). It should be expected that inequality would increase somewhat (which would be ignored...), but the higher top end salaries would increase the average income in the area (which would be roundly celebrated...). Growth, both of number of employers and firm size, and likely accompanied by population growth, would accomplish all this.

Does this begin to sound familiar? It virtually describes the urban economic development history of the United States. It explains why large cities have the highest average incomes and also the greatest concentrations of poverty—including in the last few years a startling increase in homelessness. Further, it sheds light on the fact that rural areas will have lower average incomes but less inequality. It is an obvious and much discussed fact that the preponderance of well-paid people in many major cities has resulted in high costs of living and, as we all know, higher housing costs—both before and after the housing bubble collapse of 2008. In fact, the seemingly healthy and vibrant cities (think San Francisco, Portland and Seattle) are often particularly vexed with problematic housing markets.

One result of all this is that in most large cities it has become a serious problem that the service sector workforce (which is only moderately paid) cannot afford to live near their city center jobs. Urban cores, for vibrant cities, have become the domain, employment-wise and residentially, of the upscale wealthy. And these are problems for the *employed* service sector. What if you don't have a job at all? Transportation thus becomes a key issue, perhaps especially for the homeless, but digging into this quagmire requires full-scale urban analysis—and that is not our purpose here.

TYING THIS ALL TOGETHER

Think about the development history of most major industrial sectors. The automobile industry, for instance, had over 100 firms in the U.S. in the early part of the 20th century. Now there are 3 or 4, and even they are largely integrated internationally. The continually replicated model as industrial sectors start up and then develop over time is that there are many competitive small firms early in the development process of any given industry, and consolidation gradually winnows that down to a very few large firms, each with a degree of monopoly power. And these remaining firms are put on pedestals to honor successful examples of American Capitalism. This is the lionized **success story** that all entrepreneurism should supposedly seek to emulate…! The devastating conclusion is that it is clearly a blueprint for inequality and monopoly. This idolized process is the major reason we have the inequality that vexes us today.

This empirically verifiable conclusion flies in the face of conventional economic theory, which holds that growth helps everybody ("*A rising tide raises all boats…*"). Indeed, the perfectly competitive economy—with a great many small "price taking" firms in every industry—is set out in our economics textbooks and incorporated into our citadels of higher learning as the ultimate goal and ideal of our capitalistic free market economy. (And have we spotted the Easter Bunny recently…?)

QUICK SUMMARY–AND LOOKING AHEAD

For clarity, we list, in simple bullet-point form, the logical steps developed in this chapter:

- Payments by firms determine income distribution

- Small firms tend to distribute incomes evenly

- Large firms (corporations) distribute incomes badly

- Small competitive firms tend to grow to large monopolistic corporations

- Large corporations currently dominate our economy

- Corporations employ fewer and fewer people per dollar of output

- Corporations therefore tend to cause unemployment, monopoly and inequality in local areas by "expropriating" their Value Added

All this allows us to formulate a final overriding conclusion:

Traditional capitalist economic growth and development patterns, especially as they are supercharged by globalization, have become a blueprint for inequality, monopoly and unemployment

In other words, the reason we have trenchant inequality is that we live in a society that is economically dominated by large corporations. Given that actual survey data reveal that approximately 95% of every dollar you and I spend goes through, directly or indirectly, a major corporation, our inequality is *structurally determined*. The ubiquitous presence of the major corporation as the primary economic actor in our system, whatever their advantages and benefits may be, is the primary driving force behind the pernicious and increasing inequality we currently experience. The problem and its negative offshoots are visible and much discussed. The underlying reasons are not. This (disturbing to many) premise will dominate much of what we do in this book—and it most certainly underscores our case for Localism.

We wish it were not true that our traditionally accepted (and commonly revered) systemic structure itself is our fundamental problem; and we invite anyone to attempt to prove otherwise. (*Please—test the model for yourself...*) We are confident that any instances pointed to as exceptions will be localized and anecdotal, but that the overall holistic effect of "business as usual" is to push our economic system *as it is currently structured* inexorably in the unfortunate directions indicated.

The tragedy is that conventional wisdom, in both the business community and the general public (not to mention the discipline of economics), is almost exactly opposite these conclusions. We conclude that painful times lie ahead as we struggle to adjust— with or without the overriding specter of energy constraints and climate change in the mix, which are addressed in Part Two.

Finally, we must again ask what is learned if we focus on the role of economic growth in this system? It seems apparent that connections with the negative impacts of inequality, monopoly and unemployment issues just raised are wide and deep, yet the public policy emphasis on growth as the panacea for most economic ills persists. This lightning-rod issue of economic growth is so critical to the overall arguments in this book that we devote separate chapters to its exploration. There are two directions to be taken. The first, presented next as the final chapter of this section, is from an economic (theory and practice) point of view. The second at the end of Part 2 is from an ecological resource-based viewpoint examining the effects of growth on the natural environment.

These are not intended as typical "rants" against growth, many of which exist. Rather, our coverage is an integrated exploration that dovetails with the major theme of the book. It reflects our dominant premise that this culture faces two connected crises that cannot be ignored: economic inequality and climate change. It may turn out that the solution has become the problem.

CHAPTER 8

Growth—The Economic Issue

There is perhaps no concept or issue more intricately connected to all other economic, social or environmental issues than economic growth. It is pervasive in everything we think about, from politics to community dynamics to national issues of public policy. Our view, consistent with a systems methodology, is that any worthwhile discussion—especially if it seeks to offer any new insights—*must* be integrative and systemic, lest it become just another of the many (sometimes superficial) diatribes on the topic.

It is clearly a complex issue, and there are many existing arguments for and against growth. Growth is vigorously argued as both the solution and the problem when many economic policy issues arise. Initially, it was not our strong intention to contribute to this voluminous debate. However, when topics such as inequality, climate change, globalization, the role of corporations and purposeful local responses to these issues are addressed, it is continually driven home that economic growth in many ways necessarily becomes a central part of the analysis.

Accordingly, as the project has proceeded, the necessity for our arguments of directly addressing the pervasive role played by economic growth in the entire culture, let alone the economy, has become abundantly clear. Nonetheless, we still intend the following coverage of growth to be *as an integrated issue*. How does the economic growth ethic play a role in all the other issues we address? Although little that we say is completely new, the treatment has unearthed some new insights that in our view are not immediately apparent in other existing coverages, and we hope you will agree.

IS ECONOMIC GROWTH OBSOLETE?

Sustainability as a concept began to go mainstream following the United Nations-sponsored Brundtland Report in 1989. In a popularized conceptual form, it was often described as a three-legged stool embodying the intersection of economy, environment and community. In short, a sustainable policy or act had to make sense from an economic point of view, a social, or community-based point of view, and it had to display environmental and resource integrity.

Mainstream economic thinking was indeed leery of this upstart notion, since it seemed vaguely threatening to the cherished growth ethic. In fact, economists have experimented with theoretical models designed to determine the "sustainable level of growth." (If you can't beat it, join it...) Such sadly oxymoronic efforts are not alone. In many ways the practical day-to-day economy has sought to reconcile the increasingly accepted concept into the normal business regimen so that a "de-clawed" version of sustainability can be embraced and life can continue as usual. Thus was the birth of greenwashing.

Our purpose is not to engage in the often acrimonious three decades long debate as to whether growth and sustainability can be reconciled. A few years ago a direct quote from a member in a Chamber of Commerce open forum in our city was the following: "Sustainability is a Communist plot to take down Capitalism." Such attitudes clearly indicate deeper issues, and the room for measured thoughtful data-based analysis and debate seems somewhat small. Life is too short.

For purposes here, however, the conceptual image of the 3 stools of sustainability provides a useful taxonomy for structuring our critique of the ethic of economic growth. Hence we organize our coverage within the following categories:

1. **Economic Growth and Economic Theory**

2. **Economic Growth and Contemporary Society**

3. **Economic Growth and Planetary Resources**

In this chapter, which concludes the first section of the book, we concentrate on the first category, with some allowance for the second. Attention to economic growth and potential constraints played by physical resources—including the environment—began in the early 1970's with the publication of the first Club of Rome study, **Limits to Growth**. It is clear that issues related to resource depletion and environmental deterioration are highly connected to energy and climate change. Thus, coverage of the third category, growth in relation to the limits imposed by environmental and resource scarcity, is included in Part Two, and will anchor that section.

GROWTH AS THE RELIGION OF ECONOMIC THEORY

Growth has become the assumed goal of standard mainstream economic theory. Conventional wisdom holds that a growing economy is a successful economy. This perceived need to grow in order to thrive has become a central part of the discipline of economics since the birth of Keynesian macroeconomic theory developed in response to the Great Depression of the 1930s. Our observation is that the actual *need* for growth (as well as the capacity for culturally *useful* growth) in those gloomy economic times was much greater than is the case today. This is true even though we hear vigorous arguments to the contrary. In one way or another, the leftover cultural trauma of that devastating decade seems to have inculcated into economic theory a fusion of the terms "economic growth" and "economic success."

The single most observed statistic in assessing the performance of a modern economy is Gross Domestic Product (GDP), which is (abstracting from certain wonkish statistical manipulations) the value of all the material output of goods and services produced in some defined economy in a given year. More output, according to the discipline of economics, is essentially equivalent to more human happiness. All market transactions count; and while economics texts and the professionals who talk about it give passing lip service to the fact that many "market transactions" do

not increase human well-being, the premise that more output equals more happiness remains predominant. In other words, they acknowledge that it is an imperfect measure of human welfare, but enthusiastically choose to use it anyway.

A car wreck increases GDP, as does a heart attack or a natural disaster. The Exxon Valdez oil spill in Alaska resulted in billions of dollars in market transactions to affect the cleanup, but the best that can be said about the net contribution to human well-being is that the related cleanup jobs, however welcomed as "income" by businesses and employees involved, primarily attempted to restore a previous condition of satisfaction with the beaches, the salmon runs and the pristine beauty of Prince William Sound.

This argument can be generalized. The increased attention to environmental cleanup, for example, is more accurately termed a "mitigation of bads" as opposed to a "creation of goods," as mainstream economic analysis would identify the resultant market expenditures. Hurricane Katrina dramatically increased the GDP of New Orleans, but no one would contend that it increased human happiness.

The emergent sub-field of Ecological Economics was pioneered in the 1970s by the likes of Herman Daly and Robert Costanza. In part, this led to development and estimation of a concept known as Gross National Happiness. This represents an attempt to measure *actual* human satisfaction by subtracting out losses due to the kinds of incidents identified above, and especially environmental and human health losses due to expanded economic activity. An important inclusion in the environmental realm was biodiversity and ecosystem losses. Mind you, no departure is made from a distinctly materialistic base—any production of goods and services still counts as a positive contribution to human happiness and well-being. It is simply the case, however, that clear losses are considered and netted out as well.

Obviously, if quantitative estimates are to be attained, the task of statistical measurement becomes tricky, especially when "non-economic" environmental values such as species extinction and ecosystem damage are taken into account. Nonetheless, their transparent methodology employs the best practices of contingent valuation long used in Resource Economics, and believable ranges are presented. Without belaboring the details of this process, their general conclusion is that the costs of growth may have begun exceeding the benefits as early as the mid-1970s. In general terms, it is fundamental logic that continued growth in an increasingly crowded, polluted and scarcity-prone world at some point must unequivocally create more problems than it solves. Even if the exact date when the cost and benefit curves cross is debatable, the broad conclusion is that economic growth has for some time ceased to promote the human purpose on this earth.

This is a devastating, and even radical, conclusion; but it is of course a macro level observation. Are there populations, regions, countries or underserved (presumably poor) cohorts where the benefits to additional growth would clearly outweigh the costs? Certainly, there are. The logical (ideally world level) policy implications, therefore, would clearly be to direct any additional growth to those areas—both within and between countries—and move to somewhat of a "stable state" condition for those already comfortable higher income areas of the world. (More growth in Switzerland would be of marginal benefit, but South Sudan could definitely use it...)

But the clear implication of this is that the ideal situation should seek to reduce inequality—and therein lies the problem. As we have seen, and as we will continue to maintain throughout this book, capitalism is innately an inequality producing system—it produces inequality almost as effectively as it produces wealth—or should we say **concentrations** of wealth. Furthermore, the modern globalized version of capitalism is even more hardwired to create a world of rich and poor. Globalism is little more than Capitalism on Steroids.

Viewed holistically, therefore, the overriding challenge of Localism would appear to become a restoration of more economic equality. Without overstating the issue, the success or failure of this task for our entire system may determine the difference between a comfortable economic future and economic disaster. The stakes could not be higher, and a look at one of the most basic economic tools can illuminate the challenge.

GROWTH AND THE CIRCULAR FLOW

One of the most popular and commonly used images of a capitalistic free market economy is the simple circular flow diagram. This construct puts businesses (producers) on one side of the flow, and individuals (consumers) on the other. They interrelate in two ways: First, they connect in input markets as individuals earn their income by offering their services to business in the act of production. Second, they connect in the final product markets as individuals and families spend those earnings to purchase the output of producers. (*Go to work, get your paycheck, then take it to the grocery store and the mall...*) Ideally, for a market economy this flow process is supposed to be in balance, with each participant acting as a supplier in one market, and a demander in the other—with mutual self interest comfortably hovering over the entire process. The invisible hand of Adam Smith is in full sway.

The reader should be warned:

**The following discussion is an exercise in logic.
It accesses some well-known economic theory,
but it is not economic theory. The argument develops a
critique of standard economic beliefs that results in an
apparent contradiction between logic and economics.**

Be aware—you may have to make an important choice.

In reality, this sought-after balance cannot exist. Consumers hope to take in more than they spend and thus accumulate savings, and businesses also hope that receipts exceed expenditures, thus resulting in a profit. In fact, unless consumers save and businesses profit, almost by definition you *cannot* have what is commonly considered to be a successful economy—with prosperity for everyone. They each seek to extract something from the circular flow by putting in less than they take out.

Simple logic dictates that the postulated balance cannot happen if each side spends less than it receives. The "circular flow" would shrink and disappear. Economic theory solves this apparent dilemma with the financial sector, combined with economic growth. Savings by consumers go into financial institutions (banks, stock market, etc.), which then make those accumulated funds available to business in support of investment in new and replacement capital. The macro economy is thus in equilibrium through an important identity, savings must equal investment.

And this is where growth comes in. Business spending for investment purposes is thus necessary to "sop up" the savings accumulated by individuals and families. But investment is essentially building the capacity for new additional production, which amounts to growth and expansion. THEREFORE, growth must occur if the circular flow is to be in balance. And, even then it is balanced only in a temporal dynamic sense—businesses spend their current profits by building capacity that looks to make even more profit in the following periods. Expectations for the future are key. This is the essence of the perceived need for growth, and it is an unending cycle. If expectations for business sales and profits are not met, the entire system falls apart.

At this point, an important question must be faced: **What is the purpose of growth?** Conventional wisdom, consistent with accepted public policy almost anywhere in the world, is that the purpose of growth is to improve the standard of living of people—to make us materially better off—wealthier, if you will. Economic development, in its many forms, has undoubtedly brought many people around the world out of poverty and has created hope for a brighter future where otherwise one might not have existed.

So far, so good. Where does the logical contradiction come in? Suppose that a modern economy is very successful, and creates a high standard of living for its people, which of course means high rates of saving. Growth has done its job and created an economic Nirvana, right? Wrong—the higher rate of savings of the well-to-do populace continues to require a higher rate of investment to employ these savings in order to keep this economy in balance. Thus, on the surface growth has apparently done its job of making us wealthy, but then **keeping** the economy healthy requires even higher rates of growth...!

There is no "off button." Economic theory does not allow for a stable end point, a steady state, sustainability... Once on the treadmill, you cannot get off. This is true of currently accepted economic theory even if the materialistic drive for accumulation of more goods and services remains insatiable and even if energy and physical resources remain superabundant. The exposition of these two points—consumerism as a dominant human value, and limits to growth from energy, resource and environmental scarcity—form the framework of our other two critiques of growth. The first follows presently, while, as we earlier indicated, the Limits to Growth coverage concludes the next section following the discussion of energy and climate change.

SOME IMPLICATIONS OF THIS LOGICAL CONTRADICTION

It is not our purpose to anoint a clear winner in this "Economics vs. Logic" battle. Perhaps that is not necessary, even though the practical stakes are high. There are, however, some striking implications that offer useful insights into the important real-world ramifications of the confrontation. Be clear that the following listing assumes that a world of unregulated growth will continue to create the inequality that has become ubiquitous in the last few decades.

In a world wherein the logic portion of the argument holds sway, perceptive observers might tend to see some of the following:

* Inadequate sales mark the final product markets, and businesses tend to advertise frantically, extend lavish credit, try to get consumers to spend "next year's income."

* A growing emphasis on luxury goods and exotic "niche"

services prevails, since that's where the purchasing power lies. Local and regional areas desperately promote tourism, for the same reason.

* Business, using a variety of culturally-based approaches, strongly urges people to identify as consumers, ignoring any charge to be workers or citizens. This turns consumers into "price seekers" primarily oriented toward material accumulation as a goal in life.

* Business becomes imperialistic, in light of modest or failing domestic demand and their own ability to produce many more goods than they can sell. Foreign markets are cultivated, and foreign investment results. Superficially, this appears to reinforce a globalization-trending world.

* Savings leaking out of the circular flow and returning as investment is not the only diversion from the flow. Taxes are extracted from both consumers and businesses, and returned as government expenditures. And, due to pressures to make up for inadequate demand and balance the flow as well as support those hurt by the rising inequality, governments deficit finance by taxing less than they spend. Supporting these growing deficits, the economy is perpetually seen as underperforming.

* To control costs and increase profits in the face of inadequate domestic demand, businesses begin outsourcing production. This may increase profits in the short run, but makes the problem worse in the long run by further eroding domestic purchasing power.

* Political polarization occurs because of the incessantly increasing inequality, and failure of the "Rising tide raises all boats" credo that growth helps everybody. Trickle-down economics is the stable mate of this credo, and despite lip service to its ineffectiveness, policies remain distinctly consistent with that discredited mindset.

* An austerity kick, as a policy prescription on both macro and micro levels, is a likely companion of these unfortunate political phenomena, since both rely on the mistaken assumption that government is the problem. And the true problem is corporate.

* And as a final side observation, forget tax cuts. They will be proposed as a panacea, and will actually make the problems worse, since they exacerbate inequality.

In an unrestricted free market situation wherein the above "Deadly Sins of Capitalism" types of observation might reasonably occur, growth in reality does not play a positive role. It is actually more of a compensation for fundamental flaws in the happy concept of a balanced circular flow, as opposed to the desired answer that indicates success. Its actual role in theory is as an error term that balances something that cannot balance itself, as opposed to the desired goal sought by so many governments at all levels. Of course, as long as a culture of consumerism prevails, politicians must run on a platform of economic expansion and promise to give people what they want. The growth ethic at work in the popular culture tells people what they *should* want, and then in theory promises to give it to them. There is little room for more spiritual or community-based values.

THE ULTIMATE IRONY

The point of all this hinges largely on the incessant tendency of economic growth as we know it to foster widespread inequality. A mindset that continues to believe strongly in a positive role for economic growth will likely reject most of the above points. And even if such a person tends to agree with some of those points, this one will probably finally drive them away: *Without conscious and vigorous redistribution, in some form or another, capitalism is doomed*. It will tear itself asunder within some variation of unpleasant scenarios, ranging from gated community police states, evolution into a complete banana-belt-republic format, to outright revolution. The de facto fascism we clearly are currently (not) enjoying will be the least of our problems.

Thus we are left with an ultimate "Catch-22:"

Capitalism must have vigorous redistribution if it is to survive, and capitalists currently in power see redistribution as their mortal enemy.

It is more than a Catch-22, it is a tragedy of Shakespearean proportions. If only, in attempting to return economics to its humane "people serving" roots, we could unite Adam Smith and the Bard of Avon. They were both British, but unfortunately lived a couple of centuries apart. And besides, they would probably need the help of Bernie Sanders...

CONSUMERISM AS A WAY OF LIFE

It is time to turn to growth and the popular culture. Here is where we engage with the slippery slope of human values. Critiques of economic growth along socio-cultural lines are becoming more strident and complex with each passing year. Nonetheless, outside of books, articles and certain publications, (and don't forget movies) not a great deal is heard at the national level. It is as though most mass media and prominent national and multinational corporations avoid even admitting that there is any question as to the primacy of economic growth as the common consensus of what we consider our national first priority—such admission would be bad for business...

Vigorous debates often transpire within communities, however—in places where people actually live. And, since the major purpose of this book is to energize and rejuvenate local economies, it is appropriate to focus initially on the types of arguments we might hear within our own communities. Mass media may understandably ignore the issue; thinking people concerned about their family's future do not. Next we raise some tangible issues and examples that may sound familiar, in hopes that we can then develop arguments for the entire culture by extracting the principles involved.

Before examining some hypothetical dialogues, however, one seminally important question must be raised:

To what extent is the proper focus of attention *economic growth*, and to what degree is it *capitalism itself?*

This is necessarily a prominent question. Growth is the assumed goal of the system, but market-based capitalism is the system itself. In practice, they obviously go hand-in-hand. At this juncture it is more important simply to acknowledge the relationship and raise the question than to force an answer, since it is difficult to sort out the relationship in the absence of some working examples or issues. Thus, keep the question in abeyance for now, and proceed in the hope that insights will logically appear.

GROWTH IN YOUR COMMUNITY

Most communities have a Chamber of Commerce. Their stated purpose is normally supporting and promoting local business interests. At the outset, one important point must be made absolutely clear: Business leaders in every community offer substantial benefits to their home areas. In addition to providing jobs, they volunteer, support non-profits, donate to community projects and often engage in major philanthropic efforts. Many roundly deserve the label "Pillar of the Community."

The criticisms that can be made of the growth ethic in any given community in no way should reflect on the *people* themselves. It is an *attitude*, or more accurately a *mindset*, that is the focus of concern. And, to address the "create jobs" fetish that many display, they are trapped by a creature that is not of their own making. Whether people and policies in communities fully grasp this point or not, the national and multinational corporations have quite obviously focused on *destroying* jobs in order to promote increased profits for stockholders and higher salaries for CEOs and other top management.

Major corporations do not call it "destroying jobs," preferring terms such as innovation and efficiency. Still, they pose as the "job creators" of our culture even though there is an incessant search to replace workers through automation and information technology. There is an understood imperative to replace that pesky labor input in a Wall Street-driven quest to lower costs, increase profits and raise share prices for the stockholder/owners. Localities tend desperately to try and retain or restore those slowly escaping jobs, and mistakenly look to the very source of the problem for their salvation.

Imagine a hypothetical conversation between two representative members of some typical community. The first, possibly a Chamber of Commerce member or a business person, represents someone devoted to improving the local economy, and is represented by ECON. The second, possibly a Sierra Club or Friends of the Earth member, is represented by ENVIRO. (Please note the absence of terms such as: Liberal or Conservative... More on that later.)

THE EXCHANGE:

ECON People need to realize that the first need in any local area is a healthy economy. Unless we have an adequate number of well-paying jobs, nothing else works.

ENVIRO But it's clearly the case that promoting growth for growth's sake has resulted in serious damage to the environment and natural ecosystems. Plus, there are many negative local land use impacts. Quality of life for residents of the area is lower.

ECON Economic growth makes available the range of goods and services that we all enjoy. Protecting the environment is often an expensive proposition. If the economy isn't healthy, there will be no money to effect necessary cleanup, and the environment will suffer. A healthy environment requires a healthy economy.

ENVIRO It's not just about cleanup—it's broader than that. It is about protecting natural systems from destruction in the first place. One thing we need to do is protect the environment from reckless economic exploitation with sensible regulations.

ECON Unnecessary environmental regulation has cost consumers and the economy a lot of money and also jobs. Even people who complain about pollution are being disingenuous. If pressed, they wouldn't want to give up their "good life."

ENVIRO Corporations and the aggressively "pro-business" types think that a person's entire identity is as a consumer. People are interested in a lot more than just consuming as many goods and services as possible. Relationships, family and a sense of community are probably more important. Rampant growth in an area detracts from this.

ECON But the "anti-business" attitude of many in the community drives us nuts, and it's neither fair nor accurate. Most of the people complaining are economically comfortable, and can afford to be critical, because their basic needs are met. We need to provide jobs so that those less fortunate can begin to enjoy the "good life" also. It's all about fighting poverty and inequality.

ENVIRO But where will it stop? No matter how many businesses you attract and jobs you create, it never is enough—we still have poverty. Business people are always promoting more growth—which inevitably means more environmental problems and community unrest. And inequality just seems to get worse. Poor people are hurt more by environmental deterioration than are the rich. Environment is a huge inequality issue.

ECON We all buy and enjoy many products not produced in our own area. We still need to keep growing and attract corporations to locate in our community. This results in the export-based products that produce family-wage jobs and bring dollars back into the local economy. We're not self-sufficient—we have to engage in healthy trade to meet all our needs.

ENVIRO Corporations cause most of our problems. They bill themselves as providing all our jobs plus all the goods that we love, but they often cause a loss of jobs from local businesses while foisting on us a bunch of products that are often shoddy and that we don't need—and which are environmentally destructive to produce. They're still too dominant. Self-sufficiency isn't the issue—it's more about sustainability.

Well, you get the idea... The exchange could go on, and you could probably meaningfully participate. Given the premises of this book, you have probably guessed which one we would favor. But we don't declare a winner—because it's a no-win debate. Both are operating with a dominant premise that virtually precludes there being a winner—or even solving the problem.

That premise is that the modern corporation is the central economic institution in our current system. As long as we rely on major corporations for our employment base and for the goods and services we depend on, this argument will be unending, and irreconcilable. The globalist mindset will frame the debate. But we do not have the luxury of waiting. The physical environment is threatening to force us to declare a winner—or even to redefine the contest—and background information pertaining to that point is the topic of Part Two. Before proceeding, however, some concluding thoughts along broader cultural lines may yield some useful perspective.

A FINAL PUCKISH HISTORICAL/PHILOSOPHICAL NOTE ON GROWTH

The growth ethic that has correctly been associated with the Industrial Revolution and the advent of the fossil fuel era has philosophical roots in the Enlightenment Idea of Progress, which holds that humankind is on an endless journey of improvement and perfection. The economic history of the United States suggests that growth has come to symbolize an evolutionary real-world practical side of the Idea of Progress.

To move beyond the purely philosophical notion, focus on the historic phenomenon of the American Experience. Specifically, the 19th century in the U.S. saw the acceleration of the westward movement, confronting of the ever-present frontier, the filling-out of an ostensible "empty" continent (if one ignores the laments of indigenous peoples...) and the notion of Manifest Destiny. This "cowboy economy" experience helped form much of the attitude base that defines our current culture, and that gave rise to many of the nostalgic, romantic and only partially correct elements of the American psyche that remain with us today.

We prize so-called "Yankee ingenuity," which leads directly to a strong faith in the ability of technological progress to surmount any difficulty. The notion of American exceptionalism, including a fuzzy image of a cultural melting pot embodying a land of opportunity for all, evolved from these earlier experiences. As the 20th century proceeded, the image of having bailed the free world out of two world wars injected, for better or worse, an additional element of military supremacy into an evolving self-image as the world's policeman and "protector of freedom."

The 19th century, however, produced another important stream of thought that can serve to support thoughtful alternative perspectives on the growth ethic. Charles Darwin published his paradigm-shifting *Origin of Species*, which permanently injected the notions of evolution and natural selection into the public consciousness. Clearly, we still live with pitched cultural debates that stem from competing world views based in religious versus scientific points of view.

One of the first outcomes of Darwin's (r)evolutionary(?) work was the emergence of Social Darwinism, which broadly held that the notion of survival of the fittest should apply to socio-cultural and institutional issues as well as to the strictly biological evolution of particular species.

Andrew Carnegie's famous **Gospel of Wealth** argued, among other things, that becoming rich was the best evidence of real dominance, thus injecting the notion that the wealthy should be deemed the most "successful," and were thus the organisms that deserved to be the dominant rulers. Over the years, Social Darwinism has been dissected and roundly criticized by social scientists and related intelligentsia; but it would be hard to deny that our current culture which idolizes the rich and famous and bestows obvious political power to the wealthy elite, doesn't strongly, if subconsciously, identify the economic elite with survival of the fittest.

How does this all play into the growth ethic? Return for a moment to the 19th century. A dominant theme in Darwin's theory was the ability to evolve by adapting to changing conditions. The traits that allowed species to adapt and flourish would turn out to be those that were uniquely fit to physical conditions of the time. As mentioned, the 19th century involved the notion of an "empty" planet—especially the North American continent. Abundant physical natural resources were there for the taking—waiting to be exploited.

Under such conditions—and remaining squarely within a Darwinian framework—a premium is put on traits that lead to the rapid exploitation of those resources and the ability to successfully compete for their mastery and control. Labor was the scarce resource, and technological advance our willing handmaiden. (Recall the "Robber Baron" era with steel, rails, oil...) Hence, the growth ethic emerged as the dominant paradigm and competitiveness the preeminent trait in deciding the way it is and the way it ought to be. Growth dominates sustainability or steady-state. Economic growth *trumps* (oops, sorry...) environmental preservation. Competition wins out over cooperation.

Today, thoughtful introspection, as Darwin would probably remind us, clearly reveals that these conditions have fundamentally changed. Despite our incessant yearning for "new frontiers," it is a much more full world. Resources are depleting. The environment is fighting back. Frontiers are hard to come by, and fueled by stretches of imagination longing for an earlier time, give rise to such harebrained notions as populating Mars as the answer to our "intractable" problems here on our own planet.

In a full world, the dominant traits should cease to be those that facilitate quick exploitation of low-hanging fruit and profligate use of abundantly available energy in securing economic control. Rather, the premium will be on organisms and institutions that use energy and resources sparingly in thoughtful congruence with others. Cooperation will trump competition. Steady state developmental concepts should ideally prevail over those promoting rapid growth.

To invoke a biological analogy, slow-growing and moisture-conserving grasses will gradually supplant rapidly growing and energy intensive weeds. Conserving resources and energy will become more important than conserving labor. After all, the 19th century conditions have reversed: Labor (people) is superabundant, and physical resources, including climate and a clean environment, are scarce. Darwin would approve...

Invoking this hopeful mindset and moving to a more peaceful and harmonious world will nonetheless be a heavy and contentious lift for our current corporate-dominated consumer culture. At stake is nothing less than a struggle for dominance between two competing and starkly different world views. Easing and facilitating this nonetheless unavoidable transition can be termed our main purpose for this book.

The above is a premature statement of purpose and hoped-for objectives for our society, let alone our economy. Properly, these statements perhaps belong in our conclusions. But, heck, this is not a novel, and partially giving away the ending isn't a real problem. But we still haven't told you how we think you can get there—so some suspense remains. For now, it's time to move to Part Two and check the physical health of the planet that we must rely on to transport us to some form of sustainable Nirvana.

PART TWO:

THE ECOLOGICAL CRISIS

FOREWORD TO PART TWO

Connecting the Crises of Economy and Ecology

Part One has discussed the malaise we perceive in the man-made world: the arena of human artifacts and institutions, if you will. Part Two temporarily sets aside concerns about rampant inequality, soaring public and private debt, the global corporate economy and the like, and turns to the natural world. Our subject, therefore, becomes the ecological crisis. It should be an obvious principle that the two are inextricably related, but a graphic way to describe the motivation for this book is that our culture has apparently forgotten this. The current de facto approach of treating ecology and economics separately, or even worse as adversaries, will unavoidably lead to tragic results in both the human and natural spheres.

Chapter 9 leads off by establishing our core environmental philosophy. These are the guiding tenets which must, in our opinion, direct any successful ecological reforms. Sticking to these principles will not be easy for any leaders/activists attempting to reverse the slide to ecological catastrophe, since they are clearly radical by present standards.

Chapter 10 turns to the central issue of energy. In a real sense, the energy resource is the key to understanding the link between the human and natural spheres, including both the triumphs and the tragedies accompanying the evolution of the Idea of Progress. Exploitation of "millions of years of stored sunlight" has brought us many cherished advances, but has also brought us to the brink of ecological collapse. At its core, Chapter 10 sets the stage for identifying a path that transitions modern societies to all-renewable, non-carbon energy systems that will give us maximum benefit of inventive technology without the sledgehammer effects of the present fossil fuel economy.

Chapter 11 directly addresses the hot-button topic of today's ecological debate: climate change. Climate change has commanded the attention of global leaders and the public of most countries—the poster boy of global ecological emergency. Unsurprisingly, it arouses the most contentious and bitter disagreements and strong resistance from the corporatist interests in power. As of late 2018, new authoritative reports indicate that global societies now may have no more than a dozen years to significantly reduce carbon emissions primarily responsible for the disruptions we all perceive. Contrary to those currently in power, we regard combating climate change as top priority for both America and the rest of the world. It is the "hair-on-fire" global crisis that will no longer wait.

Though much of Part Two suggests current policy failings, and how better ecological policy could be forged, Chapter 12 is the only place in Part Two deliberately concentrating on *policy*. Consistent with the theme of Localism, most recommended actions (i.e., "policies") are reserved for Part Three, since stimulating people to action in their own community is our overriding purpose. However, two centuries of public policy fixation on growth and progress has kicked the problem upstairs. Environmental policy, notwithstanding many admirable local climate change efforts around the country, (despite refusal of federal officials to address it) is by definition a national and international problem. Thus, we address it as a necessary background parameter to the activist local measures suggested in Part Three.

Part Two concludes with Chapter 13 and a return visit to the pivotal subject of growth. The growth critique ending Part One stressed its role as a foundational need of the current corporatist economic institutions. Economic growth, apart from the little understood irrational structure of economic theory, is necessary to allow monopoly capitalism to both maintain control and to continue increasing its already enormous wealth. The topic here is growth and the ecological imperative. The environment, the resource base and the energy constraints simply will not allow the economic growth imperative to persist without tragically unacceptable impacts on the planet and its human occupants.

Therein lies the main lesson of Part Two. Unless we effectively reconcile the pressing imperative for economic and ecological coexistence, both in theory and practice, our attempts to push our planetary home beyond its obvious limits can only result in disaster for all.

CHAPTER 9

Core Ecological Philosophy

We began Chapter 1 by asserting that we are in an economic crisis. Though many will still refute that, citing high Dow averages, climbing GDP, increasing real estate values and other measurements as their evidence of prosperity, our comment stands. Evaluated in the spirit in which humane criteria are stated—that is, a stable, sustaining system that satisfies the essential material needs of the most people—the American economy is indeed in a state of worsening crisis. The evidence we have laid out in Part One, which includes rampant inequality, the elimination of good jobs, the destruction of indigenous societies worldwide and autonomous communities at home, and the diversion of our workforce into risky financial speculation at the expense of real broad-based economic production, should be clear. Yet, the overseers of this economy, including their mass media apologists, possess an almost bottomless capacity for public propagandizing as well as self-delusion. Therefore, the economic debate continues: are America's best days still ahead of us?...Or, are we teetering on the edge of the economic cliff?

ECOLOGY: IT'S HARDER TO FOOL MOTHER NATURE THAN MOST ECONOMISTS

As we turn to ecological questions in Part Two, the debate over what confronts us in the future clarifies... but not by much. Scientists observing a wide variety of climate-related crises have steadily reinforced their case for several decades. Unlike much economic theory and analysis, the ecological/environmental case is based on hard scientific evidence, verified by repeated measurement. There is no longer any doubt: Living species are disappearing; glaciers melting; fresh water supplies no longer adequately supply human societies; the oceans are acidifying and heating; and good soils for raising food are being stripped away. The 7.5 billion humans now occupying earth, most crowded into ever-larger cities, are increasingly subject to unhealthy air and dangerous synthetic substances. Valuable industrial resources such as metals, wood, and minerals are depleting; rich energy supplies are also rapidly depleting. This necessarily jeopardizes all economic activity, based as it must be on energy. And, most recently, the climate is dangerously warming from human causes, casting a giant shadow over not just all human economies but all life on earth. All of these ominous facts and warnings signify the careless way human society has allowed itself to overshoot its environment.

Further, because most of them are relatively quantifiable, we have good cause to believe these human ecological missteps will contribute to a gigantic socio-ecological collapse—and well before the end of this century. However, if you thought this powerful evidence has put an end to all reasonable debate over ecological matters, you would of course be fantasizing. Mother Nature and the physical planet may indeed dance to a different sort of hard, science-based drummer, but for American leaders and the public alike, the question of ecological crisis is hardly settled. The defenders of the ecological status quo sow enough seeds of doubt to paralyze national action.

AS THE PROBLEMS GROW THE TIME LEFT TO DEAL WITH THEM SHRINKS

Each new ecological emergency complements each data-based update to clearly indicate that the problems grow more formidable and the time left to mitigate them shrinks. International Panel on Climate Change (IPCC) regular reports are a case in point. With each review of the data—even including technological improvement on how it's gathered and analyzed—the situation appears worse than projected in the prior report. Glaciers and ice fields are melting faster than anticipated. Seas are rising faster than experts thought. Methane is leaking from melting permafrost at higher rates. The oceans are acidifying more than previously predicted. The flotillas of plastic junk floating in the oceans are reaching continental scale. More species of plants and animals are dying and at faster rates. We now appear to be reaching tipping points which even previous cutting-edge research barely recognized. These tipping points could send climate change into an irreversible spiral guaranteeing atmospheric temperature rises of several degrees Celsius.

With this "one-way street" of climate change analysis—always worse, never better—it would be quite surprising if informed activists were not feeling a heightened sense of urgency, even bordering on alarm and panic. That is indeed occurring, with more and more of the climate scientific community taking the position that some combination of ecological, economic and social crises is now unavoidable.

With each new crisis, as the inevitable drift into the believer's camp occurs, it would be surprising if this increasing concern (or panic) did not lead to the proposal of some hastily-conceived solutions where the cure may be worse than the disease. We are convinced this too is happening, especially as mainstream economic actors begin to get the picture. A potential problem is that climate mitigation policies coming from currently powerful interests can be predicted to hold a goal of preserving the status quo at least as strongly as they purport to deal effectively with the real issues.

To be sure, it's crucial that America shake off its lethargy and indecision and collectively get serious about climate and other environmental threats. But inadequately or inappropriately committing money, human skills, material resources and precious time to poorly conceived proposals would be a huge mistake, regardless of how attractive they may seem and how fervently they are being peddled by corporatist interests. The imminence and the scale of our environmental problems has robbed us of the luxury of missteps: we've got to get it right the first time.

GETTING THE ECOLOGICAL PHILOSOPHY RIGHT

Therefore, we think it is vital to lay down a sound philosophical foundation before plunging into more specific ecological/environmental policies, programs and funded projects. What follows is our version of the appropriate elements of that philosophical base. As with our core economic philosophy laid down in Chapter 1, these few ecological philosophical principles represent a radical but necessary "re-do." How we view man's relationship to the physical environment in which we live will govern whether we succeed or fail in the critical transformational years ahead.

PRINCIPLE 1: KEEP IT AS NATURAL AS POSSIBLE

A necessary first realization is that we created the current ecological/environmental mess by ignoring the natural and emphasizing the manmade. The biggest messes we must clean up are those that most blatantly represent man's uncontrolled and ill-conceived anthropogenic assaults on nature.

So, while manmade ideas and technologies are certainly going to be necessary, we must keep in mind that, on ecological matters, nature remains in charge. Attempting to impose inappropriate technological fixes to problems like climate warming, fossil fuel depletion, water pollution, and ocean acidification comes with multiple built-in hazards. Without intelligent planning, we stand to make problems stemming from resource depletion—overshooting our carrying capacity, so to speak—even worse.

All human industrial/technological activity taps physical resources: energy to drive it, materials to process with that energy, and waste that is created. Importantly, this is true for cleanup technology itself as well as the technology that caused the problem. Correct decisions, as the following chapter will indicate, ideally lie in the domain of net energy analysis.

Nature has enormous capacity to recover and rebalance on her own—if we give her a chance. Pre-industrial man recognized this automatic, circular pattern of nature, and patterned his own society and behavior after the natural model. Obviously, he had no alternative. Unfortunately, the mastery of rich—but non-renewable—resources has lobotomized industrial man into believing his inventive but artificial contrivances are a superior substitute for the slower ways of nature. Success in the precarious times ahead will in large part be based on how well human beings can dial back their impulsive "control freak" drives and simply allow nature to once again take the lead.

PRINCIPLE 2: MAN IS FIXATED ON *PROGRESS*; BUT THERE'S ALSO
THIS THING CALLED *ENTROPY*

Allied closely with his compulsion to pre-empt nature and seize control, Industrial Man has come to rely on the immutability of *progress.* The enormous material wealth extracted from the planet during the fossil-fuel-powered Industrial Age has convinced many of us that the future lies in only one direction: upward, bigger, better...more. History clearly refutes this with its many tales of societal collapse. (But as Simon and Garfunkel so famously sang, Americans don't know much about history.) Here again, nature works on a completely different set of rules than those adopted by industrial society—particularly in light of our recent splurges with large oligarchic corporations, advanced technology, globalization and ubiquitous use of artificial substances.

In the next chapter, we will discuss the concepts of entropy, net energy and the manner in which physically limited entities (e.g., the planet) tend toward regression and loss of physical capability. That, in a nutshell, is what is afflicting American society and much of the connected system we now call the global economy. Instead of irreversibly progressing through the refinement of our technology, our organizational skills and our underlying scientific understanding, closer introspection finds progress running in reverse. We try to crank up the human industrial paradigm, pushing for more growth, better and more complex organization, more efficient technology.

But our paradigm is flawed, and technical accomplishments we manage to achieve seem to come at a steep price, benefiting fewer people, accelerating inequality and causing more environmental damage and social discord. As serious economic thinkers such as Herman Daly have long predicted, careful examination of empirical evidence strongly suggests that the costs of much human activity have begun to exceed any possible benefits. But because old, ingrained habits die hard—and some powerful elites are still gathering substantial benefits—we plow forward expecting that, anytime now, progress will resume its merry chase.

PRINCIPLE 3: THE CORPORATE ECONOMY ONLY DOES SO WELL BECAUSE THE ENVIRONMENT IS DOING SO POORLY

The present state of the centralized corporatist economy only looks as good as it does because of two things: first, the powerful economic elite have learned to cook the numbers and only examine data favorable to their case (e.g., the Dow Jones Average); and second, they are very skilled at *externalization.* Relying on phony, overly-rosy metrics is a universal problem, practiced shamelessly by businesses, government agencies and resumé writers worldwide. Such measurements as Gross Domestic Product (GDP), consumer spending, corporate profits and stock market averages are examples of corporate-friendly statistics that make the present economy seem much more robust than it really is. Notably, the health of the physical environment gets no mention in these familiar reports (in fact, as the numbers for GDP, corporate profits, stock prices and consumer spending go up, a safe bet is that environmental well-being is dropping in inverse proportion).

Externalization is a word coined by economists to refer to how firms foist their internal costs of operation onto some (usually unsuspecting) outside entity: a competing firm, a person, a community, future society—or the physical environment. Some forms of externalization are covert and downright sneaky; but others, such as communities trying to lure industries by offering big tax breaks, cheap land or water, or other subsidies are right out in the open for everyone to see.

Author John Michael Greer has suggested a somewhat controversial theory. Greer opines that many of today's best known and most successful corporations owe their profitability to the fact they are among the biggest, most skillful "externalizers." Technology giants such as Apple and Amazon have found ways to dump their costs on local governments and the general public, as well as on the vulnerable environment. Operating on a highly mobile, global basis, with scattered, diversified operations that employ a high number of "farmed-out," contracted functions, these firms conceal the cost burdens they foist on outside entities. Results: stratospheric profits, very high ratios of revenue to workers employed, and a reputation among the fawning public as advanced, skillfully managed companies producing products of the highest quality that everyone needs....AND, more to our point here, corporations that *appear* to have minimized their environmental impacts and thus (falsely) represent responsible, green enterprise. In short, let's hear it for greenwashing...

Stripped of their ability to disguise and conceal their many costs, and forced to internalize them into the cost of their products, many glamorous high-tech firms would no longer be the subject of such public adulation. Like the big transnational banks that dominate global finance, they would be seen for what they are: organizations that have large impacts on the human societies and physical environment around them.

PRINCIPLE 4: WE MUST TURN FROM A PHILOSOPHY OF *CLEANUP* TO A PHILOSOPHY OF *PREVENTION.*

Because the environment has heretofore played second fiddle to economic policy as devised and operated by powerful interests, the overwhelming majority of activity has been devoted to cleanup: after-the-fact mopping up the messes. This fact is clearly consistent with the manner in which economics and the environment have been posed against one another—in strict competition. Cleanup costs are largely seen as an inefficient annoyance. AND...when an overt conflict occurs, the economy has always been given top priority. *"Would you like to have a clean, pristine environment? ...Or, would you rather have a decent job and something to eat?"*

It is slowly becoming apparent that no amount of such cleanup will be adequate to stop the climate from warming disastrously, far exceeding the 1.5-degree limits of safety. Neglect has allowed the numbers to grow too large and forbidding. Prevention of what is causing the climate/ecosystem/depletion crisis is the only possible method of getting the numbers down—that is, dealing with the problems by preventing them in the first place. Either the disease or the effective cure will necessarily severely challenge corporate capitalism in its present form. Therefore, the turn to Localism that we propose represents an attempt to get some forms of a resilient economy in place before the corporatism collapse occurs. In fact, perhaps the most important role for Localism is as a "Plan B"—i.e., to construct a means of supplying necessities that cannot be supplied by the current globalized oligarchic structures and institutions if ecological collapse either occurs or (ironically) is successfully avoided.

This offers further rationale for why we insist that the economic and ecological problems can be solved together...but not separately...!!

SUMMARY–TWO OLD ENEMIES SQUARE OFF AGAIN: GROWTH VS. LIMITS

The sketches of the above four ecological principles are primarily pessimistic descriptions of what's wrong with current American thinking and practices. Turning from a negative critique to a positive set of alternatives for better ecological philosophy and principles requires some serious thinking, imagination and hard work. But, making the switch is entirely possible for America... providing we keep some fundamental values and reality-based ideas about our major institutions firmly in mind. In proceeding, no better way comes to mind than reintroducing two concepts we mention repeatedly in these pages: **growth** and **limits.**

Growth, initially seen merely as a possible path to bigger markets and higher profits, has evolved into a vital necessity for latter-day Industrial Age corporations. Without continued growth, many modern productive and financial corporations would soon collapse. Further, the promise of growth allows an escape hatch to both public and private officials facing ever-mounting crises in economic, environmental and social realms. Rising inequality, the disappearance of good jobs, climate and resource emergencies, social discord of all sorts—all are problems soluble (say our hard-pressed leaders) by pressing down harder on the growth pedal.

But, switching from a modern human-centric view of world affairs to an ecological/environmental one, growth becomes the nemesis. Nature, after all, lives by the laws of *limits.* The earth is a closed container: a finite system whose boundaries cannot be expanded. When humans or any other creature try to exceed them, natural systems react—sooner or later—with severe consequences. Any sane, permanent ecological philosophy must be built on the ecological model of limits. While industrialized, highly-financialized economies can seem to rest on a philosophy where human imagination is the only constraint (and imagination can be manufactured like processed cheese!), sound ecological philosophy recognizes and accepts limits. Further, it goes to great lengths to determine what those limits are, making that knowledge available to all citizens so that their actions may be responsible and informed.

CAPTURED BY MAGICAL ECONOMICS.

Current American ecological philosophy and policy has become the poor stepchild of *economic* philosophy and policy. Thus, a rational framework striving to recognize limits and determine how to work within them has been smothered by an irrational, magical framework where human fantasies of omniscience and omnipotence run the show. Our system tragically throws economics and environment into an impending collision. Thus, the real problem is less about finding a sound footing for ecological policy than finding one for economics and sociopolitical affairs. The age of assumed perpetual growth is ending. The meaningful limits of the earth have been reached—in many ways exceeded— and now the only avenue out of the mess we've created is to adopt the central premise of sane ecology: *limits.* Once that conversion is accomplished, then the train of priorities needs to be uncoupled and reassembled. Ecological philosophy and policy in light of carefully acknowledged limits will be the engine at the front; economic policy needs to become the caboose dutifully following along behind.

THE ECOLOGICAL PHILOSOPHERS' JOB DESCRIPTION

Turning this solid, nature-based philosophy into equally solid environmental policy and practical plans for our already developed world will require both discipline and resistance. There will be many alluring signals and attractions put forth by powerful corporatist interests. These enticing "carrots" will be both technological and institutional:

TECHNOLOGICAL.

First, productive corporations, backed by big finance and current national government agencies, will propose a myriad of technological "fixes" to environmental problems. The number and scope of these miracle proposals will be staggering, ranging from mechanical removal of CO_2 from the atmosphere, to unearthing new fossil fuel resources, to de-acidifying the oceans, to manufacturing food instead of growing it in the soil,...and endless others. (*Whatever happened to cold fusion...?*) In all cases, the underlying promises will be the same: we can still cling to the mantras of growth and progress, consumerism can happily motor onward, supported by new, green technology. Thousands of good new skilled jobs will be created, restoring vitality to rust belt communities and blue-collar families left behind by the Knowledge Economy.

Let's be clear: Some of this might work, and might help—*on the **margin***. However, officials and citizen groups charged with making environmental decisions must steadfastly resist viewing these dangling carrots as complete solutions, firmly keeping in mind the principles of low-tech, simplicity and adherence to natural limits. Approaches like energy accounting through net energy/ EROEI analysis (described subsequently in Chapter 10) will help give planners the needed backbone. Insisting that all proposals include estimates of all possible lifetime costs—energy and material costs, not just monetary!—will also help separate the wheat from the chaff and avoid technological white elephants with no chance of eventual success. In short, although new appropriate technologies will have a role, the environmental planners of the future must avoid the fatal technophilia that turns Americans and others into suckers for anyone with a high-tech scheme.[1]

INSTITUTIONAL.

Not falling prey to hare-brained technological ideas must be matched with stiff resistance to organizations with little or no chance of succeeding. Presently, the powerful organizations which control the American economy and set the agenda for most social arrangements have distinct advantages on their side. They are clearly the most economically powerful entities and have most of the available global wealth. Through this great wealth, they have clearly secured control of the political and information arenas. This buys them an undeserved reputation of competence in the minds of the general public. And lastly, but very importantly, they control and wield the most powerful technologies shaping the economic

---

1   Part Three will cover many useful ideas on organizing local environment-protecting enterprises, such as expanded organic agriculture, composting, capturing methane from waste and scrubbing carbon from the atmosphere using natural, plant-based processes.

and social agendas. Therefore, acting as modern Trojans who must beware of Greeks bearing gifts will not be easy for our appointed ecological/environmental decision makers.

There will be some advantages enjoyed by these ecological defenders, however. Many of the modern-day corporatist Greeks bearing their technological, organizational and financial gifts will be facing economic and political challenges to their dominance.[2] These challenges will be imposed by conditions in the natural world, irrespective of any human-induced "movement" pressures. Nature itself will thus likely be a powerful ally of environmental activists. Add to all this the certainty of higher resource prices and slackening demand from a consuming public without a lot of ready cash (but increasingly ready anger!) and you have a recipe for almost unavoidable loss of corporatist control.

SUMMING UP AND LOOKING AHEAD

Resisting the technological and institutional pressures of corporatist offerings will be made easier if ecological planners understand fully the scope of our environmental dilemma and the inescapable conflict between it and our current oligarchic/corporatist system. Articulating this message is a major mission of this book. But the real opportunity for forming better ecological alternatives that capture both the health of the planet and the broad support of the public will emerge from vibrant, growing Localism movements, and the new smaller more nimble institutions, including businesses, that will see the light of day.

In case you haven't been paying close attention, our image of the ideal "ecological philosophers" whose jobs we describe are *local* **citizens**. It is unlikely in the current toxic national political environment that inspired Localism leadership will develop at the

---

2   Corporations are now frequently being sued by citizen groups and even other businesses for their ecologically damaging practices. The recent 2018 suit brought against fossil fuel industries by Oregon crab fisherman is one example.

top and trickle down to the local levels. As with needed reforms in, for instance, health care or education, promising initiatives (experimental at first) are far more likely to spring up from grass roots communities and regions then "organically" emerge as concrete examples of what can be achieved. Need we say more than "Localism and Federalism are opposites" to lay bare the self interest vectors at work here? Perhaps the best to be hoped for from both the large public and private institutions holding sway in Washington is simply not to get in the way of the expansion of Localism. Is that too much to ask...?

Offering a concrete path that can lead to a sustainable lifestyle that coexists and cooperates with our physical environment is the mandate. And this path requires both a conceptual and a practical element: People need to see things happening on the ground.

Part One of this book discussed the various dimensions of the economic problems that we face—that is, the **socially constructed** portion of our world—our artifacts and institutions. Part Two addresses issues related to energy and environment—i.e., the **natural physical** world. Finally, the concluding section will make suggestions for real world projects, policies and mechanisms that can materially move our communities and our nation toward a sane, secure and sustainable future. This must necessarily involve the melding of these two worlds into an ecologically resilient whole.

For now, let's turn to the subject of energy: the driving force that makes all economic and social human activity possible.

CHAPTER 10

Energy—The Defining Resource

Peak Oil, net energy and other unlearned systems-approach lessons from the "Limits Era"

The specter of energy shortages was the first thing that alerted mid-20th century industrial America to a possible coming age of ecological scarcity. Energy depletion, bringing much higher prices followed by physical shortages, was first forecast by noted geologist M. King Hubbert in the 1950s and 1960s. Hubbert's calculations that US petroleum production was peaking caught the attention of only a few technocrats, academics and political types. Typical responses from these select few energy insiders varied from totally ignoring Hubbert to ridiculing his methodology. Needless to say, the establishment was not yet ready to concede that, to borrow from the title of Richard Heinberg's book, the hydrocarbon "party was over." When the US did in fact hit peak domestic oil production in 1970, little changed; certainly King Hubbert did not receive a formal apology from the CEOs of the major US oil companies.

EXPANDING THE PEAK OIL DEBATE

Discussions of America running out of oil gathered steam during the "Limits to Growth" decade of the 1970s. The "Peak Oil" dialogue was widened in two ways. First, oil and other sources of concentrated energy made all other physical resources of the earth—metals, minerals, chemicals, wood, water, etc.—available to the economy. These things too were finite and depleting; so as the shrinking base of fossil fuels met an also shrinking supply of these other crucial materials, how was the growth-addicted society going to obtain the ever-rising supply of materials it needed at reasonable prices?

Secondly, the '70s saw an escalating discussion of "pollution" of the environment, as it was then called. Smog, poisoned rivers, disappearing forests, vanishing animal species and more joined the everyday vocabulary of the general public. Further, it was becoming increasingly apparent that a major culprit behind this pollution was the burning of fossil fuels. Suddenly energy was seen as a key resource we couldn't live without (as the Arab Oil Embargo and rapidly rising oil prices helped point out),...BUT, it was also being seen as a contaminate perhaps we couldn't live **with.** As informed newcomers to the public stage—ecologists, sustainable/no-growth economists, alternative lifestyle hippies, computer modelers and systems-thinkers, peak oil proponents, net energy gurus—debated these contentious issues during the turbulent '70s, the power centers of the establishment were struggling to find a way to put all these energy-based genies back into the bottle.

By the 1980s, they had figured out a way. It was the Reagan Counterrevolution, a comfortable reversion to the old Industrial Age of growth, continual technological progress, and high consumption powered by the ready availability of abundant, cheap, richly concentrated energy. Where possible energy depletion had worried systems thinkers of the fretful 1970s, it was waved off as a non-problem by the cornucopians of the 1980s.

THE DORITOS SOLUTION: WE'LL JUST MAKE MORE

The lid was effectively slammed shut on the energy depletion debate in the 1980s, when the aroused corporatist establishment of the Reagan years provided the convenient escape hatch from resource depletion. Large new oil finds such as the Alaska North Slope and the North Sea were brought on line. Political events cooperated in putting the OPEC Cartel and other hydrocarbon rivals like the Russians in their place, which drove down oil prices to under 10 dollars a barrel (a big factor in shattering the Soviet Union at the end of the decade). These developments, plus a general revival of chest-beating, can-do, "morning in America" growth enthusiasm, suppressed any latent concerns about energy depletion and the inevitable fate of a growth-addicted society trying to exist on a finite planet. In effect, depletion was written off as a phony scare. Not only was there probably plenty of oil left to be discovered, but, even if normal supplies ran short, we'd just make more. Alternative forms of hydrocarbons existed everywhere; and we surely would find technologies that would make their usage economically viable. Plus, there was always hydrogen, fusion, magnetic pulses from outer space and who knows what other forms of cheap, clean energy that technology would turn up.

Recoiling from the gloomy years of the "Limits Era" of the 1970s, the new attitude was definitely one of "What, me worry?" America was back on track, confident of its own capabilities again. Surely, finding something to pour into our SUV gas tanks was one of the least of our problems.

IT'S BAAAACK...THE SPECTER OF SCARCITY RETURNS

The restoration of confidence in America's future of abundance and energy-based economic growth thus has continued for the last three-plus decades. America, in this interregnum since the Limits Era of the 1970s ended, has resumed high rates of energy consumption and related impacts on the physical environment.[3] Despite the soothing assurances of the cornucopians that fossil fuel energy consumption—and thus American Industrial Age consumption patterns—can and will continue indefinitely, new data are once again causing growing concerns. In the 1970s, the

---

3   US Energy Information Agency (EIA) data show that total US energy consumption has risen approximately 27 percent from 1980 to 2015.

forecasts of the landmark book **Limits to Grown**[4] ended when a combination of increased energy and resource depletion, industrial growth, pollution, world population and falling food production resulting in socioeconomic collapse starting in the middle of the 21st century. As sobering as these 1970s predictions were, today's previews of coming attractions arguably are much worse.

CURRENT ENERGY REALITY: YOU THINK IT WAS BAD THEN.

Any attempt to describe energy reality fully for a system as complex as the American economy risks being incomplete. However, the following lists what we see as the most important current contributing ingredients of our present energy predicament. As you will see, many of these factors never make the front pages or evening broadcasts of the mainstream media.

- **Depletion.** Pure and simple, our rich domestic energy supplies available to 1970s US society have been drastically depleted. The "low-hanging fruit" principle has left us not just with a smaller pool of remaining fossil fuels, but reserves that are less accessible, harder to extract, harder to process and refine, and thus much more expensive to make available to the economy and social activities.

- **Net energy or Energy Returned on Energy Invested (EROEI) decline.** Proceeding from the hard-to-refute premise that energy production systems should minimally produce more energy than they consume, net energy/EROEI "ratios" have been falling for some years...precipitously falling in the last two decades. Unfortunately, they will not be turned around by technological breakthroughs—not even those in the category of renewable energy systems.

---

4   *Limits to Growth*, Donella H. Meadows, Dennis L. Meadows, Jorgen Randers, William W. Behrens III (Universe Books: 1972)

- **Economic globalization.** The geographic dispersal of more economic activity (globalization) has affected many sectors, including energy such as petroleum, coal, natural gas and industrial equipment supporting these energy industries. While domestic energy depletion has affected the United States and many other industrialized nations, forcing them to look to Middle East and other foreign supplies, to some extent globalizing energy flows has been a conscious choice. For example, countries such as the US which have deliberately moved production overseas for goods and services—also off-shoring domestic jobs in those industries—have also forced the globalization of energy that supports that production. Result: much greater transportation, transmission and communications energy costs for a much more globalized economic system.

- **The introduction of energy-intensive energy sources such as hydro-fracturing (fracking).** To a considerable degree, using fracking technology to extract formerly inaccessible pools of oil and gas from shale formations is directly attributable to depletion and the low-hanging fruit principle. But, like certain other "alternate" technologies, the choice is presented by those developing and implementing them as a positive one: industry has discovered an exciting new technology to extract vast new energy resources efficiently. The new method will ultimately lead to new economic growth, new jobs, and prosperity for all. Oh, and it will be cheap and environmentally harmless.

- **Climate change.** Unlike the public conversation during the 1970s, today the hot topic has become climate change. As we will emphasize in Chapter 11, injecting climate change into the public discussion changes everything...or at least should. Because the burning of fossil fuels is such a huge, central contributor to a hotter, unstable climate, today's energy problems are immensely more complicated than they were four decades ago. And, as we will see, the solutions to them in a more crowded, depleted world will be immensely more difficult to find.

And finally, an energy problem you almost never hear about from the mainstream media, business executives or political leaders:

- **Corporatist consolidation and control.** Certainly the big corporation with far-reaching tentacles into national and transnational economic matters was a familiar institution forty years ago. Nonetheless, the proactive expansion of corporations—both productive and financial—into modern forms of globalization has been staggering. Beyond the monopoly of economic control that such "compression" of markets by a few super-giant corporations and banks has caused, the depletion of rich fossil fuel, uranium and other energy sources already mentioned has had its impact. Inevitably, large governmental and private players in the international energy business swing a lot more weight than even the powerful interests of the 1970s: the OPEC Cartel, the ARAMCOs, The Exxon/Mobils. Plus, from the consumer side, new industrial power centers like China exert considerably more influence in international energy markets than four decades ago. They do so using the same techniques as the old power players: by consolidating and cooperating at the highest levels of industry, finance and government.

DIGGING DEEPER INTO THE ENERGY DILEMMA.

The bulk of the remainder of this chapter will be devoted to a fuller examination of three of the above energy problems: Net energy/EROEI; globalization and its effect on soaring energy infrastructure; and finally the real implications of using hydro-fracturing to extract so-called "tight" resources of oil and gas. Carefully separating reality and fantasy in these three critical arenas is absolutely fundamental to finding our way to better energy policy.

NET ENERGY/EROEI

During the Limits Era of the '70s, a tool for making energy decisions was developed and proposed. At the time it was called "net energy;" more recently, adherents usually refer to it as Energy Returned on Energy Invested—or, EROEI. EROEI offers an alternative to the traditional monetary method of evaluating the viability of energy systems. The net energy/EROEI concept is remarkably simple and irrefutable: no energy production system is useful to society that does not deliver a net return of usable energy in excess of the energy it consumes. Or, energy *out* must be more than energy *in*. Proponents of EROEI point to several ways EROEI is superior to just totaling up the exchanges of money to see if a system is profitable.

For one, tracing energy use throughout a system instead of monetary exchanges is less subject to the distortion and "fudging" that has crept into money-based evaluation. As an example, certain energy systems receive little or no public subsidy, dependent entirely on market forces to deliver useful energy to consumers at a profit to producers. However, other energy systems have received substantial, even enormous, benefits of public subsidies: research and development, favorable tax treatment, direct cash grants or cheap loans, protections against environmental disasters, and so forth.[5] This uneven pattern of public financial subsidies is

---

5   Two egregious examples of such lucrative government support are the nuclear power and corn-based ethanol industries. Without favorable government treatment which has pumped billions of dollars into each, it is beyond question that neither industry could have survived on its own. Not far behind, of course, are the petroleum industry, with its depletion allowances, and large-scale hydroelectric dams, most of which were constructed as public projects decades ago (but which have at least returned large sums to public treasuries from the sale of power to consumers, industries and smaller utilities).

justified as getting valuable energy systems and technology up and running; but whatever its benefits to the energy-consuming public, it often has made inefficient, costly and polluting systems look just the opposite, while damaging the perception of better systems not as fortunate when it comes to the public dole.

KEY TERMS

Venturing into the potentially confusing, non-standard area of net energy/EROEI is made easier by understanding some of the key jargon. To begin, EROEI is usually stated as a numeric *ratio*. For example, a petroleum production system delivering gasoline for powering automobiles might have an EROEI ratio of **50:1**. That means that 1 unit of energy must be invested in that system over its lifetime for it to deliver 50 units of energy in the form of gasoline for end use in vehicles. A crucial note of emphasis: *net energy/EROEI analysis demands a **systems-approach.*** Therefore, all energies consumed anywhere in our hypothetical gasoline production system—extraction or drilling of petroleum, pumping, piping or hauling, refinement, service stations or other means of final delivery, oil company advertising, cleanups of spillage, and so on—must be accounted for in calculating input energies accurately and fairly. Only if the total input energies are less than the energy in the produced gasoline can the system then be said to have a positive EROEI ratio.

The following four terms get to the critical questions of (1) where in energy production systems—often very complex and multi-faceted—energy is consumed or produced; and (2) in what form this energy is either consumed or produced.

WHERE THE SYSTEM PRODUCES AND CONSUMES ENERGY.

End-Point. Most energy production systems produce their energy output at an obvious, easily-recognizable point in the system—which we will call the **end-point.** For example, in our above example of a gasoline producing system, this might be the refined gasoline in the storage tanks of a large number of service stations, ready to be pumped into the tanks of customers' automobiles. For a hydroelectric dam, the end-point might be either the electricity measured at the output of the dam's turbine-driven generators; or better yet, the electricity measured at the meters entering the homes, office buildings or factories of the end users. End-point energy primarily is a useful measure of the energy *produced* by the system, while the following terms are more useful when considering *input* energy to operate the system.

Infrastructure. Complex energy producing systems consume much of their necessary input energies throughout their often complicated, interconnected infrastructure. Good examples of infrastructure input energy would be energy necessary to manufacture and deliver the steel in the pipes used in oil rigs, or the copper wire transmitting electricity from the power plant to homes. Because of the complexity and number of organizations, materials flows, subsystem producers and human labor involved in today's energy systems, it is easy to grasp how difficult the task of accurately calculating—or even estimating—net energy/EROEI is for researchers. Petroleum, gas and coal systems are complicated technologies, as are nuclear power plants and even newer renewable systems such as solar photovoltaic systems and wind turbines.

THE FORM OF THE ENERGY CONSUMED OR PRODUCED.

The form in which energy is either consumed or produced by energy production systems is also a crucial factor in determining the net output of a sophisticated system and its overall usefulness to society. Two additional terms are relevant here:

Direct. *Direct* simply refers to necessary system input energy being consumed directly: burned or otherwise used in a manner we routinely recognize as energy consumption. In other words, this might be the burning of diesel fuel to drive pumps that pump natural gas through a pipeline. It might be electricity used to light the powerhouse at a hydroelectric dam, or the fuel power-ing a locomotive hauling crude oil to a refinery. Almost all direct energy consumption comes in the form of burning hydrocarbons or electricity, a factor that somewhat simplifies accounting for direct system energy input.

Indirect, or embodied. By contrast, *indirect* or "embodied" energy consumption may come in a wide variety of forms through-out the system. Complex industrial systems need lots of steel, aluminum, copper, plastics, concrete, laser printer toner, etc. Much required input energy is embodied in these materials and the services that go into producing them. Also—easily overlooked—replacement parts, tools needed for maintenance and human energy in the form of brain and muscle power is needed for the energy system to function over a long lifetime.

"ANTI-PROGRESS:" THE STEADY RECENT DECLINE OF SYSTEM NET ENERGY

Over the forty-odd year history of net energy/EROEI analyses, it's fair to say progress has been slow. This is in part due to the difficulty of the task of tracing direct and embodied energy flows throughout industrial infrastructures that can be mind-numbing in their complexity. It is also due in large part to the resistance of energy industry managers as well as financial firms backing energy development—and even government technicians and regulating agencies.[6]

---

6   The dominant energy industries and related government agencies have, for over 40 years, resisted integrating EROEI/net energy techniques into their analyses. This objection ostensibly is because of the familiarity and proven nature of "money accounting" methods; but in part it can be attributed to the results EROEI analyses by early non-industry pioneers have revealed. Many mainstay energy systems of the current economy are mediocre net energy performers; many systems promoted by powerful establishment interests may indeed be net energy "losers" (e.g., nuclear power and biofuels). Moreover, analyses show the EROEI ratios of many if not most energy systems declining rapidly in recent years—and projected to drop even more rapidly in the immediate years ahead.

The corporatist interests of the present fossil fuel-based energy industry indeed have much to fear if EROEI ratios ever are adopted as a primary way of making energy policy. Looking at some relatively recent EROEI studies reveals why.

The following two charts are taken from data presented in the Post Carbon Institute report, *"Searching for a Miracle: Net Energy Limits and the Fate of Industrial Society"* (a joint project of PCI and the International Forum on Globalization, September, 2009).

Energy mechanism	EROEI
Hydro	11:1 to 267:1
Coal	50:1
Oil (Ghawar supergiant field)	100:1
Oil (global average)	19:1
Natural gas	10:1
Wind	18:1
Wave	15:1
Solar Photovoltaic	3.75:1 to 10:1
Geothermal	2:1 to 13:1
Tidal	~ 6:1
Tar sands	5.2:1 to 5.8:1
Oil shale	1.5:1 to 4:1
Nuclear	1.1:1 to 15:1
Biodiesel	1.9:1 to 9:1
Solar thermal	1.6:1
Ethanol	0.5:1 to 8:1

FIGURE 1: EROEI RATIOS FOR 15 ENERGY SYSTEMS

Figure 1 shows the approximate EROEI ratios of fifteen energy delivery systems. Some deliver end-point energy as liquids and gases, some as electricity. There is a combination of older "natural" or traditional sources or systems, such as coal, oil and natural gas, newer less traditional hydrocarbons such as tar sands, biodiesel and ethanol, and renewable energy forms such as wind and solar photovoltaic (PV).[7]

It's plausible to look at Figure 1 and conclude that things don't appear too bad. Except for the lower ethanol ratio of .5:1, all of the system ratios shown are at least positive; we're at least getting more energy out than we're putting in. But the static data of Figure 1 do not show important developments of just the last few years. "Tight" oil and gas from fracked wells are now dominating new US production. (In fact, without shale-bound production in the US and tar sands output in Canada, new production throughout the world has declined since natural petroleum peaked in 2005.). As older worldwide fields decline and are replaced[8] by tight oil and gas from fracking or deep offshore drilling, two things are happening. One: the high energy and financial costs of tight oil and gas drive the overall EROEI ratios of these energy systems down rapidly—which, in turn, drives the EROEI of all other energy systems down because of the key roles oil and gas play in all industrial infrastructures. Two: attempts to sustain production in these older, declining fields result in higher costs and lower EROEI ratios from this older production too. Steam and water injection, drilling additional wells, and other advanced recovery techniques cost money—and added energy. The "low hanging fruit" principle means that, quite unsurprisingly, the energy industry drilled and

7   At the time "Searching for a Miracle" was written (2009), based as it was on somewhat earlier data, the overall ratios depicted in Figure 1 do not heavily represent the introduction of "tight" oil and gas fracked from shale deposits. Newer studies incorporating these less energy-efficient sources tend to show lower EROEI ratios for oil and gas, especially if they concentrate on North American production, which also is now incorporating greater amounts of Canadian tar sands-derived oil, also a very low net energy producer. Both fracked oil and gas are currently estimated to have EROEI ratios of approximately **5:1**.

8   Despite the hype, fracked gas and oil are insufficient to replace the decline in "naturally-drilled" gas and oil. Presently, even with depressed worldwide demand for energy due to the stagnant economy, the decline of older gas and oil fields is 2 to 3 times the volumes being added by new production—including that from fracked wells.

dug the richest, most concentrated, most accessible, cheapest to extract resources first. Now, as those rich energies are depleted, it's also not rocket science to expect that finding new resources and wringing the last few barrels, therms, lumps of coal or car-loads of fissionable uranium from old sites will only come at high energy and monetary costs.

Our next chart, Figure 2, is also from *"Searching for a Miracle."* It depicts the change in critical petroleum EROEI over the last 80 years. Between approximately 1930 and 1970, depletion of old, rich reservoirs and the need to replace them with energetically more expensive new discoveries dropped domestic oil EROEI ratios from about 100:1 to around 30:1. During the subsequent 35 years—up to about 2005—the same effects of depletion, replace-ment, and increased recovery efforts in existing fields drove oil EROEI down to about 15:1. (By 2005, the EROEI ratio impact of fracked oil was barely being felt. Over the last decade, however, it has become a major influence driving this ratio down even further and faster. Some analysts estimate that domestic US oil's overall EROEI ratio, combining traditionally-drilled and fracked oil, is now no more than 10:1.)

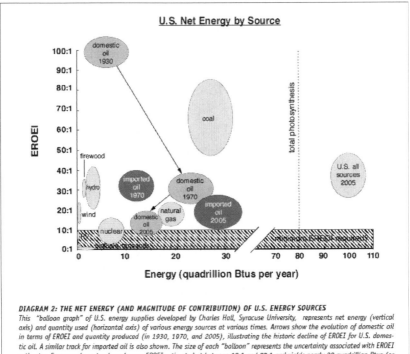

DIAGRAM 2: THE NET ENERGY (AND MAGNITUDE OF CONTRIBUTION) OF U.S. ENERGY SOURCES
This "balloon graph" of U.S. energy supplies developed by Charles Hall, Syracuse University, represents net energy (vertical axis) and quantity used (horizontal axis) of various energy sources at various times. Arrows show the evolution of domestic oil in terms of EROEI and quantity produced (in 1930, 1970, and 2005), illustrating the historic decline of EROEI for U.S. domestic oil. A similar track for imported oil is also shown. The size of each "balloon" represents the uncertainty associated with EROEI estimates. For example, natural gas has an EROEI estimated at between 10:1 and 20:1 and yields nearly 20 quadrillion Btus (or 20 exajoules). "Total photosynthesis" refers to the total amount of solar energy captured annually by all the green plants in the U.S. including forests, food crops, lawns, etc. (note that the U.S. consumed significantly more than this amount in 2005). The total amount of energy consumed in the U.S. in 2005 was about 100 quadrillion Btus, or 100 exajoules; the average EROEI for all energy provided was between 25:1 and 45:1 (with allowance for uncertainty). The shaded area at the bottom of the graph represents the estimated minimum EROEI required to sustain modern industrial society: Charles Hall suggests 5:1 as a minimum, though the figure may well be in the range of 10:1.[14]

FIGURE 2: EROEI/NET ENERGY BY SOURCE AND OVERALL US CONTRIBUTION

Figure 2 also shows a 40-year change in imported oil's role in the US economy. Over that time imported oil has contributed between two and three times as much total energy to the US economy; but, like domestic oil, its EROEI has dropped, declining to its present calculated level of approximately 19:1.

This decline in EROEI ratio in imported oil is not nearly so severe as that of domestic oil, however. In 1930, some three-quarters of a century ago, natural petroleum was in its net energy heyday, producing about 100 units of available output energy for every unit input. (Some researchers even estimate that in the early

20th century of giant Texas and Oklahoma oil fields, oil EROEI may have reached 200:1.) The Figure 2 bubble for domestic oil in 2005 shows that, while overall energy output was almost tripled in the 75 years, domestic oil's EROEI had plummeted to somewhere around **15:1.** A bit of straightforward math reveals this sobering result: to produce the same amount of usable oil energy that the oil system of 1930 was capable of supplying, the domestic oil system of 2005 required burning *between **6 and 7 times** the total gross input energy.*

Falling EROEI ratios. Thus the big story for the present US energy industries should be the ***rapidly falling net energy or EROEI ratios***. Despite the accelerating, precipitous fall of EROEI ratios across all energy production, and the somber news that holds for the US and all other economies, you only find the occasional net energy/EROEI story in specialized media at the fringes of public debate. The big drops that spell special trouble for industrial life are coming in oil and gas, where the twin effects of rapid "orthodox" resource depletion and the switch to fracking and "unorthodox" hydrocarbons such as tar sands and biofuels will continue to pull down oil and gas EROEI ratios at an increasing pace. Oil and gas, of course, are the co-anchors of modern economies and lifestyles.[9] (Coal EROEI, while also dropping due to depletion of the richest deposits and more energetically-expensive infrastructure, remains higher than oil and gas at approximately 50:1.)

Despite the chest-beating ballyhoo of corporate PR, researchers and government officials—which ***is*** given extensive coverage in the friendly media—the occasional technological breakthrough has no chance of halting this downward net energy spiral. The development of a more efficient generator turbine blade, or a

9   Coal, in most industrialized nations with the exceptions of China and India, has been relegated primarily to the generation of electricity. In the US, the "big three" fossil fuels of petroleum, gas and coal accounted for 68 percent of all electrical generation in the US in 2012. The largest segment of this was coal: 37 percent (or, over 54 percent of the fossil fuel-generated contribution). By 2016, preliminary data indicate gas has supplanted coal as the top fossil fuel-fired method of generating electricity.

marginally better pump for gas pipelines, or a better way of mapping possible oil deposits from satellites are pitifully ineffective against the steady depletion of remaining rich supplies of orthodox fossil fuels and their temporary replacement by unorthodox, "tight" substitutes which come at much higher energy, monetary and environmental costs. One final note here: many EROEI experts such as Charles Hall of Syracuse estimate that within a decade oil and gas EROEI ratios will fall to **1:1**. In blunt terms, we will be pumping one unit of assorted energy down the well or into the pit to extract one unit for our use. Essentially, the entire economy will be devoted to the energy industry.

Finally, fracked oil and gas, now viewed as the saviors of the American economy that will turn us into the energy suppliers to the world again, will be non-factors within that same single decade. The remaining supplies of shale-bound oil and gas will not be extractable at a cost our economy can afford.

INFRASTRUCTURE

Another big story of present-day US energy, one revealed by the lessons of net energy/EROEI, is *infrastructure.* The systems-approach of net energy analysis clearly exposes how rising overall infrastructure costs totally overshadow any technological advances or other isolated improvements made at scattered "end-points" in the energy systems. Once again, because this is bad news corporatist interests do not want us to hear, almost nothing is heard from the mainstream media controlling the public dialogue. Presently, industrial infrastructure is supposed to be a positive part of the storyline of progress: as technology progresses, as materials and techniques get more advanced, as these developments are carefully rationalized and dispersed around the globe by efficient corporations, productivity will rise. Growth will occur. Systems will get more efficient. Energy use will drop, and with it pollution and the threat of climate change. Instead, as infrastructure has risen sharply over the last century, so has energy use, depletion and the damage to ecosystems.

During the early 20th century peak of energy efficiency, infra-structure was all but invisible. In the heyday of American fossil fuels, with 100:1 or even 200:1 oil EROEI ratios, we rarely gave a thought to the energy input demands of relatively modest infrastructure. All the attention was on gigantic Spindletop-like discoveries, where you could almost poke a sharpened stick in the ground and get a gusher. No one thought or talked about terms like "embodied" energy, or "infrastructure."

One reason infrastructure has shouldered its way into the conversation is obvious: it has increased enormously over the last century. One reason for that increase is also obvious: the low-hanging fruit has been pretty much picked over, necessitat-ing much greater energy and dollar investments in discovering, extracting, transporting, refining and delivering all fossil fuels. Environmental protections and restoration, though hardly ade-quate in the minds of many, are also now a much larger infrastruc-ture cost charged against the gross energy output of all systems. New energy sources unknown in the early 1900s—nuclear power, alternative hydrocarbons like tar sands and biofuels, renewable systems such as solar PV and wind—have come along, requiring large energy investments in supporting infrastructure.

GLOBALIZATION

The case of the second big energy story of recent years also involves an information gap. This gap causes both officials and the public at large routinely to overlook an important reason for soaring infra-structure: the *globalization* of the modern economy. Institutionally and structurally, energy like almost all other aspects of economic life has been geographically expanded, organizationally integrated, and infused with high-tech in ways which, whether by design or not, have caused mushrooming infrastructure costs. Partially, it was inevitable and unavoidable that energy had to become a more global industry, if it were to continue to supply soaring industrial society demands. As local fossil fuel reserves were being depleted, only gigantic new oilfields like Ghawar in Saudi Arabia could supply the voracious new demands of a globally dispersed economy. Similar trends in gas and coal were happening, leaving only a few places in the world where abundant fossil fuel reserves remained. One of the axioms of the modern global economy is that consumption centers need not be anywhere near production centers; and production centers (think China and Japan) need not be co-located with the necessary energy to fuel them. Hence energy, like the physical raw goods and final products it makes possible, must be constantly on the move. Thus energy transportation and transmission are two areas where infrastructure is extracting much higher energy and monetary costs—but only two.

The "devil made me do it" defense. Energy depletion and the uneven global distribution of remaining reserves are big causes of costlier energy infrastructure and transport, to be sure. But controlling corporatist interests would have you believe that, therefore, globalization of energy is unavoidable and beyond human control. In truth, like globalization in other areas such as manufacturing, energy globalization has largely been a conscious decision by powerful interests who not only profit from it but are powerful enough to pull it off. In energy, just as in other economic sectors, the vast cost differentials available across the globe have been too enticing for globalization proponents to resist. The "devil made me do it" defense, whereby globalization is some sort of exogenous cosmic force that cannot be reversed, is a simple convenience whereby transnational energy interests, like other globalizers, can dodge some of the blame.

SEARCHING FOR A COHERENT ENERGY POLICY

Energy would seem to be the classic case of a highly technical subject where it's desirable to have producing industries and regulating officials possessing the highest technical skills. Yet, in the recent past, technical expertise clearly has proven to be inadequate in making American energy policy that effectively confronts the rapidly mounting energy problems we and the rest of the world face. Where technical data and evidence-based decision making have clashed with entrenched institutional control and material self interest, the "best science" hopeful Americans always expect to win the day gets consistently tossed under the bus. Like the Harlem Globetrotters versus the hapless Washington Generals, the established corporatist energy interests of the Big Three fossil fuels, the electric power industry and (perhaps most concerning) even the slowly emerging renewable energy sector win hands down.

BIPARTISAN CONSENSUS: TRASHING THE SCIENTIFIC METHOD

Little noticed is the manner in which this confrontation is not even a partisan one typical of today's bitter American political gridlock. These days most Democratic leaders and other liberal politicians supposedly believe in fossil fuel depletion, the urgency of converting to renewable energy, and the dangers of man-caused environmental damage, including climate change. Likewise, many pay homage to the scientific method, research, and decision making based on the facts it produces. Further, liberal decision makers predictably support systems-based thinking and decisions which necessarily integrate all related subjects that will affect, and be affected by, the outcome.

But in the realm of energy, the scientific method has routinely received little or no respect. Conservatives who spurn concepts like peak oil, resource depletion and climate change predictably continue to ignore the grim numbers of energy. But quite unexpectedly, liberal policy makers who regularly trash conservative deniers for their disregard of science, also trash the scientific method. Both parties support remarkably similar status quo energy policies those ugly numbers discredit, making the goal of "best science" a joke. Whether it's the numbers of peak oil, plummeting EROEI ratios, the real reserves and brief lifetime of gas and oil from fracking, the potential for renewables to take over the load now carried by fossil fuels, or any of dozens of other topics: if reality threatens the continuance of the status quo... well, so much for the scientific method, holistic thinking or saving the planet. "All of the above," "drill, baby, drill" energy policies have become something on which bitterly divided Republican and Democratic leaders can at least agree.

STEP ONE: UNITING THE FRACTURED FIEFDOMS OF ENERGY

To adopt more holistic, systems-based approaches to energy analyses and decision making we would first have to change the way the sweeping energy sector is run. This would amount to a unification of the fractured, isolated carrels of the current industry. Because of the historical path by which they developed, the separate energy sectors—coal, petroleum, gas, nuclear power, electrical utilities, biofuels, renewables, etc.—are owned, run and regulated by separate businesses and regulatory institutions. They are run as separate, isolated fiefdoms, making it much harder for any publicly-minded regulators to control the actions of the powerful, for-profit businesses. Perhaps more important, it makes it extremely difficult to implement systems-approach analyses such as net energy/EROEI, or consistent ways of assessing environmental impacts. Finally, the present compartmentalization becomes a huge barrier to integrating energy and climate change policy, as we are now witnessing—to our national chagrin.

The different corporate power centers now dominating each of the energy fiefdoms of course resist any attempts by federal, state or local public regulators to unify research or policy making across the scattered pieces of the current energy landscape. Any attempt to treat a btu produced or consumed in one system as a btu produced or consumed in any other—as, say, net energy analysis would do—could endanger the autonomy and ultimately the profit potential of an energy fiefdom. Thus, maintaining the system of "regulatory capture" by which key personnel in public regulatory agencies become little more than agents of their regulated energy industry is a high priority. In this atmosphere where maintaining the hegemony and the power to make economic decisions that protect all industries' enormous assets, revising policy to meet depletion realities or climate protection needs becomes impossible. The numbers are too great; the chasm between reserves we can affordably burn, the demands of a fossil fuel-demanding global economy, and what the warming climate can tolerate are just too vast.

The first order of business, therefore, is to unify the disparate energy fiefdoms, adopt systems methodologies that integrate reserve realities, comparative abilities to produce useful amounts of net energy into the future, and conform with the strict limits of climate warming. It's a daunting task, from both technical and political standpoints. Suffice it to say, no influential leader of either mainstream political party currently is stumping for such a radical, integrated new energy policy. Nor is the US Department of Energy, or most similar energy regulatory bureaucracies at state or local levels, currently attempting to integrate individually regulated energy fiefdoms and conduct their vital oversight in a more holistic manner. Neither leaders nor regulatory agencies effectively integrate energy policy decisions with tough climate change decisions.

PIPE DREAMS: THE SPECIAL CASE OF GAS AND FRACKING

Finally, we must mention a third element of the confused, failing current energy policy: the turn to alternative or "tight" supplies, and specialized technologies they entail—most notably, **fracking.** Recently when the Obama Administration made natural gas the centerpiece of its main climate mitigation policy, many activists celebrated: at last, the blindness of a fractured energy policy that ignored climate change was being reversed. Plus, when President Obama celebrated "a hundred years of clean gas" he seemed to be signaling a much more scientific-based energy policy. If technology was making a bonanza of abundant, cheap, clean gas available, allowing declining, dirtier fuels like coal to be retired, surely this decision was backed up by sound science as well as good economics. Other plans to jump on the gas bandwagon—Boone Pickens' idea to convert the nation's cargo truck fleet to gas, new pipelines, ships and port facilities to liquify gas for profitable export, and a gas-based revival of domestic manufacturing that would "bring back the blue-collar jobs"—showed that our government and businesses were ready to make the tough decisions and act like systems-thinkers. Finally some of the untouchable fiefdoms might be inconvenienced or even broken up as American leaders sought energy with longer lasting reserves, higher efficiencies, fewer emissions and lower costs.

Ugly production numbers. Unfortunately, much of the optimism is already proving premature. Any energy advantages of natural gas are quickly disappearing as objective research cuts through sanguine information coming from the industry and the chronically optimistic data of the Energy Information Agency. As production of fracked gas already sinks into decline in the most productive early areas, it is clear an impossible number of new wells must be drilled over the next two decades to keep overall gas production from falling. And, of course, the low-hanging fruit principle means equally productive new wells will be hard to find, given the best ones have already been exploited.

Ugly economic numbers. Economically, the gas fracking industry is proving to be its own worst enemy. The early spike in production as fracking got underway glutted the market with new gas, driving down prices. Prices have remained low—often too low to return a profit to marginal producers. As drilling moves from the best wells to less productive ones with even faster depletion rates, losses to drillers and developers as well as investors will mount even further. (Both drilling and economic trends in the fracked gas industry closely parallel those in the fracked oil industry, as high necessary drilling rates, rapidly depleting wells, and rising development costs drive early developers and speculators to take their profits and run. This leaves the more marginal latecomers never likely to produce much gas at a profit or, in the case of the investors, get their money back. So while there's a lot of gas out there on the market, and prices remain quite low, fewer and fewer of the technical or financial players are making any money.)

Ugly EROEI numbers. Turning back to net energy, as we've already seen EROEI ratios are falling rapidly for fracked gas due to depletion and soaring infrastructure costs. The remaining gas reserves that are drilled in the old traditional manner continue to have a reasonable EROEI: in the neighborhood of 20:1. But with traditional gas reserves declining (now at a rate estimated as 2 to 3 times as fast as new fracked gas production can replace them) overall gas EROEI is almost certainly below 10:1...and falling.

In sum, the problems of dwindling reserves, disastrous bubble-like economics and plummeting ability to produce net energy make it problematic that natural gas could continue to supply for much longer the needs it now serves. The incredibly Pollyannaish new demands that are being proposed for gas—transportation, a foundation for an American manufacturing revival, and taking over production of the nation's thermal electrical generation load—simply turn the improbable into the ludicrously impossible.

Finally, as if any further nails needed to be driven in the gas coffin, gas has been touted as the solution to keeping the atmo-spheric temperatures within livable levels. Here too the numbers are ugly, as we will discover further in Chapter 11 when we take a closer look at climate change. When regarded as a whole *system,* natural gas does not promise to save the planet by taking over the production of American electricity now supplied by coal. Rather, it may well *increase* overall CO_2 levels, if and when fac-tors of net energy, soaring infrastructure and methane are ever taken into account.

Fracked and fractured. *Fracking* is, of course, a key difference in both the current gas and oil sectors—though this distinction is lost on American policy makers obsessed with "end-point" thinking. The optimistic planners of a new Great Age of Gas, or even a temporary gas-powered transition to a renewable energy future, forget they are not just talking about natural gas systems. They are talking about **fracking** natural gas systems. Failure to make such critical systems distinctions is an important reason why American energy planning remains fractured, dysfunctional and wholly captive to the centralized corporatist interests.

As we turn to the emergency-level problem of climate change, sadly we will see more of the same fractured, narrow self-interested thinking in action. However, with climate change seizing the position as Ecological Problem #1, the stakes for healing these fractures of industry autonomy become dramatically higher. Where energy issues alone have never been able to do so, the ominous realities of climate may make system thinkers of Americans yet.

CHAPTER 11

Climate—The Defining Constraint

Introduction: a short history of the Ecological Limits era

In the 1960s and 1970s, the early days of awakening to ecological problems and beginning to think of remedies to them, *energy* became the synonym for scarcity and *pollution* was the poster-boy for environmental damage. As serious as the threats of ecological crisis were seen to be—and analyses such as the **Limits to Growth** forecast some very dire consequences indeed—most experts believed society still had time. If we heeded the warning signs and reformed our consumption-addicted economic and social practices, human societies could once again live sustainably and harmoniously within planetary limits.

Much has changed in the half-century since. In those early formative years, most of the recognized examples of scarcity on one side and damage on the other were relatively geographically confined. By that, we mean that energy depletion or the growing scarcity of key metals, minerals and other resources was seen as a problem for individual nations—or smaller regions within those nations. *(If Bolivian tin deposits run out, Bolivia's export-based income will drop. Poor Bolivia....)*

Similarly, damage we inflicted on the physical environment affected specific, often small areas and specific ecosystems within those confined spaces: a Love Canal where lethal chemicals had been dumped; an area of Northern California where redwood trees had been over-cut; an area of the French coast where an oil tanker went aground and broke up; a part of the Ukrainian countryside irradiated by a failed nuclear plant.

Globalizing ecological damage. One of the biggest changes over the last four decades is the manner in which both the scarcity half of the ecological crisis and the ecosystem damage half have been globalized. This change has dramatically adjusted the way we now view energy and material scarcity, and the optimality of any potential policies designed to mitigate them. Plus, the change to a more global view has also affected how the counter-attacks of status quo interests determined to block ecological action have been organized and deployed. In other words, politics and economic structure, a point we make repeatedly in this work, have become all-important in virtually all "depletion and destruction" debates.

The last 30 years in particular have had massive impacts on our response to human-caused damage to physical ecosystems. This revolution of awareness, policy formation, and the resistance of opponents, can be attributed to one thing: the emergence of the specter of catastrophic *climate change.* During these last decades, the focus of concerns about how man is impacting the planet has shifted from small-scale, often localized episodes of pollution to that granddaddy of undeniably global ecological impacts, global warming or climate change. Before, it seemed like there could be peaceful coexistence between energy policies framed on the Doritos ("We'll just make more") solution and restricted pollution problems where a workable solution was frequently seen as big doses of money and advanced technological clean-up. Now, with climate change elevated to Problem Number One, and astride the whole world, any potential solutions would seem to doom the world to perpetual scarcity. The knotty question is usually posed as something that would fit comfortably in the classic movie Catch 22: *"How can we prevent the climate from collapsing and still burn enough fossil fuel to prevent society from collapsing?"*

In this chapter, we will profile the major characteristics, issues and challenges of runaway climate change that America faces. As a final objective, we will try and clarify the tortuous and troubling relationship between a climate that is rapidly warming to emergency levels, and energy, which supports the major threats to climate but must continue to be the mainspring of how all useful work gets done.

CLIMATE CHANGE REARS ITS UGLY HEAD

The "Limits Era" of the 1970s was overturned by brute force. By pumping remaining fossil fuels at a furious pace, and by spreading corporate-based globalization backed by free-wheeling neoliberal economic policies, America and much of the rest of the world has been able to keep the economy afloat and in effect ignore the ecological warnings for over three decades. But, even though the public policy of continued growth and consumption forged after 1980 still largely prevails, it has not been without challenges. Near the end of the decade of the '80s the new crisis was introduced to American leaders and the public. Like energy depletion, it also received a sometimes lukewarm, often downright hostile, reception. Its title was originally "global warming." Today, just as "steady state" re-emerged as "sustainability," the term has morphed into *climate change.* (If the public or the powers that be sours on something, just rename it....)

Many trace the beginning of the global warming debate to June, 1988, when Dr. James Hansen, NASA administrator and scientist, testified before a US Senate hearing. Hansen asserted that global warming was already occurring, and that the chief cause was the greenhouse effect created by humans pouring warming gases into the atmosphere. We are learning now that concern over human conversion of fossil fuels, plus the discharge of other warming gases, was known and being discussed by energy companies like ExxonMobil, and by the US Department of Defense, much earlier than Hansen's testimony. But a comprehensive follow-up story by the New York Times summarizing Hansen's findings put the issue in the public spotlight for the first time in summer, 1988. (Often now forgotten, there was NASA and NOAA research on climate impacts of CO_2 and other global warming factors for at least a decade before James Hansen's testimony. Much of this research, sponsored by congressional members such as Al Gore, was discontinued during the 1980s by Republican cutbacks in energy and atmospheric research.) Stay tuned for a "déjà vu" event with President Trump...

A QUARTER CENTURY OF GROWING CLIMATE CONCERNS–AND GROWING RESISTANCE TO ACTING ON THEM

By the early 1990s there was growing international consensus among most experts that climate change was not only a real problem, but was anthropogenic (man-caused) and capable of enormously broad and severe damage to natural and man-made systems. Consequently, acting through the United Nations and through individual actions, the international community has taken many climate mitigation steps over the last 25 years. Conferences such as Rio, Kyoto, Copenhagen and most recently Paris have sought universal commitments to cut carbon emissions. A series of reports prepared by the multi-disciplinary Intergovernmental Panel on Climate Change (IPCC), organized by the UN, has attempted to gauge the seriousness of the problem, project the likely impacts on planetary ecosystems and human societies, and identify solutions.

While it is not our purpose here to present an exhaustive account of the various climate-related international activities of the last quarter century, a few general trends should be noted. Each IPCC Assessment Report (the fifth, AR5, was released in 2014) has grown more scientifically sophisticated, as improved research has yielded better data. Notably, each report has become more pessimistic and alarmist in tone, predicting advancing atmospheric warming and related climate emergencies that are more frequent and severe than anticipated. Polar ice sheet melting has advanced much faster than previously forecast, as has the melting of the critical Greenland ice fields. The same is true for permafrost in northern latitudes resulting in accelerated release of trapped methane, a climate warming gas many times as lethal as carbon dioxide. Ocean acidification is happening faster than was originally forecast, meaning, among other things, the ocean cannot store nearly as much carbon dioxide as was hoped. Some facts underscore the mounting scientific evidence that climate change is anything but a liberal hoax:

- **Some 97 percent of climate scientists now agree climate change is real and human-caused.**

- **Polar temperatures are increasing twice as fast as in more temperate and tropical zones. This raises the danger of the rapid rise of sea levels due to melting ice as well as interruption of longstanding ocean currents (for example, the warm Gulf Current that is responsible for Northern Europe's moderate climate).**

- **As 2016 ended and, as expected, became the hottest year on record since 1880 when record keeping began, sixteen of the seventeen hottest years will have occurred in the 21st century (the other year was 1998).**

DENIERS DIG IN

Despite many indicators suggesting effective climate change action is gaining ground, a well-organized (and equally well funded!) opposition continues to fight back just as effectively, especially in the United States. The climate change deniers are undeterred by mounting scientific evidence. The gathering consensus represented by five generations of IPCC reports and numerous other studies, backed up by recorded data, may have rocked the denier movement back on its heels somewhat, scientifically speaking. But it has failed to dent their prodigious political and economic influence. Certainly it has not swayed the disproportionate climate denier politicians who do their bidding in the US congress, state legislatures, governors' offices, and, with the ascension of Donald Trump, the White House.

Blocking Paris. Thus, when the newly-elected Donald Trump describes climate change as a Chinese hoax invented to make the

American economy uncompetitive, he's preaching to an already well-organized, well-funded choir of deniers determined to block American climate mitigation efforts. In following through on his campaign promises, one of Trump's first actions was to withdraw America from the commitments reached during the 2015 Paris agreements. At that conference, international leaders, including President Obama acting for the United States, pledged to take action to contain total temperature rise to 2 degrees Celsius. (In a moment of even greater determination, they agreed to a more rigorous "aspirational" goal of a 1.5-degree rise, a level many scientists now consider the maximum that can be safely tolerated.) In accordance with the agreed-upon terms of ratification by a significant number of the world's biggest emitters of warming gases, the Paris agreement formally went into effect in November, 2016.

Though the Paris accord was greeted with widespread enthusiasm by many US and global climate change activists (it represents the first such deal to which the US has agreed, after all), the cheers of some closer observers were more muted. Limiting the temperature rise over pre-industrial times to 2 degrees C is to be accomplished by individual countries taking individual, voluntary actions. There are no quotas or mandates handed out by the UN or any other central body. There are no monetary or other penalties for missing any carbon reduction or other targets on any particular dates. Signatory nations simply are committing to do their best—and even strive to meet the tighter 1.5-degree standard. But each nation must determine its own particular strategies for reaching its goals.

COAL-TO-GAS POWER PLANT CONVERSION

In the case of the US, the Obama administration pledged to reduce our carbon emissions by 26 to 28 percent by 2025, based on emission levels in 2005. It was pinning much of its hopes of meeting these Paris commitments on one action: converting coal-fired electrical power plants to burn natural gas. However, as we will soon see, that strategy faced a number of stumbling blocks that threatened to derail it before it could even be put into action. Obviously, the political hurdles posed by a powerful denier community, soon to be led by a new president who never saw a scrap of carbon he didn't want to burn, are substantial to say the least. But, more importantly, the technical inadequacies of the plan— its failure to meet overall emission reducing requirements and its lack of a systems approach that would have highlighted fatal miscalculations—promised to doom it before it could break out of the starting gate.

SO HOW BAD IS THE CLIMATE CHANGE PROBLEM?

In understanding the enormity of the climate change predicament, it is necessary to review some technical projections. Although a quarter century of increasingly precise scientific data and comprehensive analyses of it still have not swept away the cloud of misinformation and **dis**-information surrounding climate warming, the data really do matter.

Perhaps the best summary of the real dimensions of the climate change problem comes from the veteran environmental activist Bill McKibben. In an August, 2012, essay published in **Rolling Stone,** McKibben described the crux of the climate problems America and the world faces in terms of three critical numbers:

- **2 degrees Celsius**

- **565 gigatons of CO2 and,**

- **2,795 gigatons of CO2**

NUMBER 1: 2 DEGREES C

McKibben's first number, **2 degrees Celsius**, is the now-familiar ceiling for how high we can let the average global atmospheric temperature rise and still maintain some reasonable hope of not disastrously cooking the planet. As said, the Paris conference was the latest example of the international community acknowledging this maximum tolerable warming—a level many scientists now question as too lenient and likely to cause catastrophic damage to human communities and other ecosystems. But despite these possible inadequacies, it is a hopeful sign that the 2 degrees warming limit was formally recognized by the international community. In Paris, in December, 2015, 167 countries, including the US, for the first time made the pledge to constrain emissions consistent with that limit.

NUMBER 2: 565 GIGATONS OF CO2

McKibben's second number is what the best scientific evidence now indicates is our near-term "carbon budget" necessary to cap warming at 2 degrees C. After repeated, increasingly sophisticated computer modeling runs and other analyses, climate scientists determined that we can burn **565 gigatons of CO2** by mid-century and maintain a "reasonable" chance of keeping climate change from reaching catastrophic levels. ("Reasonable" translates to four chances in five; although the more pessimistic scientists like James Hansen now insist that the rapidly deteriorating climate situation points out that any warming above 1-degree C carries risks.) Since the 565 GT figure cited by McKibben was estimated more than five years ago, reruns of increasingly complex computer simulations of the world's climate have essentially confirmed that ceiling; the fifth IPCC assessment report, released some three years later than the initial 565 GT estimate, contains similar numbers.

Carbon budget for eternity. Thus, decades of scientific effort have now settled on somewhat under 600 gigatons of carbon dioxide as our "carbon budget." The estimate of 565 GT is the maximum we can release by 2050; but there's no respite after mid-century. Since released CO2 persists in the atmosphere and raises the temperature for decades or even centuries, and because we are irreversibly committed to processes that cannot avoid the release of substantially more carbon in the immediate years ahead, the 565 GT amount actually becomes our *eternal* carbon budget. Overspend it in just the next 30 to 35 years and the risks of climate disaster soar, regardless of what we do after that. We're likely to collide with a catastrophic array of climate crises in the years beyond—crises that will make those we are already encountering look like child's play.

NUMBER 3: 2,795 GIGATONS OF CO2

Finally, Bill McKibben rolls out his third number, which he describes as the scariest of all. It tells us the approximate amount of carbon humankind has "in the bank." The Carbon Tracker Initiative, a UK-based group concerned with the probable impacts of climate change on world investments, meticulously calculated the total global reserves of oil, gas and coal which energy corporations and governments list as their ***proven reserves*** (i.e., already found and waiting to be extracted).

Translating these volumes of hydrocarbons into CO2 yields **2,795 gigatons of CO2.** In other words, the global holders of our fossil fuel energy reserves claim they have, ready to deliver and burn, some 2,795 GT of CO2. Even allowing for estimation errors (and deliberate exaggerations of reserves encouraged by how corporations derive their stock values and net worth and countries their political and economic power) this is a lot of carbon ready to be torched. As Bill McKibben soberly emphasizes, ***five times*** *as much burnable carbon as our eternal budget!* The bottom line of all this? *Any expenditure of time, money or energy in exploration for new untapped fossil fuel resources is sheer wasteful folly.*

Postscript: the dollars. Having revealed how woefully out of balance our carbon budget and our carbon bank account are, Bill McKibben rubs salt in the wound by citing one other set of painful numbers: the dollars involved. Using the estimates of the Capital Institute, McKibben's 2012 article puts the total monetary value of those 2,795 GT of oil/gas/coal reserves at approximately **$27 Trillion.** A little more back-of-the-envelope math reveals that, given we can only safely burn about 20 percent of all that fossil fuel in the bank (565/2795=20.2%), approximately **$20 trillion** worth of currently ready-to-go energy assets are at risk of being stranded. Between the energy corporations, the energy-supplying countries and regions within them, and the financial institutions which all tie their worth to this gigantic pool of fossil fuel wealth, the impact of leaving 80 percent permanently in the ground would be, shall we say, financially "inconvenient." A not-so-hypothetical question begs to be asked: ***Does it boil down to a choice between stranding $20 trillion of corporate wealth or ruining the planet...?***

REVISITING CURRENT POLICY

Notably, policy makers in countries both disposed to limit climate change and those generally disposed to ignore it have studiously ignored Bill McKibben's article and subsequent similar ones. To acknowledge it, after all, would be to vividly underscore the bankruptcy of current climate policies—policies already in question not just by knowledgeable climate experts but by many in the general public. Blatant examples of areas where this policy dysfunction is ignoring climate reality are easy to find. Here are two of the most influential:

1. THE DISCONNECT BETWEEN CLIMATE AND ENERGY POLICY.

The biggest failure of American policy in recent years has been keeping the inseparable subjects of energy and climate separated. The energy policy of both recent Republican and Democratic administrations and congresses has been "all of the above." If it can be found, and looks or smells at all like a hydrocarbon, well, let's dig it and burn it! While the Republicans have at least been consistent in opposing climate change mitigation, Democrats generally have expressed concern over a warming climate and a willingness (granted, mostly rhetorical) to combat it. Plainly, this policy choice leaves Democrats in an awkward position: How does a political party which values a healthy environment also stand for the continued consumption of a substance which has been clearly implicated as the major enemy of a stable climate? Further complications arise with the fact that this hydrocarbon energy is rapidly depleting, leaving the inferior remaining supplies exploitable only at huge economic and ecological cost.

For Republicans and other corporatist-leaning deniers, the choice has been simple: deny that both fossil fuel depletion and climate change are happening, and lay down a smokescreen of pseudo-science to help keep critics at bay. For this strategy, they have taken modest heat from an undemanding public for ignoring science. Understandably—and convenient for the Republicans—this public for the most part does not itself understand the complicated science of either energy or climate.

But for the Democrats, the choice has been much harder. A longstanding key constituency of the Democrats has been the progressive left—a motley crew of environmentalists, social critics, anti-corporatists, holistic systems thinkers, and other quarrelsome radicals. In the last quarter-century, this left edge of the Democratic Party has formed the core of the climate change activist movement. The party has been loath to simply brush off the gathering science and warnings supporting climate change coming mainly from this direction—and thus join the Republicans in denial. Yet, the Democratic mainstream remains committed to continued economic growth within the current globalization model they see as the only solution to inequality, rising debt and other economic problems America faces.

Nurturing this world view depends on having copious amounts of energy to feed the American economy and our high-consumption lifestyles. (And try running on a platform calling for a lower lifestyle and you'll be banned from your local party precinct committee, and don't even think about higher office...) Further, if more of this energy can be exported via oil and gas fracking and coal shipments, reviving the good old days when America was the oil supplier to much of the world, it would help our gigantic balance of payments problem. Much of this trade imbalance is due to our decision not to make most of our own stuff anymore, but to export raw commodities then buy back the energy and materials embodied in imported goods and services.

Exporting more fossil fuel energy (and carbon) would help relieve some of this outflow of dollars. Unfortunately, exporting the carbon in no way exports the climate disruption capability on a world-wide scale. In fact, given the differences among countries in regulation and pollution abatement technologies, it probably makes it worse.

An energy-climate policy apartheid. The only solution for conflicted policy makers trying to combine the growth addiction of neoliberal economics with the growth aversion of efforts to save the planet has been to separate the two realms of energy and climate policy. In short, pretend that no connection exists. Only by pretending that the two need not be connected has it become possible to extol policies ostensibly limiting climate-warming emissions to levels necessary for a healthy planet while continuing to push other policies extracting ever more fossil fuels seen as necessary for a healthy economy. *"Let's all support higher economic growth...but let's keep it clean!"*

2. RELIANCE ON GAS AS AN ENERGY "BRIDGE TO THE FUTURE"

On a less abstract level, the previously mentioned US commitment to lower carbon emissions made at the 2015 Paris conference strategically relies almost entirely on converting coal-fired electrical generation to burning natural gas. With "orthodox" (non-fracked) American natural gas production in decline for approximately 20 years, that means that keeping the atmosphere below the 2 degrees C threshold vital to saving the planet depends, with no small irony, on fracking.

Gas pipedreams. Power plant gas conversion is just the latest scheme lining up to take advantage of America's imagined new bonanza of fracked natural gas. We already noted that investor/oilman T. Boone Pickens has promoted a plan to convert much of America's trucking fleet to natural gas, reducing the demand for oil and supposedly lowering overall national carbon emissions.[10] Other technical and economic experts are stumping for plans to revive American manufacturing based on abundant supplies of cheap fracked gas. We are promised the fracked gas bonanza is just the dangling carrot American corporations and their financiers need to bring those off-shored industries and good jobs back to America. And finally, as if our own outsized domestic demands for more gas weren't enough, plans for exporting gas proceed apace. Readers may recall the promises made by gas extractors and financiers a few short years ago at the height of the Ukraine crisis: American liquified natural gas terminals would be built to supply the gas demands of America's Western European allies, rescuing them from the clutches of Russian gas oligarchs pumping gas to the west through pipelines running through Ukraine. Meanwhile, as LNG facilities to save Europe were being built on the East Coast, others would be constructed on the West Coast, supplying the Chinese and other growing Asian nations also scrambling for more gas.

Catching up with reality. There is just one catch...well, maybe more than one. As discussed in the last chapter, the ugly energy realities of advancing depletion, net energy decline, and mushrooming technical infrastructure make building a prosperous economy on the foundation of natural gas a fool's errand. The fact that gas from hydro-fracturing—*affordable* gas—will almost certainly be in decline within at most a decade is just another straw on the camel's back of a shortsighted set of energy policies.

Turning back to climate realities from energy and economic ones, gas is emerging as anything but the low-emission, climate-saving miracle proponents are still promising. The primary reasons are two-fold: *net energy* and *methane.* While gas enthusiasts constantly rave about how it produces only half the carbon emissions

---

10   US Energy Information Agency data puts CO2 emissions for burning natural gas as only 72 percent of those from diesel. Coal is even dirtier. Burning natural gas emits just 55—57 percent of the carbon produced by bituminous coal producing the same energy output.

as coal, they either fail to mention or fail to understand crucial cold hard facts of gas as a *system*—a system where "naturally-extracted" gas is being replaced rapidly by *fracked* gas.[11]

EROEI/net energy facts about fracked gas, with its much higher infrastructure costs and environmental impacts, and much higher well depletion rates, are anything but encouraging when fracking systems are compared to traditionally-extracted systems of gas production. Likewise, comparing the EROEI ratios of fracked gas to those of coal systems rudely contradicts the simplistic notion that coal is dirty while gas is clean.[12]

The specter of methane. As if the facts regarding rapid depletion, low net energy, excessive demand and likely economic collapse weren't enough to torpedo the myth of a hundred-year bonanza of fracked gas, turning to the topic of methane would seem to seal its fate as a climate savior. Between 2002 and 2014, scientists noticed a dramatic rise in global methane levels. Over these years, measured methane emissions rose by some 30 percent, causing surprised governments and academic experts

---

11   US Energy Information Agency data show that by 2014 almost all new US gas production was coming from fracking; and fracked gas already comprised almost half (48%) of all domestic gas production.

12   *Searching for a Miracle: Net Energy Limits and the Fate of Industrial Society*, published in September, 2009 by the Post Carbon Institute, places the net energy/EROEI ratio of natural gas systems at 10:1 (that is, over system lifetime it takes 1 unit of combined energy input to a typical natural gas system to produce 10 units of usable energy as output). But those estimates were made almost ten years ago, before fracking replaced much of traditional gas extraction. More recent estimates by PCI and research such as that of Charles Hall at Syracuse University place the EROEI ratio of *fracked* gas as no higher than 5:1...and dropping fast due to the "low-hanging fruit" principle. *Searching for a Miracle* also calculates the EROEI of coal systems as 20:1. Thus, if these estimates are reasonably accurate, comparing gas to coal systems gives coal an advantage of producing four times the output energy for the input energy necessary to feed system infrastructures over their lifetimes. It's wholly unreasonable to believe, given that EROEI one-to-four deficit, that gas systems generating electricity could have any overall CO_2 advantage over coal systems during system lifetimes of at least several decades. Even a two-to-one CO_2 emission advantage at the single end-point of combustion in the power plant turbine could not overcome such a huge EROEI disadvantage.

to hurriedly initiate studies to find the causes. Two Harvard University studies, released in early 2016, offered probable answers. The data were gathered from carefully sampled measurements conducted both on the ground and from satellite instrumentation. The US was heavily implicated, with estimates of as much as 60 percent of the rise in methane coming from American sources. Two sources in particular were seen as producing most of this additional methane: One, deteriorating natural gas infrastructure; and two, the conversion of US natural gas production to fracking.

In the first case, aging and poorly maintained natural gas delivery infrastructure—well equipment, pipelines, pumping and compression stations, storage facilities, etc.—was pinpointed as the primary cause. Instead of the 2 percent that the EPA had long predicted leaked into the biosphere, researchers estimated the actual methane leakage to be at least double that. Some estimated the leakage to be triple: 6 percent.

Methane from fracking. The implication of fracking was more controversial. Fracking has become a significant factor only since the mid-2000s, when the boom began in earnest for both oil and gas produced with fracking technology. The nature of that technology produces significantly more risk of methane escaping than does traditional drilling and pumping. In December, 2015, a two-year peer reviewed study backed by the Environmental Defense Fund was published. Focused on the key gas fracking Barnett Shale area of North Texas, the study found that methane emissions were some 90 percent higher than estimates by the EPA. The EDF study used a substantially different methodology, employing many more airplane flights measuring actual emissions from above, as well as more careful measurements of the "superemitters"—i.e, the production sites responsible for the majority of area methane leaks. Thus, most scientists regard it as much more accurate than earlier estimates made by the EPA, many of which were based on industry-furnished data.

When the emission attention thus turns to methane, a gas estimated to be 80 to 90 times as lethal as a short-term contributor to atmospheric warming than CO_2, the prospects for gas suddenly appear more dismal. Even very small increases of released methane can have dramatic impacts on atmospheric temperature, completely erasing any advantage in CO2 emissions gas enjoys over other fuels (which we have already seen are largely mythical, when examined using full life cycle cost accounting).

Furthermore, methane leaks are extremely hard to control. Clearly, urban and other existing gas infrastructure can and should be upgraded and maintained at higher standards. However, it appears quite difficult to obtain better methane leak control resulting from extraction, processing and delivery with current gas and oil hydro-fracturing extraction. Installing the technology to significantly reduce methane leakage might be technically possible; but with gas and oil fracking entailing thousands of small production wells operating over a relative short lifetime, it's not likely to even approach being economically feasible. As the best wells rapidly deplete and are replaced by many more marginal wells necessary to maintain gas production, both the technical and economic viability, like the EROEI ratios, can only get worse.

CONTEMPLATING BETTER ENERGY POLICY – A FIRST TAKE

Many veteran environmental activists, whatever their differences with each other or with climate deniers, at least saw the rise of the climate issue as a relief from the long-standing, bedeviling conflicts over energy policy. Climate crises, whatever else they portended, would solve our battles over energy depletion and environmental destruction. If you are to save the climate from overheating, you will have to stop burning nearly as much fossil fuel. The arrogant reign of the behemoth energy industries and their captives in government would be finally ended. RIP. End of story.

The resultant big sigh of relief, however, appears premature. If anything, the making of energy policy over the next crucial 30 years, as we attempt to cross the precarious bridge to an all-renewable, electrified future, will be even more technically demanding than it's been. And politically, it's certain to be even more contentious.

We will reserve our more in-depth discussion of specific policy issues for the next chapter, where we address the combined policy needs of climate, energy and other ecological realms. Further, we discuss them in the larger context of **economic** policy, which now dominates and renders most present ecological policy making inconsequential. However, because fossil fuel burning is so complicit in damaging the climate, three elements of energy policy are worth mentioning as vital to saving the planet from climate disaster.

Lower energy levels. First, overall energy usage will certainly need to be much reduced; not only must we squeeze into the 20 percent budget straightjacket forecast by Bill McKibben and others, we must devote a very large portion of burnable remaining fossil fuels to fueling the transition. An all-renewable infrastructure—almost certainly dominated by solar and wind energy, along with smaller additions of bio-fuels, hydro, ocean wave/tidal power, and a few others—must be built on the back of the infrastructure that the remaining fossil-fuel supplies can support. And, of course, the availability of these bedrock fossil fuels that must carry us across the bridge to the renewable future will be constantly, irreversibly dropping, meaning constantly, irreversibly higher costs and heavy environmental damage. (Supplies of petroleum and gas will take a significant hit well before mid-century, as fracking peters out and no longer produces significant volumes of affordable fuels.)

Conservation. Secondly, to divert as much of the old hydro-carbon economy as possible to building the renewable bridge, we will be forced into very serious programs of conservation. The impacts on everyday levels of consumption and activities American have been used to may well be draconian. One result: the failure of many businesses and an accompanying loss of jobs as less vital industries have their energy and carbon budgets slashed. Another result: a serious testing of public levels of support for tough, belt-tightening policies necessary to navigate the transition in the short time left to us to do so.

And of course, there's always net energy.....Finally, the ever-present problem of net energy/EROEI will put a premium on careful energy planning and tough policy making decisions that will be politically unpopular. Choices will have to be made that are guaranteed to gore the oxen of multiple energy industry power-houses and the many economic sectors that presently rely on their products. Many current energy sector practices (e.g., biofuels, nuclear power, fracked oil and gas, ...even possibly some promising renewable systems) will come under hard questioning: Do they really produce more usable energy than they consume? Is a net energy loss tolerable and necessary to obtain a vital, unique flow of energy essential to building the "renewable transition bridge?" Assuming we get the all-renewable, electrified energy future built, (a large and problematic assumption in itself) will it have adequate net energy and self-sustaining power to keep it running? ...at what levels of total energy production?

In short, the tough decisions of energy did not go away when the 900-pound gorilla of climate change lumbered into the room. In all likelihood they got even worse, although the climate change issue, due largely to increasingly frequent and severe natural disas-ters, may have a perverse benefit of convincing the public more definitively that something truly needs to be done. Nonetheless, energy policy makers of the next 30 years will have a constant stream of agonizingly difficult decisions to make.[13]

SUMMARY–CLIMATE CHANGE AS A CORPORATIST GAME-CHANGER

The seemingly endless argument over climate change puzzles many Americans who are not themselves members of the 10 percent of hard-core deniers.[14] After all, the scientific evidence of climate

---

13   A new 2018 analysis examined the decline in "natural" fossil fuels as well as oil and gas from fracking that likely will occur before mid-century. It found, to avoid a serious crash in the American economy before 2050 caused by a shortage of energy, we should be installing solar and wind power at a rate **10 times** what is actually occurring.

14   According to a March, 2016, Pew Research poll, 90 percent of Americans now believe human-caused climate change is already happening

change has been mounting steadily for over a quarter century, arguably reaching overwhelming, no-brainer levels. Looking further back to the Limits Era of the 1970s, methodologies such as peak oil, EROEI/net energy and other ecological, systems-based approaches laid the foundation for understanding the connections between ecological crises such as climate and human addiction to economic growth and physical consumption. During the intervening four decades, exhaustive statistics have been collected and published on the rising use of fossil fuels, their discharge in the form of CO_2 and other pollutants, and, more recently, the warming of the atmosphere. It's been a long slog, but the evidence finally seems clear on at least a few key associations—and particularly the connection between profligate hydrocarbon burning and climate change.

Why then, many logically ask, does climate change policy remain so disconnected from energy policy? Why can even more progressive politicians urge strong climate mitigation policies and actions, but still talk about growth and support essentially "drill, baby, drill"/"all of the above" energy policies? How can ostensibly enlightened political leaders, with access to all the facts and expertise, subscribe to such incompatible, inimical policies disastrously pitting climate against energy imperatives?

In her recent books and essays, the noted climate activist and author Naomi Klein offers one plausible answer. It has little to do with often-heard mainstream media chatter about deniers being ignorant of the scientific method, or of innocently misreading the real scientific evidence. Thus, it dismisses the usual liberal chimera that a little more data, a little better presentation of facts, or a little more persuasive discussion of the consequences will finally do the trick, convert the deniers, and enlist them to help save the climate.

Naomi Klein asserts that the powerful climate deniers—the same powerful corporatist interests which control the economy

---

or will at some point. Only 10 percent are convinced it will never happen, the lowest denial rate since 2007. During the same month, a poll of the US Congress found that a third (182 congressional members, or 34 percent) described themselves as committed deniers of climate change.

and make the political decisions that make that control possible—know full well what the real scientific evidence is and what it portends. They understand—even more clearly than many liberal activists who believe the climate can be saved and the current corporatist/global institutional structures preserved as well—that if effective climate mitigation policies are ever instituted at the top level of American and other national governments, the jig is up for Corporatism as we know it. In the words of climate scientist James Hansen, it's "game over."...Only in this case, the loser would not only be the planetary climate but the corporatist dominion of American and global economies.

If this proposed scenario is true, it means that multinational corporate interests are willing to risk the very health of the planet for one last measure of political control and profit—even though they basically understand what they're doing. This is nothing less than a tragedy of Shakespearian dimensions. Forsooth—would that the Bard were alive to chronicle its unfolding...

Oh my, here comes the conspiracy theory...! Though some will recoil at this narrative (it does in fact smack heavily of conspiracy based on crass short-term self interest) there are no other current plausible alternative explanations. Quantitative research and analysis, whether it's Bill McKibben's three numbers, the unmistakable and irreversible decline of net energy/EROEI ratios, the real facts about fracked gas and oil, or other nasty little problems like methane lurking in the wings, reality is clear and irrefutable. Deniers among the general public may indeed be confused by the scientific data, largely dismissive of the scientific method, or displaying that familiar American cultural trait of blind faith in technology; but they don't count in what passes for current American "public dialogue" on climate change. (Incidentally, neither do the liberal optimists who are convinced renewable energy will save the day and the climate without requiring any drop in high-consumption lifestyles or energy availability.)

The simple reason self-identified progressive politicians can embrace diametrically opposed policies on climate and energy is that their power and position require it—if only to get re-elected.

They may believe the grim climate change numbers; but they also fall in line with the corporatist model which ultimately destroys the climate with its own commitment to growth, continued consumption—and ecological damage. Saddled with a schizoid set of energy and climate positions and allies, liberal politicians have decided to come down on the side of more energy and consumption...as quietly as possible, of course. On the climate side, they say the right things, offering large supplies of rhetoric and the occasional tepid action to appease their climate activist constituents. There is, of course, a pathological rationality to all this, since even their supportive constituency would have trouble accepting the full implications of the actual situation. And, apprising them of it would dramatically impair re-election chances—*first things first...*

But the numbers won't go away; and they are clearly destined to get worse.[15] Corporatist institutions and structures offer no way to relieve them. Instead of sane policies that effective politics would be implementing *right **now***—that is, aggressively deciding how we are going to keep 80 percent of fossil fuels in the ground and most sensibly allocate the other 20 percent to the creation of a society with a future—we continue to hunt for more fossil fuels we can never safely burn. Until we take the first step and demand that climate policies and planetary survival must drive and integrate with energy policies, the lemming-like rush toward the edge of the ecological cliff will continue.

---

15   In fact, they did just get a lot worse. In an interim report released in October, 2018, the IPCC forecast that only immediate, severe economic and social measures can now avoid exceeding the old estimated temperature rise limit of 2 degrees Celsius. The IPCC contends that to avoid exceeding the 2-degree ceiling, we must cut carbon emissions 45 percent below 2010 levels... *by no later than 2030.* Further, to keep from exceeding the lower 1.5-degree limit—now recognized by most scientists as the maximum safe level—we will probably have to double those cuts.

CHAPTER 12

Ecological Policy—Past, Present and Future

Why this chapter?

This book is dedicated to the ultimate goal of energizing *local* efforts in the search for effective *local* actions that speak to problems largely created by globalism writ large. Globalism, therefore, looms as a parameter we must accept rather than a phenomenon we immediately seek to change. Nonetheless, the first two parts necessarily deal with broader conceptual and global issues as we attempt to identify what we feel citizens must understand so that they may act effectively in their own community.

In other words, we feel compelled to speak to the question: *What is the global and theoretical framework within which Localism must necessarily proceed if it is to be effective and create positive results?* Treating any problem demands a clear understanding of the roots of that problem—even if those roots are far removed from your sphere of personal influence. Accordingly, the third important section of the book is dedicated to proposed local initiatives apart from anything the federal government or major corporations might do or say. In our view, Localism demands this—it must ideally proceed apace no matter what mischief the Feds or corporate lobbyists might currently be up to.

Consistent with this, we have held that national level policies are not our primary `concern. However, the realm of environmental policies poses a dilemma. (*We're talking about the climate here, folks, and that ain't local...!*) Fortunately, there are many resource use policies, such as local food and energy production, composting and recycling, that both individual citizens and local governments (we, the people) can productively stimulate and support. Indeed, that has been happening. But there is a background of planetary reality, along with national policy, that is the 800-pound gorilla in the room. Recycling your cans, bottles and newspapers doesn't help much if climate change proceeds unabated and the seas are rising—or if income and wealth inequality rages onward.

Consequently, before turning to the strictly local perspectives and actions in the final section of the book, some further observations on environmental policies are necessary. Although we earlier promised not to dwell on national policy—We Lied. Full disclosure requires at least a quick survey of where we've been, where we are and where we might be going in the relatively new realm of environmental policy. It is appropriately placed here, since as you may have noticed in the previous two chapters, any largely scientific and technical discussion of energy and climate begs the injection of political and policy perspectives. This chapter builds on the energy and climate policy ideas introduced in the previous two chapters. It knits together both the subject matter of energy and climate and the temporal span of past, present and future. Successful ecological policy making is going to have to combine not just the elements of energy, resources, climate and other ecosystems, but will have to overcome the problems that made past and present ecological policy largely ineffective.

First, we discuss the checkered history of environmental activism—its successes and shortcomings. Second, this leads to the current status of attitudes and environmental policies, and how they fit in with broader economic policies. Finally, we look to the future by identifying some potential initiatives—both culturally and policy-based—that in our opinion would be compatible with effective local actions, proposed here or anywhere else. It qualifies as our "wish list," although we do not speak to how to get there.

Ironically, in the current national "tone deaf" milieu, it appears that any promising directions are those that may emerge from state and local governments. Much as it seems to be with health care, the paralysis of the federal government means that most promising initiatives will be "bottom up" experiments that citizen awareness has stimulated. Then, given the magic of the internet and its unruly stepchild, social media, these innovations can hopefully set examples for others across the country, and ultimately spread to the nation as a whole. The upshot of all this is that meaningful political change will occur in the reverse order suggested by mainstream organization theory logic. Instead of broad top-down policy providing a framework for state and local action, exciting piecemeal local experiments will drag national policies and priorities along kicking. Perhaps this is as it should be—and will have to be...

THE PAST: FORTY YEARS OF UNDER-PERFORMING ENVIRONMENTAL PROTECTION

Over the last four or five decades many initiatives to save the planet and the organisms living on it have come and gone. Needless to say as a body they have had mixed success. The proof is found everywhere around us; witnessing the American landscape and reviewing a few of the "ugly numbers" of environmental crisis is proof enough that the physical planet is in bad shape.

Nonetheless, concerned Americans in large numbers continue to join various energy conserving, species saving, pollution cleanup, and—most recently—CO_2 emission reduction efforts. It is easy to take a disparaging view of their aggregate effectiveness— as many climate deniers and environmental critics regularly do. More to the point, we need to examine why so many determined efforts, well-populated by dedicated people, drawing substantial funds from individual and even corporate donors, have had so little success. During this last half-century of environmental activism, total energy use has continued to climb, CO_2 and other warming emissions have continued to climb, overall consumption has continued to climb, the number of threatened or extinguished living species has continued to climb—in short, the efforts of environmental activists appear to have had little or no effect in stemming the advance of ecological disaster.

Why is the environmental record of the last few decades so poor? With so much research and data behind it, presented by so many logical and persuasive arguments, and with the stakes for failure being so potentially catastrophic, why has environmental activism been able to make such a small impression on the way America treats the environment?

General causes: the economy rules the roost. Some general causes have already been offered. An economy built on the possibility and desirability of continual growth, material consumption and ever-higher standards of living cannot go easy on the physical environment. Despite suggesting other, less material human standards for success, economic attainment arguably will hang onto the top spot of American goals for the foreseeable future.

Deindustrialization and rapid financialization seem to offer a way to have a thriving economy without so much physical consumption and impacts on the environment. But, in fact, they are simply ways to disguise continued growth in material consumption by hiding it behind the curtains of globalization and indirect demand, allowing us to believe we are "going green" without really reducing the burden on the planet. "Faux green" and "greenwash" thus become distracting corporatist tools as economic power centers step up efforts to placate consumers and keep us buying.

Explanations of why formal environmentalism has thus far proven so ineffective all follow a common thread back to a single origin: the economy. A dab of environmentalism is tolerated—like any socially aberrant, but non-threatening, behavior. In fact, well-channeled environmentalism can actually be a positive source of economic growth, boosting sales of such things as electric cars, organic foods, solar smart phone chargers and eco-vacations in Costa Rica.

But let those efforts expand to structural challenges that threaten the economic status quo and they must be discredited, put in their place and controlled. This clearly has been the experience for some environmental causes and movements during the last four decades. (*Are you keeping up your membership in Greenpeace...?*) The message is clear: Serious environmental policy and public practices threaten the prosperity of an industrial economy. Even "environmentalists" are not to forget that the environment and the economy are diametrically opposed. When one goes up the other must go down, and prosperity is everyone's goal...

But even this message is mixed and contradictory. One moment the economic-environment relationship may be portrayed as the familiar confrontational face-off. But in the next moment, ortho-dox economic methodology and assumptions may be employed to signal that the economy and the environment may peacefully coexist. In fact, the bottom line "holy grail" position for corporat-ism—of course after lecturing nervous citizens about economic primacy—is to establish a widespread "soma" assumption that they can indeed co-exist. *(Don't worry yourselves about the environment—just put your newspaper out on the curb and head for the mall...)* What's more, sound environmental behavior may be encouraged by using economic tools that are mainstays of free markets working on the familiar principles of supply and demand. Sounds comforting, but where does that leave us?

THE PRESENT: DOUBLING DOWN ON MORE OF THE SAME?

As the ecological time bombs of energy depletion and a deterio-rating climate continue to tick, the U.S. federal government has decided that better policy to meet the impending crisis is no longer needed. The Trump Era marks many detours in the normal course of modern American life. But none is so potentially consequential as its decision to end all national and international-level attempts to forge a livable ecological policy that assists humans and the planet itself to survive. This has left a few states and many locali-ties, acting almost as subversive rogues defying authority, to carry on the national business of ecological activism and reform. These dogged activist survivors must surely see their role as similar to the monks of the Dark Ages: they alone must struggle to keep rational policy making alive until a wider renaissance wakes up American leaders and the general public.

But while much of the public slumbers, the Trump adminis-tration is indeed imposing its policy priorities—and even though these policies are being roundly castigated, all Americans should immediately recognize them as a familiar model. Trump, albeit in a particularly obnoxious manner, is simply reaffirming that in the modern USA, *the economy comes first*. And those that get to pick and choose what economic policies will be are the same old corpo-rate power-wielders that have been in charge for a long time—inci-dentally through both recent Republican and Democratic regimes.

Thus, what is really taking place in the ostensibly shocking reversal and rejection of environmental policies is nothing more than a firm (*brutally* firm, some say) reaffirmation of the econo-my's top spot in the nation's list of important priorities; as well as a reaffirmation of what and whom that economy serves. The clear message: The economy rules, and when ecological interests threaten to get in the way, the smackdown that occurs is an unmis-takable reminder of the opposed, irreconcilable juxtaposition of that relationship. Trump hasn't ended ecological policy making as much as he has bluntly restated the dominance of economic priorities in a late-Industrial Age society.

Some in the more extreme environmental community contend that canceling four-plus decades of efforts to save the planet won't matter much. This view reflects the sobering fact that, despite all manner of policies and programs to preserve species, ecosys-tems, save energy and more recently cut global warming, little has been accomplished. The planet is on a much more perilous crash course with disaster than it was at the turn of the 1970s, when the environmental movement was just getting started. In this hyper-critical view, there are few or no crusades available to save modern man from his own foolishness. A few spotted owls may have been saved, (*and they're not doing that well...*) but overall, when viewed in light of current depletion and climate crises, environmental protection policies and programs have been a flop. When push has come to shove in the neoliberal age in which America still finds itself, economic exigencies have always trumped the environment.

THE FUTURE: DISARMING THE ECONOMY VS. ENVIRONMENT SHOWDOWN

We ended Chapter 11 by explaining why climate change, the most serious threat now facing America and human civilization, must subsume and define energy and other ecological policies. Unless the present U.S. *"drill, baby, drill"/"all of the above"* energy policy is brought to heel, it will make a farce of any attempts to keep the climate in a safe range. Just as climate, arguably the greatest threat civilized human societies have ever faced, must dominate energy and natural resource policies, *energy/environmental policies per se must now trump economic policies*. The necessity of priority setting must venture out of the enclave of environmentalism and cross the border into economics. Only when that border is crossed and ecological and economic policy are considered as an inseparable whole will we be able to disarm and deescalate the current showdown between the two now hostile spheres.

We will start modestly. While it is true that environmental preservation efforts thus far have had only limited success, focused as they often have been on narrow problems, they should be examined for what value can be salvaged. All may not be hopeless. Constrained by higher economic priorities and resisted by powerful environmental doubters and deniers, environmental activists have always faced stiff resistance. Arguably, they have only been allowed to operate in narrow causes and in ways that did not threaten the economic interests of the powerful corporatist status quo. As long as actions were confined to relatively trivial crusades—saving a few snail darters or cleaning up old abandoned gravel pits—they have been tolerated and even given modest financial and philosophical support. Our brief examination covers both what environmental movements have chosen to tackle as well as how they have chosen to conduct their efforts.

First Things First: The Market or Not? Many of the policies designed over the last forty years have touted the use of the old tried and true American fallback position: *market incentives*. These amount to monetary enticements designed to elicit good environmental behavior from either producers or consumers. One immediately can think of policies regarding automobiles, public transit, buildings, home appliances, and such waste handling practices as recycling. Various kinds of market-based incentives offer either monetary rewards for saving the planet or penalties for continuing to harm it.

By injecting the implication that the market can handle our problems, this hopefully calms American ideologues suspicious of any radical public sector action challenging to the status quo. (Read: *oppressive government regulation.*) Despite being a nation of both corporations and individual consumers who—in theory, at least—self-identify as sharp, parsimonious decision makers, market incentives have conspicuously under-performed as ecological policies. They haven't really had much impact.

Still, policy makers continue their love affair with "carrot and stick" monetary incentives, even though structural changes over this last half-century make it even less likely that they will succeed in saving the environment. Anywhere you look in America's highly diverse economy, you tend to find more influences acting to counteract and defeat efforts to establish environmentally-friendly behavior than to promote it.

Inequality as Environmental Despoiler. One feature worthy of mention, if only briefly at this juncture, is our old friend inequality. There have always been many flaws in market-based incentives as a way of eliciting better social behavior. The best things for the physical environment are not always those that earn producers the highest profits or save consumers the most money. The reasons that people buy certain products are not always the careful calculations of "economic man," but a range of murky influences ranging from rationally conceived needs to blatantly irrational luxuries. The high levels of income and wealth inequality we now see segregating the bulk of Americans from a small extremely affluent minority create severe problems for effective use of monetary incentives—whether targeted at either the rich or non-rich.

First, a small very rich elite always distorts a market-based/ supply-demand economy. When a small elite possesses a disproportionate amount of the wealth (e.g. spending power), a market economy responds by producing a disproportionate amount of luxury goods and services. As the famed bank robber Willie Sutton knew full well, it's called going where the money is. Quite unsurprisingly, an economy skewed toward luxury goods forfeits any claim to greenness; yachts, private jets, 40,000 square foot mansions, etc. Big shares of the demand-driven financialized economy are anathema to socially efficient resource use or ecological purity. 2017 statistics reveal that the richest 1 percent of Americans owned 35.5 percent of our national wealth, while the bottom 50 percent held only 1.1 percent.[16] With so much demand in the hands of so few super-rich at the very top, it's small wonder the laws of supply and demand channel enormous resources toward wasteful, environmentally damaging goods and services.

At the other inequality pole, where half the US population is squeezed into a demand pool holding less than 2 percent of national wealth, environmental values are also being shredded. If the "have's" enjoy their lavish flow of luxury goods and services and jet-set lifestyles, the "have-not's" also get a consumption lifestyle pre-packaged by today's globalized economy. It's the modern version of mass production and marketing: globalized, technologically intensive, highly monopolized and dominated by a small number of giant corporations. As middle-class incomes stagnate and national wealth is diverted to the few percent at the top, the majority of Americans are forced into this standard pattern of consumption that offers little real choice.

Most characteristics of this mass consumption pattern are familiar to Americans, having been the subject of endless water cooler and dinner table talk over the last few decades. They usually include a wide range of economic and social gripes: cheap floods of foreign-produced goods instead of domestically-produced ones (read: Made in China); common synthetic materials that are hard

16   OECD analysis indicates expanding the affluent elite from the super-rich top 1 percent to the merely very rich top 10 percent raises the holdings at the top from 35.5 percent of all US wealth to a staggering 75 percent.

to dispose of (read: plastic); excessive packaging also hard to dispose of (that often seems better made than the product it holds); highly automated processes that minimize production labor (as they force wages down toward rock-bottom). Most marketing is by retail chains owned by large national/multi-national corporations rather than local retailers (soulless big-box stores that bid goodbye to Mom-and-Pops); selling practices that facilitate the universal use of credit rather than cash (buying chewing gum on your Visa, which adds convenience but also exploitive interest and fees)....And the most recent innovations: "stay at home" shopping via mail order and telephone sales—or, better yet, Amazon-like automated on-line sales (read: RIP "brick and mortar").

And finally, all of these cliched insults and aggravations of modern consumerism are sold to the defenseless public with high-pressure advertising—glitzy, 24/7 media blitzkriegs. With the commercials come assurances that, contrary to our gut reactions, modern production and marketing practices are a veritable consumer's paradise, offering the highest quality products, the widest choices, and (the best part for hard-pressed people feeling the brunt of rising inequality) the lowest possible prices.

Just as the luxury economy catering to the every whim of the super-rich forfeits any pretensions of environmental responsibility, the globalized, debt-supported mass economy for the rest of us also makes any environmental effectiveness excruciatingly hard. Many of the causes are somewhat subtle and seldom recognized as environmentally destructive: "virtual" organization which highlights one manufacturer (the name on the label) while disguising the vast, inter-connected infrastructure of suppliers, sub-suppliers and subcontractors beneath; marketing in vast big-box outlets owned by distant corporations (where "brick and mortar" is still hanging on); or alternatively, marketing through long distance mail order and internet sales (where "brick and mortar" can be disposed of).

Other features are well known as plainly damaging to the environment: long travel distances for everything from raw resources, energy and finished products; elaborate over-the-top packaging, processing, protection and preservation, made necessary by those long distances and the need to protect fragile and/or perishable goods shipped all over the globe. And finally there are the mountains of waste produced by all these global goods and packaging, of which only a small share can be recycled, reclaimed or made into something useful.

IMAGINING SOME ALTERNATIVES

As we warned you, the coverage so far invokes many factors well beyond our ability to implement easily. Some might be partially treatable with full-bodied changes in policies at the national level. Others would depend on wholesale changes in cultural values and attitudes. Most would require a mix, but in any case the prospects for attacking needed social and regulatory change head-on appear daunting to say the least, and would no doubt require some sort of an organized social movement.

Nonetheless, we press on. The remainder of this chapter suggests some features that in our view would be compatible with the level of cultural and environmental renaissance that may well be needed if we consider the seriousness of the climate challenges we face and look ahead to crafting an effective strategy for survival.

MARKET INCENTIVE POSSIBILITIES

Despite the sabotaging effects of inequality, three market incentive-based ideas offer potential for saving energy, capping emissions and adjusting consumer behavior. These ideas, probably familiar to most Americans, are carbon taxes, fossil fuel taxes, and general product pricing.

Carbon tax. Carbon taxes, as well as similar (but significantly different) carbon-cap-and-trade schemes have been suggested, and implemented, for some time. The latter cap-and-trade experiments have not been encouraging, as they have led to various subterfuges by which powerful corporations and others have gamed the system while providing no measurable decrease in carbon emissions. However, carbon tax proposals, such as that offered by

Dr. James Hansen, the former NASA administrator, which would tax carbon entering any economy at either its source or point of entry, have real potential.

Carbon taxes would act to make the burning of carbon much more expensive across the board to all consumers, and not just to selected major contributors. Ideally, the proceeds would largely be returned to the general public, offsetting much of the added cost to consumers of higher direct and embodied energy costs in the short term. Some funds should support technological research and/or grants to business innovation in converting operations. Consequently, both businesses and citizens have incentive to modify their behaviors toward conservation and reduction of ecological footprints.

A well-structured carbon tax system should Ideally direct the proceeds downward on the income ladder, and thus also counteract inequality while helping to restore true choice for ordinary consumers seeking to make sound environmental decisions. It would necessarily establish a form of "energetic accounting" similar in concept and operation to other Net Energy/EROEI schemes. By taking us away from standard monetary accounting methods that allow corporatist controllers to distort benefits, hide and externalize costs and otherwise game the system, careful and comprehensive carbon taxing would measure important physical flows—carbon and energy—through the industrial system.

An important advantage of a carbon tax would be to highlight the destructive practice of **externalization.** By revealing where carbon was being used and emitted throughout the industrial system, the public and political leaders could see where true environmental costs were being imposed, and by whom. In that way, we would have a clearer picture of where and how these costs were being shifted, and hopefully ways to "plug the externalities leaks" could be devised.

Higher fossil fuel taxes. In contrast to standard gasoline taxes, a series of "smarter" fossil fuel taxes could be levied by a variety of political jurisdictions and on all forms of fossil fuels that emit carbon. Whereas they are currently untargeted and lack any real ecological "reform" purpose, such taxes could build in incentives to use energy—and related processes—that produce few if any direct emissions. Further, coupled to carbon taxes, graduated taxes could be levied on fuels depending on their levels of systemic warming emissions. Taxes could be higher on fuels not produced domestically, since these entail higher transportation energies to import and distribute. This almost smacks of a tariff, in that it would introduce the positive concept of providing incentives for locally-produced energy and disincentives if that energy must be brought in from long distances.

Truly ambitious variations could include tax schemes that raised taxes on energy forms with a low net energy/EROEI ratio, while rewarding relatively efficient energy sources with high EROEI ratios. Yet another variation might be to add a level of taxation for any energy source that is non-renewable: that is, energy sources such as solar, wind, geothermal or hydro power would not pay the same level of energy taxes as fossil fuel-based systems such as oil, gas and coal.

As with carbon taxes, fossil fuel taxes would need to be structured very carefully to achieve optimum environmental and societal results. Proceeds could also be directed toward Americans of low and modest income, or could expressly be set aside for safety net programs to deal with economic disruptions stemming from predictable but random climate change impacts.

Pricing "cheap" products. (*What do you mean "too cheap?" I can't afford things now...!*) Our current inequality-ridden economy threatens to become one whereby only globalized, mass-produced imported products in the current corporatist mold are affordable by today's economically marginalized American public. A seeming contradiction looms—too cheap or too expensive? Our view is that, with notable exceptions, the bulk of consumer products in today's advanced societies are *too **cheap.*** That excessive cheapness lowers incentives to do the right thing for the environment.

Let's be clear. By "cheap" we mean priced so as not to cover the real and fair life cycle costs of producing them, including a reasonable profit to the producer, fair wages for workers, and ultimate waste disposal. When goods are priced too low to incorporate full direct and indirect costs, something must give. Too often, in today's global economic arrangements, that something is the environment. So, while many economically hard-pressed ordinary Americans may feel compelled to shop at Walmart, there are environmentally destructive reasons that these mass market outlets stuffed with imported goods appear affordable.

Operating with globalized mobility and technology, producers find the places with lowest possible wages and environmental standards for producing their products. This facilitates their favorite sport: *Internalize the benefits and externalize the costs.* Thus, many of the exorbitant global energy and environmental costs are externalized to people world-wide and to the planet itself, including to future generations. Finally, after exploiting workers and shedding these human costs, the sticker price may appear low, but should probably still be higher. Ironically, a monopolistic markup may still exist—but it is not shared with consumers, and producing corporations get to keep it. Perhaps that is a major reason that the corporatist one-percenters are so much richer than the rest of us—and they get to shop at Macy's and I. Magnin...!

RANDOMLY SELECTED URBANIZATION FACTORS

This section is difficult to organize. Actually, the proper heading is probably "four other things we need to mention." They are not individual items, but rather *systems* requiring focused attention if serious energy use and climate mitigation progress is to be made, as opposed to specific climate-related policy suggestions. Our purpose here is to identify the general need, and perhaps more importantly, to argue for policy that *treats them as systems* rather than simply as "to-do" lists. We mitigate our guilt for omitting any detail by noting that specific action suggestions *consistent with these important areas of concern* are presented in the third part of this book. Thus, you should view these categories as ripe for policies that would support the actions suggested later—actions which are good ideas with or without the policies. The four are: 1)

The food system; 2) The transportation system; 3) The urbanization process itself; and 4) The waste treatment system.

A new food system. The present globally-dispersed, corporately-dominated, fossil fuel-dependent industrialized food system provides a classic example of an ecological problem area which is unfixable in its present form. It is so structurally and institutionally stacked against ecologically sound operation that it needs to be scrapped. Minor modification and tweaking is a waste of time, money and human effort. Of course, we need to avoid starvation while a conversion is made to something better! And that is perhaps why a visible and obviously preferable parallel system has been so slow to expand.

Alongside the broken industrial system is a useful model that has operated for some decades. (Actually, *centuries*...) This alternative food system, an organic and local one, exists today—albeit in a prototype almost miniature form. Though it commands only a small amount of the present market, it is expanding. Today's organic farmers and gardeners use organizational methods, technology and concentration on local resources and local markets in ways that are directly supportive of an ecologically sound future. As industrial food systems falter, victims of energy shortages, transportation costs and the heavy impacts they impose on water and land ecosystems, we will need a ready and viable replacement. Activists can quickly take advantage of the guidelines established by these organic/local models and their existing footholds all around the country. They provide a valuable starting point—why wait for the current one to fail?

Little more will be said here, since we devote an entire chapter to food and another to energy in the final section of this book. However, the burgeoning literature on local food production is rich with good ideas that we can't wait to share. Therefore as a "preview of coming attractions" to Part Three, we offer the following eight points as a (highly incomplete) to-do list for concerned citizens. Consider these suggestions as *personal environmental policies* that will strengthen local movements and facilitate a comfortable escape from the many disadvantages of our current industrial system. As we will emphasize in Part Three, such reforms also provide a path to much more healthy eating while at the same time stimulating valuable enterprises and jobs in local economies that badly need them.

1. support local CSAs (community supported agriculture), farmers markets, and locally-owned groceries selling local products

2. grow more of your own fresh food and support community gardens and urban gardening movements

3. take public/political action to limit and regulate ecosystem-endangering chemical use

4. promote local-based energy systems that support an alternative food system

5. support universal local composting that turns sinks into sources

6. support and patronize other related local businesses that can contribute to more complete local-based food networks (e.g., small-scale food processors, marketing, agricultural input supply)

And two that corporatists *really* don't want you to see:

7. eat less packaged/processed food

8. eat less meat

The measuring stick of a new, environmentally sustainable food system will be its success in making two transformative changes: reducing the massive transportation needs of the current global-ized system and reducing the consumption of animals and animal products. Both are huge users of energy and resources, both can be changed for the better, and each will present monumental challenges to any reform efforts. The barriers will come from entrenched corporate interests, along with our own ingrained consuming tastes and those of almost all global cultures.[17]

Rethinking transportation. The basics of a more environmentally friendly transportation system have been exhaustively researched and discussed for decades. They include the electrification of as many vehicles as possible (personal automobiles, trucks, trains and other forms of public transit); transitioning away from dependence on private vehicles for human transport; transitioning away from aircraft and trucks as primary modes of carrying cargo, and—sure to alarm many used to today's mobility patterns—the abandonment of un-salvageable mass commercial air travel. ("You mean we're going to have to bike to Disney World, Grandma...?")

A keystone of these reforms must be a resurrection of America's long-neglected rail systems. Rail travel—electrically powered—will become the most environmentally effective means of carrying both human passengers and cargo in the years ahead. Likewise, rail transport will be the centerpiece of travel at all levels: local, regional, nationwide and even to some extent international. As some commentators such as James Howard Kunstler have envisioned, we may yet see not just the revival of ship travel, but trans-oceanic voyages and cargo using modern versions of wind-powered sailing ships.

The new electrified, rail-centric transportation system must solve some difficult "crossover" problems. Chief among these will be transporting food and agricultural goods. Even if the vast preponderance of the food system is made local, there will still be substantial energy needs to move productive inputs to farms and move the food to local customers. Add to this the on-farm needs

---

17   Animal agriculture critics, such as Dr. Richard Oppenlander, estimate that all activities related to raising and consuming animals and their products is responsible for up to 52 percent of all global warming emissions. If this continues until 2030, the animal food industry alone will emit more than 565 gigatons of carbon. That is, fossil fuel use could be eliminated entirely for all other uses and mankind would still exceed our carbon budget simply by eating animals and their products.

to power tractors and other equipment and it becomes clear that energy needs—and subsequent climate warming emissions—won't disappear even if the food system shifts from globalized and industrial to local and organic.

Localizing transportation equipment, whatever technological directions it may take, is an example of an industrial sector that will be the last to "de-globalize." We use this fact to again make the point that complete detachment from a global economy will never happen, nor should it. One can hope that the ultimately more localized economy brings into the local sphere everything that is feasible. The more stringent energy budgets of the future should reserve for the global economy those needs that cannot be met without centralized (high tech) corporate involvement. Use corporatism only when necessary, but don't let it run your life. Basic (lower tech) needs as well as luxury products are best left to local control, which leaves everyday citizens maximum choice and freedom to optimize in a more scarcity-prone world.

Challenges of Urbanization. Throughout the Industrial Age, rapid urbanization has become the accepted, expected settlement pattern in virtually all nations, certainly including the United States. In fact, urbanization is often the proxy for "developed" (superior) as opposed to "undeveloped" (inferior). From our early agrarian times, when almost everyone lived in rural settings, to modern times where patterns have reversed, the swing from rural to urban over time has been dramatic. The 1790 census showed that 95 percent of Americans resided in the countryside, but by 1990, 75 percent of Americans were urban dwellers. Over half lived in metropolitan areas of over one million.

Historic analysis attributes this urban migration to industrialization. As mechanization of agriculture freed up farm workers, and factories in and around cities created the new jobs of the Industrial Age, workers and their families naturally flocked to the cities and the life of a wage worker. The de-industrialization of many American industrial production areas (read: rustbelt) of the last 40 years has not stemmed this rural-to-urban tide. Though many domestic urban dwellers are moving outward to the suburbs and exurbs (creating a false image of rural re-population), America's immigrants continue to flood into the cities. The overall motivation seems clear: Cities and suburbs now offer the overwhelming majority of new jobs. An economy that now emphasizes service employment—a vast, diverse collection of jobs ranging from hedge fund manager to big box store shelf-stocker—creates its jobs in urban settings. Almost all college graduates head straight for the big cities; American higher education has to a great extent become a prep school for late Industrial Age, urbanized jobs.

This large-scale migration has had monumental implications for energy use and environmental impacts, and unfortunately the trend is not easily compatible with the worsening twin problems of energy depletion and climate change. Negative environmental impacts threaten to override all the urban positives of more jobs, higher incomes, better schools, cultural advantages and just plain harmony with the glamorous Information Age. After all, much more than their counterpart cities centuries ago, the modern American city has become a seemingly irreversible *energy sink*.

This means that cities and their surrounding metropolitan areas require vast inputs of energy, associated raw materials, finished goods, water and other "inputs" to survive. At the other end of the pipe, cities require that their profligate waste products all be carried away. Unable either to generate the massive inputs to make modern urban/suburban living tolerable, or to absorb the equally massive waste which would also make living impossible, cities depend on the outside world for an environmental "subsidy."

The conventional wisdom contends that this parasitic relationship is more than repaid by the positive products of cities: e.g., jobs, higher incomes, GDP, organizational and financial resources, educational opportunities and other cultural advantages. But, from an environmental standpoint, the sprawling US metropolitan areas are a dead weight: a draw on the resources and ecosystems of nature's primary economy as well as large parts of the human economy called on to provide the subsidy.

Ironically, this situation is more true for the great cities of the developed world than for those in lesser-developed nations.

There is a popular notion that great first world cities (think New York, Paris, Rome) are exciting vibrant places that engender all the exciting events and ideas, while large third-world cities (Cairo, Calcutta, Jakarta) are environmental disaster areas. On superficial examination, that appears true, but it is only allowed because the Western World cities exact a much higher burden on their surrounding areas to supply resources and dispose of wastes. In the big picture, the wealthy cities are undoubtedly harder on the planetary environment because of that wealth.

In recent decades urban environmental specialists and activists have attempted to reverse this dynamic by which larger and larger cities become more dependent energy sinks (and climate-warming "engines"). They have advocated policies and programs such as urban gardening, rooftop gardening, solar and wind generation on skyscrapers, urban tree planting, higher residential densities and infill, improved mass transit, and many other measures that would facilitate movement in the right direction. Thus far none has stopped or even slowed the rapid rise of energy use and increasing emissions, much less their continued growth. Many "showcase" good news projects are highlighted, but, as positive as they are, do not confuse them with fundamental change. Meanwhile, as the activists' modest urban ecological policy reforms continue, so do the efforts by corporatist forces and growth proponents to continue their traditional expansion of cities.

At work is a straightforward application of the old axiom "Follow the Money." Economic development programs still revolve around attracting major corporate employers to the largest cities; land use planning in all but a few "enlightened" cities still favors constructing single family housing in sprawling suburban peripheries. Transportation budgets continue to be heavily skewed toward more freeways, street improvements, parking and other accommodations of the automobile as the prime means of urban transportation. Vested interests in both the private and public sectors remain hard at work.

Thus, the overriding question remains: If current projections are accurate, how are future planners and decision makers going to counteract the stubborn allegiance to urban growth and development as a primary American economic and social policy? Or, put in a slightly more activist manner: As carbon budgets shrink to a small percentage of current levels, do we systemically attack current forms of urban expansion as a crucial source of climate change? ...Or, do we concede that, despite environmental damage, cities are an irreversible fixture of modern American life and must be subsidized whatever the cost?

The choice can be concisely expressed as: *Back to the land or green urbanism?* We could attempt to virtually evacuate existing cities, offering incentives and other measures designed to get urban dwellers to relocate to small towns and relatively rural settings, or we could aggressively implement a much more environmentally sustainable, comprehensive policy for the cities themselves.

The first path seems fraught with huge problems. The immense size of current US metropolitan areas means that many thousands—or millions—would seek to migrate, giving up their homes and lifestyles and then trying to duplicate them in their new rural surroundings. The impact on the rural environment for all typical services would create many infrastructure crises. The waste and unsustainability of the abandonment would alarm environmental activists and deniers alike, raising much bitter opposition. Economically, many urban employers would find it difficult or almost impossible to relocate; and small town/rural destinations would be paralyzed with the problem of how to employ all the new immigrants—many with inappropriate skills. In short, any large-scale "back to the land" movement is likely to be emphatically rejected on environmental, economic, infrastructure and social grounds.

That leaves the second basic alternative: implement a much more environmentally sustainable, green urbanism. Where cities today are huge energy sinks and sources of climate-damaging emissions, clean up their act to make them much more resource independent, less energy intensive, and especially able to control their various ecosystem-impacting wastes. That is, sever the physical cords by which the modern industrial city parasitically depends on outside subsidies.

Although the green urbanism alternative seems to be a prefer-able choice, there will be many pitfalls. Noting that the job is easier said than done is the understatement of the year. While existing efforts to grow more urban food, plant more trees and shrubs, etc., can certainly be expanded and improved, conversion from a dependency on outside, transported inputs and reductions of emissions will be slow. As Part Three will attempt to show, here is where a resolute commitment to Localism could help. By con-sciously working on the vibrancy and stability of local economies, we create a "carrot" of attractiveness of smaller cities to accom-pany the "stick" of fleeing the larger ones. The environment—and social cohesion—can only benefit.

And what about waste? Handling the inevitable waste of modern life is clearly an indispensable component inherent with the first three topics of this section: food, transportation and urbanization. The current systems to process and supposedly "manage" wastes are reactive, after-the-fact efforts that must respond to whatever the industrial economic and social systems drop into their lap. In terms of achieving real energy, environmen-tal and resource use gains, many are mostly ineffective—though often very financially expensive and problematic in terms of energy use and emissions themselves. They are also incapable of reform-ing the broader industrial systems which make them necessary.

American waste handling systems proceed from the conviction that the overall economic and social systems which produce these wastes are inviolable. You can tinker and try to refine how wastes are handled, processed, recycled, de-toxified and stored; but the overall system that creates the waste is mainly off limits. Waste handling thus remains a reactive, ineffective, after-the-fact activ-ity—at the end of the industrial pipe, so to speak. Forced to react to overwhelming events and practices "upstream," crises such as the seas of plastic now clogging the world's oceans will continue. Further, relying on world markets to process the recycled "stuff" can be a fool's errand, as China's recent ending their acceptance of our plastics has demonstrated. (Too dirty for China—but we'll have to take care of it ourselves...)

Quite obviously, waste collection, recycling, decontamination, storage and the rest are in such chaotic disarray because the entire industrial production/consumption system is not seen as such—a *system*. As we will discuss in concluding this book, modern societies have viewed the economy as a linear throughput process of extracting and transforming natural resources into human satisfaction, and casting off wastes at all stages of the process: **Sources to Sinks**. This in effect assumes infinite resources, and an economy that can grow forever.

Future environmental policy must overturn that approach. The economy must be treated as a closed system, even developing ways of using wastes as valuable inputs. The alternate economic paradigm of a finite planet has been labeled as **Spaceship Earth** or **Circular Economy**. Such decisions as the choice of products, the materials to be used, choices in packaging and processing, etc., must be considered as an inherent part the overall waste handling decision making process. It may seem heretical to suggest that waste handling policy makers should influence whether a product should even be produced, and what raw materials can go into it, but continuing along the present path will ensure that waste handling will remain in crisis.

Reforming the entire waste handling issue, complete with promising technological options, is a task beyond our pay grade for this volume. However, we suggest one immediate policy change that would elevate the waste problem in the consciousness of both decision makers and the public alike: **Make the handling of waste a mandatory public utility**. At present, communities of all sizes have accepted that having fresh, safe water as well as effective sewage treatment are necessary public utilities. They establish a baseline for a safe, sanitary, quality community. Further, although many valuable public services have foolishly been privatized in recent years, Americans in all geographic regions continue to view water and sewage systems as sufficiently important that they must remain publicly operated.

We propose that all American municipalities, from the smallest village up to giant metropolises like New York City be required to open publicly-operated facilities to effectively handle all their own wastes. The exact composition of these wastes will vary considerably, of course, but local waste utilities should be capable of handling whatever the local citizens, businesses, factories, adjacent farms, etc., create.

Composting, for example, would get a real boost from the imperative the utility would create for the municipality to be "self-contained." In fact, the need to locally process all kinds of materials might suddenly get people thinking of some new job possibilities. Even though processing technology for used materials is known, the ethic is that it must be done on very large scales to be economically efficient. (clearly, left-over thinking from corporatism...) Smaller scale efforts could create new products and create jobs. Many would have to be subsidized, but what better way to spend economic incentive money—and do climate mitigation at the same time?

The bottom line of all this, as we have emphasized, is that a comprehensive systems approach to the entire local area (waste and everything else) is likely to yield new ideas and new job possibilities that recession-proof your community through increased self-sufficiency, make it more ecologically sound and probably even combat income inequality. Community social cohesion will also be the beneficiary—just ask school children for their best ideas and stand back...

BOLDER OVERALL ECOLOGICAL POLICIES

The following three "big picture" policy suggestions deviate from traditional narrow environmental and energy policies as America has treated them in the past—as if we haven't already. Once implemented, they would help create a framework for a permanent platform for an ecological/environmental peace treaty: a coexistence with nature. They are essential features of a "full system" sustainable society.

Energy is at the heart of all economic activity, and our current fossil fuel-centric energy systems doom the planet to climate disaster if used permanently on anything like their current scale. The foundation for this new economy and society must therefore be renewable energy resources. The current fossil fuels which provide some 85 percent of all US primary energy have two crippling effects: they are both poisonous to the atmosphere in the way they raise climate temperatures, and they are non-renewable. We are sentenced to depletion and certain economic disaster within less than a century regardless of whether or not climate collapse gets us first.

1. TRANSITIONING TO ALL-RENEWABLE ENERGY

In the immediate next few years the most critical task for global societies—including America—is to lower the flood of carbon into the atmosphere well below the current level of over 400 parts per million. The only path to doing that, short of a total collapse of world economies, is to consciously and aggressively transition from our present primarily fossil fuel-based culture to one based on energy sources that are both renewable and non-carbon. An entire systemic commitment is required. A tepid "semi-voluntary" effort has no chance of working.

The renewable energy transition "bridge," as Richard Heinberg, David Fridley—and others—surmise, must be crossed by approximately mid-century if the worst effects of both resource depletion and climate crises are to be averted. A useful start has been made in designing, manufacturing and installing large numbers of wind and solar electric energy systems. But it is only a start. At present only slightly more than 10 percent of American electricity is generated by renewable sources, and about half of that comes from hydroelectric dams largely built in the mid-20th century.

Heinberg and Fridley, in their book *Our Renewable Future,* point out what is often overlooked even by many avid renewable energy advocates: despite obvious signs of ubiquitous electrification, America is still a fossil fuel-addicted nation. Only approximately 20 percent of our end-use energy is consumed in the form of electricity. Heinberg in recent essays points out another sobering estimate: if America is to have the renewable electricity by mid-century required to avoid serious economic contraction, we should be building solar and wind capacity about 10 times faster than we are.

Clearly the renewable "bridge" can only be built and crossed by overcoming very serious challenges. And, somewhat less clear, the bridge will only lead to a better life on the other side if the lion's share of our industrial, commercial, residential, agricultural and transportation infrastructure can be rapidly weaned from fossil fuels and made to run on electricity. This leads directly to a second top priority project for the next 20 to 30 years.

2. WIRING AMERICA: CONVERSION TO AN ALL-ELECTRIC ECONOMY AND SOCIETY

Renewable energy systems are distinctive in how all but a rare few produce their energy in the form of electricity. Systems like solar photovoltaic panels, wind turbines, hydroelectric dams, and wave and tidal energy devices all exemplify the dominance of electricity generation among the currently most developed and proven alternate technologies. This is a hopeful sign. Yet, if virtually 80 percent of our present energy use is *not* in the form of electricity, it is uncertain how America is going to convert the bulk of that 80 percent before we simply grind to a halt from lack of available energy.

Some answers come easily. Homeowners can swap out their gas furnaces and water heaters for readily available electric substitutes. Cars, as we are seeing, can run on battery-powered electric motors (hopefully helped along by continued improvement in battery technology and battery materials that are more renewable). Electric locomotives have long been the standard in many parts of the world—though this creates certain electrical infrastructure challenges across America's long rail distances.

However, in other areas such as construction, mining, heavy industry, agriculture and transportation, the outlook is not so sunny. While in theory technology can provide electrical methods of doing what is now done by fossil fuels, the conversion costs—in terms of precious energy, capital and raw resources—will be great. Fossil fuel technology which now seems perfectly functional will have to be abandoned for new electrical technology which often will seem expensive and unproven. Using the traditional short-run economic context for such decisions, many environmental choices confronting us will seem downright crazy.

In extreme cases, the combined push toward an all-renewable, all-electric energy society will spell the doom of currently familiar features of modern life. One example is widespread commercial air transport—for both human passengers and cargo. Presently, the imagery conjured up by electrical airplanes (with either revolutionary new generations of lightweight and enormously powerful batteries, solar panels, or very long cords…!) is ludicrous. Currently unknown technology may come along to partially bail out and extend the life of mass air travel and cargo hauling; but with a mid-century deadline looming as inflexible, any rescue of today's air transport industry is more apt to come from the world of politics and not technology. Political decisions will have to set aside the fossil fuels—and a good portion of our meager carbon budget—to keep the most critical planes in the air. In any case, air travel faces severe restrictions.

3. A CARBON BUDGET

Why a carbon budget? The essence of its importance is not so much what it says, but rather the initial agreement that we need it. No technical, scientific or public participatory work may start until the collective will within the body politic makes it happen.

The all-renewable transition, along with conversion to a predominantly electricity driven society, should ideally be accompanied early on by our third high priority project. That is the development of a comprehensive "carbon budget." The basic numbers of how much total fossil fuels we can safely burn are already well known through IPCC-sponsored and other independent research. The difficult challenge for the budget makers will be to allocate—then enforce—this budget among all the supplicants seeking a slice of the carbon pie. A related crucial challenge will be to determine the sources from which the carbon will be drawn. For example, how much petroleum, natural gas, coal, tar sands and "unconventional" hydrocarbons like ethanol and biodiesel are to be used. These decisions will have deep implications for the environment, and also for the health and profitability of private owners and energy sector businesses.

The job of the budget makers obviously will be very controversial. To many, it will look a lot like the workings of a Soviet-style planned economy. Because of the contentious, highly-politicized nature of the task, several things appear essential. The budget process itself must start with a comprehensive re-calculation of the upper limits of carbon that can be emitted over time. Much of this work has been done, but should be reviewed and updated to form as strong a consensus as possible. Different parts of the overall budget making should be carefully delegated to decision makers at various jurisdictional and geographic levels.

Next, it will be important not just to allow the public to review the final budget-making decisions, but to actively participate in making them. Whatever the composition of the various institutions and individuals who contribute to developing the final overall budget, it is vital that currently dominant corporatist institutions—that is, large corporations, financial giants and a few federal government agencies—*not* be allowed to dominate the process. In our current polarized political environment, it is difficult to see this going smoothly...!

Needless to say, this is an immensely complex task, and will put great pressure on both domestic and international ability to integrate technical, economic, social and political considerations into some sort of rational, purposeful effort. No useful American "budget" could or should be drawn up unilaterally. Close communication and cooperation must be established between Americans taking part in the effort and responsible groups around the world. The overall goal is the elusive notion that has loomed since the Rio conference a quarter of a century ago, and it couldn't be more critical: *forge a global agreement on what we all must do to save the planet from climate disaster.*

But, as we said at the start of this section, the first step is **agreeing that it needs to be done.** Forging the plan will be difficult enough, but it cannot even start until the need is broadly acknowledged within our political economy. That is what is now missing, and that is the greatest tragedy of our current leadership.

SUMMARY: BOOSTING PUBLIC PARTICIPATION

As with so many current environmental matters, viewing the halting efforts of four frustrating decades of environmental cleanup and preservation, it would be tempting to just give up. Though progress has indeed been modest, it has helped save many species, reduce serious cases of pollution/contamination, and has made life a bit safer and better for many people. So, despite the temptation to dismiss 40-plus years of environmental efforts for not having miraculously saved the planet, it would be the wrong move. More to the point, it would probably set back vital near-term efforts to mount new, more effective, more comprehensive environmental policies when we need them most.

Presently, the environmental movement, like many worldwide activist efforts, is suffering from an inevitable case of "crisis fatigue." People who are engaged and already concerned about climate change problems see each new intense wildfire, devastating flood, hurricane that exceeds any past experience, and their beliefs are reinforced. One can hope that at least out of the devastation of each new event come a few more converts to the belief that serious measures must be mounted. Working against this, much as with the increasingly frequent and tragic violent shootings, the public could (and perhaps already has) become numb to each new headline. The real tragedy would be for our culture to accept all this as the new "business as usual" normal.

That would be ensuring the ultimate onset of dire consequences.

Yet, if headway is to be made against the various entrenched institutions and cultural attitudes blocking progress, it arguably will be made by grassroots efforts of ordinary people organizing to solve local problems. Climate itself cannot be individually and directly affected. These concerned people, in their awareness of what's not working in their lives, will, if determined and persistent enough, find ways to make necessary things work better. Where progress has been slight, or effectively stalled by entrenched power, environmentalism is no different from other social justice causes. Attempts to force high-level, top-down change through wielding political power have, for the most part, not worked. While voting for the right people to represent strong environmental values in the congress or the White House is certainly important, taking direct actions on your own with family, friends and neighbors is much better.

It would be wonderful if something approaching the suggestions in this chapter could become part of our national policy and collective world view. That would add substantive structural support for innovative efforts in your own community. However, you could justifiably view these measures as "wishful thinking," since you're probably going to have to do it yourself. At least, when the Big Boys notice something working in your community and plaintively ask: "Can we be of any help?" you'll have some specific suggestions to offer....

CHAPTER 13

Growth and the Ecological Crisis

The clashing of the 3 economies

As the "specter of scarcity" overtakes both America and the industrial world, our initial assertion becomes even more urgent: Given all the pressing economic, social and environmental challenges America faces, **the key issue is growth.** In Chapter 1, we laid out the quandary for those economic theorists and policy makers defending the current status quo. Although it is normally billed as the solution to economic woes, the growth obsession exacerbates many economic problems, starting with rapidly increasing income and wealth inequality. Further, a few dominant monopolistic corporations trample on the interests of workers, consumers, communities and small businesses, all of which is abetted by their virtual lock on political processes. It becomes increasingly awkward to rationalize the failure to solve problems in which more growth is proposed as the solution. To date, neither business nor political leaders have come up with new economic models that can reconcile the broad economic needs and faltering institutions while preserving the mantra of endless economic growth.

THE RIGID PHYSICAL LAWS OF THE ENVIRONMENT

Even though the occasionally impenetrable abstractions of economic theory might appear to allow the door to remain open for positively defining the growth-economics relationship, that door slams shut when it comes to the environment. There is no such intellectual wiggle room—the geophysical laws governing the workings of the planet are by comparison immutable and crystal clear. The old saying, first proposed to the general public in the tumultuous 1970s, sums it up well: ***Infinite growth in a closed, finite system is impossible.*** The laws of physics are not negotiable in defining the relationship between the physical biosphere and human economies. Acknowledging this immutable fact, an inevitable collision becomes painfully obvious. The pertinent question: When does the collision occur and what does it look like?

Despite this reality, industrial economies, with America in the lead, have studiously ignored or denied its validity. The rationalizations have paralleled those offered to defend economic theory and practice itself. Modern American leaders of all political stripes have developed novel ways to contend that continued growth can, should and even must continue. What lies behind this position, which is both anti-science and anti-common sense? We need to probe beneath the endless growth hypotheses and attempt to understand what makes clinging to a sinking lifeboat so irresistible and ubiquitous in modern industrial society.

THE THREE ECONOMIES

For the last few decades economists have expanded their thinking about how many economies are actually in play shaping all life on Earth. It may seem a superficial question, but the exercise serves to shed light on the critical subject of ecological crisis and how our mania for perpetual growth affects our survival.

1. THE SINGLE ECONOMY OF MAN.

Until the 1960s and 1970s when the modern ecological debate emerged, Western economic theorists recognized only a single economy. The economy of humans was organized to produce the goods and services mankind required and desired. This straightforward and decidedly anthropocentric approach pretty much ignored nature, in failing to question both its ability to provide an endless reservoir of physical resources and also to remain healthy in the face of human impacts. With humans fully in control and calling the shots, it is no surprise that perpetual growth was viewed as a given, and completely within our grasp. Moreover, to many respected and influential economic thinkers of today, the single human economy is where it all still begins and ends. Humans make the important economic decisions; a prudently "managed" nature simply provides and reacts.

2. THE SINGLE ECONOMY OF MAN BECOMES TWO ECONOMIES.

A major transformation of the turbulent 1970s was the definition and recognition of a second economy. Pioneering ecological economists such as E. F. Schumacher, Herman Daly, Robert Costanza and Nicholas Georgescu-Roegen joined with systems thinkers and ecologists to propose the idea that the economy was in reality two economies. Because the natural world provided essential support in the form of physical resources to supply human (and all other) life, as well as healthy ecosystems that absorbed waste and provided other vital support, the economy of nature was accorded recognition (by some...!) as a full-fledged economy. In fact, it was argued that the natural world should be recognized as the primary economy; with the familiar human economy, totally dependent as it was on nature's largesse, demoted to the secondary economy.

This "dual economy" thesis quickly became a popular foundation of the blossoming environmental movement, limits to growth proponents, etc. Traditional economic orthodoxy, however, reacted in two main ways. First, some paid no noticeable attention and continued to maintain that human decisions were all that mattered. The physical environment could continue to be taken for granted, since the resource pool was adequate and resiliency of ecosystems were not a problem. Second, other orthodox thinkers insisted that the theoretical and practical structures of the single human economy already adequately take the physical environment into account.

Economists dislike admitting that the market system does not or cannot handle virtually any contingency. Market pricing

and other practices would satisfactorily compensate for ecological scarcity or damage—should these things ever become
significant problems. It is classic technological optimism: Rising
prices, resource substitution and technological innovation were
all that was needed to deal with any ecological issues and ensure
that nature will keep supplying human needs. Thus, we could
continue rapid growth without the concerns being expressed by
overwrought environmentalists...(who, frankly, just needed to take
a deep breath and chill).

3. TWO ECONOMIES BECOME THREE.

But the amoebae-like division of the economies was not
yet over. Recently, powered by strong empirical evidence, the
notion has emerged that the two economies—human production anchored by nature—are in fact now *three* economies. The
tertiary economy is, like the secondary economy of produced
goods and services, an artifact of man. It is a former subset of that
secondary economy, and in light of both its newfound size and
wealth, deserves to be declared independent from the traditional
operations of the secondary economy. The tertiary economy is the
financial sector, now operating under new management in many
developed economies, and with special prominence and influence
in the United States.

We have earlier pointed out that the financial sector has
hijacked much of the effective economic policy decision making
at national and global levels. Employing their sheer size and eco-
nomic/political power, the big banks and other "FIRE" "(Financial,
Insurance, and Real Estate) sector firms have diverted income and
wealth into their own pockets, creating in their wake rampant
inequality. But our focus here is on two other factors. First, we
explore how the actions of the financial tertiary economy dangerously contribute to our ecological crisis, complicating efforts
to deal with the problems of energy/resource depletion, climate
change and related environmental degradation. And secondly, in
conjunction with the main issue of this chapter, we examine how

the tertiary economy throws up these barricades to dealing with ecological crisis by encouraging that old bugaboo: *growth.*

ECOLOGICAL CRISIS: THE THREE ECONOMIES SQUARE OFF

The greatest challenge now facing the US and similar industrial economies is to rapidly reduce the burden on the primary economy of nature. If there is one clear result of the late-Industrial Age binge we've been living through since the lost promise of the 1970s, it is the degree to which the natural primary economy is threatened by human economies. Extreme dependence on fossil fuel energy, continuous flows of physical resources and the viability of vital ecosystems has created this urgent mandate.

Jumpstarting growth. Significantly reducing the primary economy pressures would naturally seem to require—among other policies—curbing growth. But instead, *jumpstarting* growth remains high on the agenda of most modern nations. With many economies continuing to stumble and stagnate following the Great Recession, leaders are obsessed with regaining short-term economic health. This is of course understandable. When facing incessant population growth and grinding poverty, it is difficult, as the saying goes, to remember that your job was to drain the swamp when you're up to your neck in alligators.

As an aside, it appears obvious to most observers that the fundamental challenge for the human race is certain to be a final reckoning with the question of population growth. Economic growth may appear to be the presenting problem, with resource scarcity impinging on that in a variety of ways, but the ultimate limit is the inability of the planet to support an infinite number of people. We unequivocally assert our agreement with this premise, but that is not our area of expertise, and one more uneducated polemic would serve no purpose. Thus, out of prudence (or cowardice) we proceed.

In the immediate short run, therefore, growth-fueled prosperity trumps green transformation on virtually all political agendas.

This is more justifiable in the developing as opposed to developed world, but however it unfolds, it maintains and even increases the existing burdens on the primary economy. Paradoxically, the only relief granted the primary economy comes when the two human economies under-perform—for some reason staying stuck at sub-par levels of performance. Thus, given our current economic structures, recession appears to help the environment. This is most unfortunate, since it reinforces the common perception that it's "the economy vs. the environment," a ruinous mindset if there ever was one... One major purpose of this book is to demonstrate that Localism can turn this around.

Blaming the secondary economy. Though largely confined to empty rhetoric, current modest economic policies attempting to lighten the load on the primary economy usually target the secondary economy of goods and services. It seems a natural and intuitive choice; the productive economy is virtually synonymous with physical ecological impacts of all sorts. Secondary economic production evokes images of raw resources and energy being scraped from the Earth, of smoking factories with humming assembly lines producing endless goods from these materials, and of fleets of trucks, trains, ships and planes hauling all these products to giant malls and retail outlets across the globe. Secondary production is also seen as the big polluter, pumping emissions of all sorts and the waste from consumption into the environment. Though they're still seen in a more benign light than manufacturing, the service sector has gradually also become recognized as a source of heavy energy and materials use as well as ecosystem damage. In short, the twin damages to the primary economy—resource depletion and ecosystem degradation—appear to be coming almost entirely from the extraction/production/consumption/disposal chain of the secondary economy.

Regulating the secondary economy. Accordingly, for over forty years almost all activist pressure and resultant government regulation has focused on the secondary productive economy. As environmental activists have won hard-fought battles, traditional enterprises have had to stop pouring so much effluent into the skies, rivers, oceans and soils. Secondary economy mining and energy firms have had to find less destructive ways to extract materials. Automobile makers have been required to reduce the fuel use of their cars. Manufacturers have had to limit or even stop selling dangerous substances and products. Consumers have been urged to cut down their waste, recycle, drive less, etc. Almost all the attention of reformers as well as government regulatory response has been aimed at the secondary economy.

The faux-greenness of the tertiary economy. While ecological reform slowly has been applied to the secondary economy, the fast-evolving tertiary economy has pretty much drawn a free pass. Criticisms of financialization abuses, schemes and damage to the secondary economy have been many—especially since the 2008 disaster of the Great Recession. But even bitter liberal critics of Wall Street seldom mention any ecological effects of the tertiary economy. There's a curious and deceptive phenomenon going on here. In a similar manner to how globalization-driven de-industrialization has allowed proponents to portray the off-shoring of much of America's old manufacturing dominance as a green—and thus, good—thing, tertiary economy partisans celebrate the parallel shift to a much more financialized economy in the same way. The physical, geographic displacement of America's old manufacturing economy is used to disguise the fact that mass production is still hammering the primary economy. Only, it's happening somewhere else, out of sight and smelling range of Americans, and out of the reach of carefully limited American energy, materials consumption and emission statistics. As in the old saying, out of sight, out of mind.

In assessing the ecological footprint of the tertiary economy, emphasis is placed on the *direct* use of energy and materials as well as the *direct* carbon and other emissions attributable to tertiary economy firms. Lacking strip mines, factories, power plants, fleets of 18-wheelers, or big-box retail outlets, FIRE sector firms look like ultra-green enterprises. In the rigidly compartmentalized manner in which such statistics are kept, the tertiary economy comes off as a modest consumer and emitter: an ecological winner, a positive and profitable basis for a new post-industrial, ecologically sustainable economy.

This superficial conclusion could prove disastrous. It would be misleading enough If globalization succeeds in disguising the ecological impacts of the secondary producing economy, supposedly tucked out of sight through transparent tactics like off-shoring and outsourcing. However, it would be much more serious if failure to look behind the screen overlooks the more subtle manipulations that serve to hide the ecological impacts of the tertiary economy. The effect it has had in driving the secondary sector to engage in the visible ecosystem damaging activities cannot be overstated— especially in this globalizing world.

ECONOMIES OPERATING UNDER DIFFERENT ECOLOGICAL RULES

To get a more balanced and accurate view of the true nature and size of tertiary economy ecological impacts on the threatened primary economy, we turn to John Michael Greer. In his 2011 book, *The Wealth of Nature,* Greer succinctly explains the subtle ways the modern, expansionist tertiary economy puts destructive pressure on nature. The key is understanding the different ways in which each of the three economies are limited, both within and by factors operating in the other two economic realms.

Supply-limited: the primary and secondary economies. Nature's primary economy and the secondary economy of human production hold one crucial characteristic in common: they are both *supply-limited.* This means, the output and availability of things each economy produces is limited—as is natural for any closed ecosystem. The primary economy has only so much petroleum, copper or iron ore, fresh water, fertile soils and ocean fish it can supply. Its ecosystems can absorb only so many toxic chemicals or endure so much global warming. Turning to the secondary economy, much the same is true, although it may not seem as obvious. The human economy has a limited amount of human labor and human mental ingenuity from which to draw. Productive resources that augment human effort, such as machines and warehouses, are similarly limited.

Attempts to rapidly increase the capacity of any primary or secondary economy resource are usually very difficult or even impossible, often resulting in costly imbalances that upset system equilibrium. For example, if fossil fuel energies are in short supply, additional exploration, mining, drilling and refining come at high capital, energy and environmental costs. If human labor is short, increasing the population or diverting trained workers from other areas might take many years. And critically, attempts to expand the supply of resources in the secondary economy are clearly contingent on primary economy resources being available and affordable.

Self-correction and negative feedback. Because of this common dependency on supply-limited rules, the primary and secondary economies have tended to be somewhat self-regulating throughout our industrial history. When certain plant and animal species over-breed or over produce (usually due to some unusual and temporary abundance in their food supply) nature reliably responds with unfavorable conditions that cause a die-off—and a sustainable balance is restored. Analogously, in human secondary economies, producing too much of something (for example, over-priced houses being marketed to under-qualified buyers) will have similar results. Production is usually cut or stopped altogether, often not without severe impacts on the general economy, until supply and demand are more balanced again.

Such self-correction—which John Michael Greer points out is the operant principle with Adam Smith's Invisible Hand—ideally occurs in both primary and secondary economies because they are governed by *negative feedback.* Apologists of the current system would like to think this happens automatically in every case, and that market price adjustments will always restore a healthy equilibrium. (*Leave it to the private market...*) If valid, this process allows the primary and secondary economies to work together, creating an acceptable balance between the two without outside regulation or control.

For example, if too much demand for iron ore threatens what nature's iron mines can supply, the price of ore goes up. This drives some marginal iron consumers from the market, no longer able to afford the higher price. Pressure on supply then relaxes a bit. Plus, marginal old mines, new mines and higher production from existing mines may be brought into play by devoting more capital, human labor and other resources. Prices drop and the system again finds some equilibrium. Technological change normally plays a critical role.

Using a slightly different example, if the demand for airline flights is increasing, putting baggage handlers in short supply, the wages of baggage handlers might be bid up. This may cause workers in other fields to acquire baggage handling skills and seek better-paying jobs in the airline industry. This causes other employers to raise wages to keep from losing workers, slowing the labor stampede to baggage handling. Wages and employment levels stabilize and eventually the baggage handler shortage is ameliorated.

The powerful connection between the primary economy—the ultimate source of all vital resources—and the secondary economy, based as it is on supply-limited physical reality moderated by negative feedback loops, is the basis for standard economic theory and analysis—as you may have noticed. Without the ultimate supply-limited constraints along with the discipline of countless negative feedback loops, the supposed ability of economic systems based on markets, supply and demand to self-regulate would make no sense. They would have no chance of withstanding the many unbalancing, de-stabilizing forces inherent in modern economies, and would have long ago collapsed. Even now, the relationship is tenuous. Onset of the Age of Scarcity in a continuing political environment of incessant pressure for economic growth may have already permanently impaired the ideal primary/secondary relationship. But it gets worse.

Demand-limited: the tertiary economy. Enter the upside down, contrary workings of the mushrooming tertiary economy. While the primary and secondary economies are supply-limited and controlled by the finite availability of real, valuable things, the tertiary economy is **demand-driven.** The tertiary economy, which revolves around the creation and manipulation of artificial tokens of wealth, is only limited by the demand for such tokens. This demand, increasingly disconnected from the finite supplies of real, essential things, can, like the artificial tokens themselves, be created out of thin air.

For example, if bank officials observe the demand for houses—and thus for 30-year mortgages to help people buy these houses—banks create more mortgages. If the process seems limited by the availability of qualified buyers with good incomes, recall the recent history of the Great Recession. By appealing to home ownership as the culmination of the American Dream, and by less lofty practices (emphasizing the millions to be made by monetizing the rapid appreciation of houses, conjuring up all sorts of sub-prime, untraditional mortgages, openly ignoring existing industry standards of buyer qualification, etc.) the home building/selling/financing industry was able to create mortgage demand far beyond reasonable levels consistent with the real economy.

If Greece or the United States determines the only way to pay off rising national debt is to print more money and/or issue more treasury bonds, it prints more money or bonds. The notional value represented by the electronic dots on some investment banker's hard drive does not necessarily represent "real" value. It is not physical goods coming from nature, processed into valuable goods and services by human workers, using capital accumulated from producing real assets in the past. A simple stroke of the pen, a press of a key or click of a mouse is all that is required. Paraphrasing P. T. Barnum, if the sucker of the moment can be found, the tertiary product can be peddled, no matter how ephemeral it might appear to those of us not schooled in the financial mysticism of tertiary economics.

At this stage, the willing buyers for the national or corporate bonds, sub-prime mortgages, derivatives, credit default swaps, pork belly futures, platinum credit cards, 72-month RV loans, options on gas fracking lease sites or whatever, appear bottomless.

Despite a long history of lost fortunes and induced catastrophes going back to Tulip Mania in the 1630s, demand, the only requirement for tertiary tokens, remains strong. Fueling that demand for tertiary wealth, of course, is human greed—a durable commodity obviously able to survive any economic crisis.

The ecological danger. As destabilizing to the secondary economy as a runaway demand-driven tertiary economy can be, the present danger is predominantly ecological. That is, the stress put on the secondary by the tertiary is immediately passed through to the primary—and in all likelihood amplified. There is a deep irony here when one takes note of common perceptions. An ordinary citizen/observer will conclude that it is the productive activities (mining, industrial production, disposal of waste, etc.) that are the chief despoilers of the environment, while the financial sector is "good clean" economic activity. In truth, the excesses of the financial sector are likely the real culprit. In the current globalized version of the modern economy, the financial sector incessantly drives the secondary to ecologically destructive behavior. Clearly, this realization has profound implications for any attempts to regulate or mitigate environmental damage.

The chief reason why the tertiary economy is so dangerous concerns feedback. While the primary and secondary economies operate predominantly with negative feedback, the tertiary economy responds to *positive feedback.* As we earlier pointed out, the primary and secondary economies tend to be largely self-governing, because negative feedback loops dampen the extremes and bring imbalances back toward equilibrium. Exactly the opposite is true in the tertiary economy.

Consider the housing bubble of the mid-2000s, a big contributor to the Great Recession. Did the rampant sale of overpriced houses financed with risky and excessive mortgages sold to underqualified buyers set in motion natural forces that acted to limit these sales, lower house prices gradually, or otherwise lower the risk and avert crisis? Hardly. Just the opposite happened; more marginal buyers rushed into the market, afraid of being left out. More investors poured in more money to capture the high profits (before the market crashed). And the industry marketing cashed in on the "buy now!" hype to woo both buyers and investors. Much the same happened at the end of the high-tech bubble in the late 1990s: investors were enticed to sink their money into any technology/internet/computer scheme with a pulse, so to speak. That didn't work out well, except possibly for those who made a living from transactions fees—i.e., the tertiary economy "bottom feeders."

Leading up to the 2008 crash and the Great Recession, the tertiary economy even doubled down on that. By creating new exotic financial instruments such as derivatives, bundled mortgages, credit default swaps and the like, Wall Street sought to monetize and gain from the home equity buildup (temporarily) enjoyed by individual homeowners. Employing hitherto unimagined financial leverage, the tertiary sector managed to squander much of the equity buildup previously held by individual homeowners. As an aside, it is nothing less than criminal that the gains from the recent rebound in housing prices are enjoyed not by those who first lost the equity, (some $6 trillion in homeowner losses by some estimates) but in large part by the big financial institutions which caused the problem in the first place! Individual homeowners are having to buy back in at the rebounded prices.

These examples illustrate how positive feedback works to reinforce the forces and trends that are causing the problem. As signs of trouble appear, instead of tempering the things contributing to the trouble and bringing the system back toward stability, positive feedback loops cause a strengthening or speeding-up of the contributing factors. Financial overshoot, such as the high-tech bubble or the housing bubble that followed it, cause more money to be committed—more investors (often less able to stand the inevitable loss) to be drawn in.

An obvious and proven dangerous ramification of the tertiary economy's positive feedback loops is to the secondary economy. As we saw in the Great Depression, the high-tech recession of 2000-01 and the housing bubble preceding the Great Recession of 2008-09, the blow to the secondary economy of production, jobs and vital output is often disastrous. The costs in human suffering from job losses, unemployment and foreclosures are huge. The fallout for the public sector in terms of costly bailout and stimulus programs and lost tax revenues is equally serious. Of course, in the current political climate, the public sector virtually saved the economy—and got criticized by many for doing that.

But less recognized is the damage that occurs, usually through the intermediary vehicle of the secondary economy, to nature's primary economy. At first glance, the slump in secondary economy production may seem to be an ecological benefit. Ironically, energy use, the consumption of raw materials and even emissions into the biosphere drop during recession. But, because overshoot followed by collapse is the pattern of positive feedback systems, falling resource consumption and lower discharge of wastes comes at a steep price. For instance, the mid-2000s housing bubble caused many more homes to be constructed than could be bought under healthy, sustainable conditions. Many of these houses stood vacant for an extended period when the bubble burst. (Some are still vacant in the hardest-hit areas; others were simply torn down or bulldozed without ever being occupied). The waste of physical resources, valuable land, infrastructure, human labor and useful capital was enormous.

In the case of other financially-based bubbles which ultimately burst, the excess wasted resources were largely in industrial infrastructure, such as internet-related capacity, telecommunications networks, electrical power plants and grids, software development (much of which ultimately went unused) and similar investment. As is typical, much of this sunk investment, because it causes GDP to rise, is viewed positively as productive growth. The opposite approach, based on recognizing the current highest human economic priority as lightening the load on the hard-pressed primary economy, produces a much less sanguine view. Such dead-end financial ventures waste precious energy, finite physical resources, time, labor, capital and ecosystem health. They should never have been made; the tertiary economy greed that inspired them, and the positive feedback loops that reinforced them once in progress, could and should have been avoided by smarter policies.

The tertiary economy gains control and flexes its muscle (again). Much of the world of finance—investment banks, private speculators, etc.—has always operated according to demand-driven rules. But big differences occur when, occasionally, the financial sector of various countries grows powerful enough to set itself apart from the supply-driven secondary economy where finance normally plays second fiddle to productive economy interests. These "break-out" periods of uncontrolled dominance of a powerful, autonomous tertiary economy invariably have ended in severe financial crises. And these crises always feed back markedly to the operation of the secondary economy—and with increasing intensity and disastrous results onto the primary/natural economy. The severe boom-bust roller coaster rides of the Robber Baron era, the 1920s (ending with the onset of the Great Depression), and the revival of neoliberalism of the last three decades are all examples of America allowing its economy to be seized by tertiary economic control. And finally today, the reality is that ***finance is crippling the environment***. As academic/author Joel Kovel says, capital has become the enemy of nature.

The current American tertiary economy once again has gained enough wealth and political power to control not just important government economic policy making, but much of the strategic operation of the secondary productive economy from which it has split off. Most critically, when an ascendant out-of-control tertiary economy makes the rules, the "pass-through" pressures on the primary economy of nature, already at dangerous levels, can imperil much more than economic stability. It can imperil the planet.

Finally, it is important to emphasize just how excessive financial sector power and rule setting translate into ecological damage to the primary economy. Though Wall Street bankers and hedge fund managers don't have unblemished reputations with many Americans these days, we hardly tend to think of them as big energy and resource gobblers or as big polluters. Following are two examples of indirect tertiary economy ecological impact focusing on something other than the sterile statistics of sector energy use or carbon emissions.

1. GLOBALIZATION AND THE TERTIARY ECONOMY.

Globalization is normally viewed as a product of the secondary economy. Manufacturers, seeking cheaper and more compliant labor, fewer government controls, lower environmental standards and closer proximity to overseas resource supplies and end markets, outsourced and off-shored their factories. To the extent that advancing technology has allowed, suppliers of services have followed suit, putting additional downward pressure on jobs, wages, and remaining domestic productive firms.

It's a familiar story. The secondary economy does indeed still produce the goods and services; and it now does so on a much wider, interconnected scale. In extolling the scale economies and labor cost advantages of this new global economic "world view," occasionally ignored are the ecological (primary sector) impacts of this transition. They occur mainly from the additional use of fossil fuel energy and electricity (also largely fossil fuel-based) necessary to power all the additional cargo hauling and communications across vast global distances. Much more energy is needed to close the wider distances between producers and all the whistle stops in the global economy. Many American secondary economy manufacturers, both those that have off-shored and those who have stayed home, have seen their profit levels jump. The ones that left have lower labor costs and the ones that stayed home use the outsourcing threat to bargain for lower domestic wage and benefit packages—a win/win for corporations and a lose/lose for common folks.

Workers and consumers (ideally the same people...) are "bribed" into accepting this inequality and environmental disaster by pointing out the cheap goods made available by the whole arrangement. (*"Just head for Walmart and it will all work out fine...!"*) The bottom line is that a societal addiction to consumerism is used to inoculate the general public against the realization of the equity implications of the big picture. The story becomes complete when the offending corporations are lionized as the prime creator of jobs for our chronically underemployed population.

The missing part of the story is the change in strategic decision making. Increasingly in recent decades the crucial decisions on how this would all be organized and set into operation have come from tertiary economy decision makers more than those in the secondary economy. Today, that transition is virtually complete—finance rules the world. Tertiary policy makers have seized opportunities primarily in two areas: 1. Global trade agreements that have marked the last twenty-five years; 2. Exploiting their own demand-driven rules by the simple act of...you guessed it, creating more demand.

Global Trade Agreements. Trade pacts such as NAFTA, CAFTA, the WTO and the more recently proposed Trans Pacific Partnership (TPP) are in large part the brain children of powerful decision makers within the tertiary economy. Arguably, such trade agreements and similar international negotiations have been more lucrative to transnational banks and other big financial interests than to transnational productive corporations. And, since the well-being of common citizens is much more dependent on a flow of needed goods and services than on understanding an impenetrable financial sector, the same is true for the public. By prying open formerly insular foreign banking systems, the big financial firms have developed a wealth of profitable investment opportunities. Such "deals" often prey on the hunger for foreign investment in particular nations, as well as the favorable light in which that sort of capital transfer is viewed by major nations and the international financial institutions.

These opportunities are often more profitable than those available in traditional secondary economy investments at home, subject to less regulatory oversight and are combined with mergers, acquisitions and other lucrative "fee-based" financial manipulation. The particular product(s) involved may be of only incidental consequence—it's all about the money. Under the terms now agreed to by many nations, rules were relaxed and international markets opened in ways that have greatly increased the mobility of money—and greatly enriched the fortunes of the biggest tertiary economy firms which control much of that money.

Occasionally, as in the Great Recession following 2008 and the Asian crisis of 1997, all this mobile hot money, acting with its positive feedback loops, has created severe crashes. This, too, has become an opportunity for higher tertiary economy gains and increased control. As Naomi Klein so thoroughly documents in her book **The Shock Doctrine,** the crises induced in formerly insular economies have become excuses for converting these economies into dependent, vassal state of the centrally controlled global economy. In exchange for debt refinancing and extension, (usually organized through such tertiary economy "hit-men" institutions as the World Bank and International Monetary Fund) debtor nations have agreed to privatization, austerity measures through public program cutbacks, and foreign control aimed primarily at paying back tertiary economy creditors.

The main effect on the primary economies of these debtor nations has been to require a more rapid exploitation of their valuable raw resources, alongside attendant damage to their eco-systems. Shamefully, corporations often eagerly pursue practices that are clearly not allowed in their home country. Previously, where longstanding domestic secondary economy enterprises had restricted production to levels the primary economy could bear, the twin grim realities of becoming a debtor in the high-stakes game of globalization quickly throws massive new burdens on the debtor's primary economy. Hundreds of millions of dollars of debt to foreign tertirary economy creditors can only be paid off one way: through new exports.

That necessary capital can only be earned by cranking up domestic production by setting aside old moderating supply-based limits on the primary economy and converting the country's secondary economy to a modified tertiary economy. They oper-ate under demand-driven, positive feedback rules, maximizing domestic production to earn crucial foreign exchange needed to pay off their mountainous debts. Production is pushed beyond the reasonable levels signaled by any supply-driven alarm bells, no matter how low the prices for exports are pushed nor how serious the damage to local ecosystems.

2. CREATING DEMAND IN A DEMAND-DRIVEN ENVIRONMENT.

The second way tertiary economy decisions and profit-motivated pressures have acted to increase ecological damage is through the creation of additional demand—and hence stimulate growth. We've spoken of the ways in which mature industrial economies like the US and Western Europe naturally offer less opportunity for tertiary economy investors. Profits are far higher in the developing world, where labor is cheap and non-union, government regulations sparse or non-existent, and natural resource pools relatively unexploited. But there's an obvious problem: the combination of massive global industrial capacity that has been installed thus far, along with the lack of demand from end consumers with money to spend, has already produced a substantial glut of global productive capacity.[18] Normally, one would think that the inherent supply-driven negative feedback of the secondary economy, working with similar feedbacks in the resource-stressed primary economy, would kick in to drive down this excessive capacity. Secondary economy suppliers would mothball some of their unused assembly lines and factories, bringing productive capacity back in line with true demand and reducing pressure on primary economy resources.

And some of this has happened. Following the Great Recession, a steady stream of bailouts, stimulus packages and Fed efforts cre-

18   The vast majority of third-world populations never have had the cash to become middle-class consumers on a significant scale; over one billion people [some 15 percent of world population] are estimated to live on the equivalent of one US dollar per day or less. Many first-world consumers in the US and elsewhere, who thus far have been the cash cows for the globalized high-consumption economy, are losing this capability, their incomes ironically depressed by the inequality effects of globalization and technology.

ating essentially free money for tertiary firms to (hopefully) loan to expansion-minded secondary producers has occurred. Most have had limited success, especially when it comes to remaining US domestic production. Firms, with ample capacity to meet the modest demands of constrained American consumers, and with new foreign consumers not appearing in nearly the numbers optimists expected, have often chosen to sit on the cash generated by present operations. And, to a measurable degree, this scenario has both reduced a small portion of the productive over-capacity and lowered demand for primary economy resources such as petroleum. In short, the supply-driven negative feedback loops of both the primary and secondary economies are working...to a small degree.

But countering efforts by the demand-driven tertiary economy have limited the positive effects any normal supply-driven negative feedback might have had on closing the supply-demand gap. Furthermore, heavy-handed tertiary economy intervention in secondary economy decisions makes a joke of the fabled ability of open markets to automatically adjust for such imbalances. Tertiary economy decision makers, having won (or seized) the authority to make secondary economy decisions, have decided that demand and production are inadequate to meet their insatiable demands for profit. They thus have decided to take the logical step to bolster those profits: create more demand. In an economic sector used to dealing primarily with token, notional, non-real symbols of wealth and value, that's no problem. The means of doing so? **Credit.**

Of course, excessive credit was a major contributing factor to the recent Great Recession. Lenders made bad loans to overly optimistic tertiary economy speculators who, when the bubble de jour burst, had no way to repay. Lenders also banked secondary economy schemes around the world that either were incapable of ever turning solid profits, or got caught up in the crash induced by the bursting of other bubbles. First world consumers took on debt through expanded mortgages, credit cards, car loans, student debt and other means. Again, when bursting bubbles in high-tech, foreign banking, or bundled sub-prime mortgages caused the various houses of cards to collapse and spread closures and layoffs throughout the secondary economy, consumers had no way to make repayment.

Certainly, the world of credit and debt has vastly expanded over the last 100 years and that, without this expansion, overall levels of consumption—and overall levels of growth and wealth—would be far lower. Of course most of us Americans celebrate this as a key, positive element of economic progress. Liberals typically emphasize it as a great boon to ordinary, non-rich people; credit enables them to live the good life of material abundance without being fabulously wealthy. Conservatives and the well-to-do investor class typically embrace credit because, well, it's one of the big reasons they are so well-to do. In a world where someone's credit is always someone else's debt, the affluent can reliably be found among the creditors.

Credit equates to ecological depletion and damage. Whatever our individual views about credit—and our individual dependence on it—it is crystal clear that easily available credit is a primary contributor to the current depletion and undermining of the physical environment. Whether caused by third world nations borrowing huge sums for risky development schemes or by first world consumers maxing out their platinum Visas, the ultimate outcome of liberalizing credit has been increasingly ruinous demands on the primary economy. Thus, despoiling of the Ecuadorian Amazon for oil extraction, as well as traffic congestion in your community around the neighborhood Walmart can both be said to emanate from common roots.

Since the credit "business" is the lucrative centerpiece of the modern tertiary economy (with secondary corporations morphing into tertiary companies to take advantage of these profits), no one expects runaway credit to be reined in voluntarily anytime soon. Indeed, economic experts, consumers, and political leaders across the spectrum all praise the general purpose of credit. Both the developing poor world and the rich industrial world crave more credit. But in recent years the primary purpose has disturbingly morphed from a facilitator of human well-being by its support of the secondary economy into its own out of control reason for being. Further, its universal popularity does not change one ugly fact: Tertiary sector credit encourages incessant growth pressures, and the continual necessary flow of physical resources leads to disastrous negative impacts on primary economy ecosystems. Expect this fundamental and irresolvable predicament to bedevil mankind far into the future.

SUMMING UP: PEDDLING THE GROWTH GOSPEL WINDS DOWN; TRANSITIONING INTO THE POST-GROWTH ERA

America's corporatist, centralized economy remains committed to growth, which has become vital to sustain the high profit expectations of the financial system. Intensive criticism, reinforced by mounting evidence of the problems growth causes, has done little thus far to dent the armor of the growth gospel. Whether these problems are experienced in our current muddled and conflicting economic policies, or in the "harder" sphere of measurable ecological degradation, the growth march trudges inexorably onward toward the cliff's edge.

Obviously, an economic system hell-bent on such a dead-end objective as perpetual growth needs an engaging (and diverting) storyline from its PR departments. This has been achieved by disciplined strategies in two areas that are fundamental parts of the current American economy: globalization and rampant financialization. Globalization and financialization are both peddled as beneficial and irreversible foundations of a new and better economy. They represent the secondary and tertiary economies of the future: able to extract the primary economy resources needed for the swelling global population and deliver them efficiently through carefully designed global systems of management coordination and finance. In the everyday economy, the PR barrage has had substantial success; many Americans continue to buy the proposition that globalization is the best (in some cases, *only*) way to supply prosperity to a world population soon to number ten billion people. And only mobile transnational Big Finance can provide the capital and organization for that huge task. If this combination of a secondary and tertiary behemoth has become a bit "too big to fail,"...well, so be it.

But, given the obviously deteriorating planetary environment and climate health, globalization and dominant financialization are becoming an increasingly hard sell. In response, the spin establishment has devised strategies that put distance between the real ecological impacts of globalization and financialization on one hand and the public's perception on the other. In brief, here's how these strategies work:

1. Globalization: *spatial* distance. Globalization, in moving economic activities around the globe, puts ***spatial*** or ***physical*** distance between how environmental matters really work and how we think of them. TRANSLATION: we are encouraged to think that because environmental impacts have been moved far away they have been eliminated entirely.

Off-shoring and de-industrializing activity is of course primarily designed to make corporations more money. However, it's a convenient byproduct that exporting our production facilities and jobs has also exported the resource extraction and production effects of these activities. When tangible environmental impacts are moved beyond our senses of sight and smell, corporatist greenwash efforts take giant steps toward mission accomplished. It takes only a little more ingenuity from the public relations department to sell this as a deliberate move to enhance post-industrial sustainability.

2. Financialization: *causal* distance. Financialization, by shifting the focus of growth from "hard" goods production to abstruse financial manipulation, puts ***causal*** distance between human environmental impacts and people's perceptions of their root causes. TRANSLATION: we are encouraged to think that environmental damage is being caused by organizations and policies other than the incessant financial imperatives that are really driving it.

As in the old shell game, tertiary economy proponents want us to believe the environmental impact "pea" is under the secondary economy "walnut shell," not their own. Financialization is, of course, eager to accept the mantle as the sector with the most rapid, positive growth (rapid growth still being defined as "winning" by most of the public). It also willingly welcomes the unearned reputation as an ultra-green economic sector, consuming little direct energy and emitting little direct waste that damages the climate or other ecosystems. What it doesn't want people to understand is how important decisions of the powerful tertiary financial institutions cause *indirect* damage to the planet. It is content to hide behind the skirts of the productive secondary economy, leaving people to believe the secondary economy of real goods and services—including consumption by all of us—is obviously the source of depletion, climate change and other "pollution." Importantly, government is content to direct virtually all of its environmental regulatory and cleanup activities toward the secondary economy.

In fairness, the secondary economy is clearly the front line of visible environmental impacts. But a better use of scarce environmental cleanup resources and efforts might be to curtail the damaging demand-based activities of the tertiary economy. Sadly, but predictably, this never seems to occur to public regulators.

A GROWTH POSTSCRIPT

The net result of these distancing policies has been to prop up the reputation of growth and to allow politicians of all persuasions to continue promoting it as the cure for America's economic/environmental ailments—at least for now. The failures of the growth ethic are mounting rapidly in the economic arena: inequality, monopoly, mounting public and private debt, the failure to provide enough good jobs for a growing population, and on and on.

But, it is in the ecological realm that the most severe dangers exist. Having already stripped the planet of the richest resources (low-hanging fruit), the obsession for growth is now taking aim at the remainder—which will only be available at enormous energy, capital, human and environmental costs. The critical area of climate gives us our clearest warning signs. Having to survive on a "20 percent carbon budget" in order to keep temperature increases below 2 degrees Celsius is both a stark signal of danger ahead as well as the last rites for unbridled economic growth.

Despite this grim picture, America allows the economic practices of its dominant institutions to escape blame relatively scot-free. Business and political leaders continue to play both sides of the street, pushing pro-growth policies to increase consumption, that demand more resources, that damage climate. The ultimate irony is that they somehow often end up being billed as signs of our commitment to "go green."

R.I.P growth. As uncomfortable as it will be for some, it is past time for America to hold a requiem for further growth. Developing a future economy that can effectively provide for material needs while respecting a fragile ecosystem must delicately juggle a number of awkward and conflicting realities. This transition has an incredibly short deadline and must occur in a human environment short on public understanding and long on disagreement among powerful entrenched interests. Nonetheless, one thing is clear: growth in the way we have described and expected it in the past will be impossible. In sheer quantitative terms, the American economy and most other developed economies around the world must certainly be predicted to shrink over the next immediate decades—the result of attempts to keep carbon from cooking the planet, and also having to pay much steeper prices for dwindling physical resources.

Corporatism: a fish out of water. Against this prospect of an inevitable end of growth, one more thing is clear: America's current corporatist economic institutions are not the ones for the job. Huge central corporations, operating within the current globalist environment and relying on their usual ubiquitous application of technology, have no way to adapt to a world which must forsake growth. They can play no effective part in the countless ways regions and small communities must find to piece together the economies that will provide their needs while conforming to constricting ecological limits. Similarly, the central government, long used to running interference for corporatist banks and producers to compete in the global economy, has little experience in building the patchwork of economic/social/political structures that will prove most resilient and productive in the future of scarcity. Without the growth sledgehammer at their disposal, both the present corporatist private and public establishments will be fish out of water. To continue to rely on them to lead us out of our dilemma—a dilemma their shortsighted policies largely created— would be both unwise and ineffective.

It is time to turn to Part Three. In this final section of the book, we develop practical ideas for institutional and structural arrangements which, in our opinion, offer the best hope for a changing future. To describe this alternative, we use the familiar term **Localism.** It should come as no surprise that our recommendations for a new, stabilized more resilient economy center around local organization. The vast majority of critiques of our present centralized, corporatist system point toward some form of a more local alternative.

In Part Three, we hope to deal in specifics. We will strive to provide some significant examples of organizations, plans and tangible actions that local people can be doing immediately. Time to transition American society into the post-growth era is short. To this point we have assumed it is important that people understand the economic and ecological challenges that suggest the value of something called Localism. It is now imperative that without delay we move beyond vague concepts and statements of the problem to the many real tasks of building a better society.

LOCALISM—TAKING MATTERS INTO OUR OWN HANDS

Crossing the Bridge from Corporatism to Localism

The dismal numbers and dead-end dynamics of current economic and ecological directions can easily create a despondency bordering on despair. While there is no honest way to soft-peddle the potential economic and ecological disasters should America fail to respond to these twin crises, a positive way of dealing with them is at hand. The task of Part Three is to define that path, estimate what will be required of all of us, and energize as many readers as possible to take up the challenge. That challenge, simplified to a single word, will be a transition to an economics and lifestyle built around *Localism.* Part Three begins putting the building blocks in place by which local living in America will be re-invigorated—and hopefully the impending collapse of both corporatist-style economics and an over-burdened environment can be averted.

The path will not be an easy one, nor will it be cheap or quickly completed. Part Three strives to make these obstacles clear; but at the same time endeavors to emphasize the positive economic benefits, the relief of environmental stresses, and even the public enthusiasm and closer human relationships that could and should again become possible. While in no way a total road map of steps to take in implementing Localism, the individual chapters of Part Three should provide valuable guidance in establishing new local enterprises, generating our own energy, using resources close at hand, providing our own planning, management and investment, and other steps as we cross the bridge from Corporatism to Localism.

As with the first two parts of the book, Chapter 14 begins Part Three by setting down some key guiding principles. Chapter 14 proposes we revert to a basic economic principle which has largely been ignored as huge, centralized corporations have dominated and globalized the economy. *Value Added* must again be a cornerstone of economic organization. Chapter 14 will explain how, by keeping resources, money and focus on supply and demand within our communities, we can wring much more prosperity from our precious resources, human skills and environmental limits.

In Chapter 15 we address the most fundamental need of any economy: food. Movements to again feed ourselves have caught fire in recent years, embodied in the organic farming/gardening and eating healthy movements. Despite progress, however, food production, distribution and consumption remains one of the most highly industrialized economic activities—and a centerpiece of Corporatism-style economics. By bringing food back under local production and control, we can lessen the risk of economic and ecological crisis, plus provide many opportunities for solid enterprises and good jobs within our communities.

Chapter 16 carries on the theme of bringing the production of essential material needs back into local communities. Energy is vital to all human (in fact, all *living*) activity; and Chapter 16 argues that the renewable, non-carbon energy systems of the future can best be implemented locally. Not only can they be organized, financed and operated with local resources by local people, but both the economic and technological performance of Localism-based energy systems will be clearly superior to the highly centralized, grid-connected systems typically proposed by corporatist interests.

The manufacture of needed local products is often seen as an Achilles heel of Localism. Chapter 17 argues the opposite, contending that even high-tech products and very specialized services can be part of a Localism-based economy. Chapter 17 will stress one of our main tenets for the Localism concept: that supplying basic needs must be the focus of a Localism-based economy. The rewards in terms of value added and money kept circulating in the local area will be great for the locales which persevere and keep production at home wherever possible.

Financing local enterprise development is another area where critics have bad-mouthed Localism advocates. After all, financing businesses costs an arm and a leg these days, necessitating going hat-in-hand to the big banks or other deep-pocketed capital sources (read: Wall Street)...or so we are led to believe. Chapter 18 will again turn this tired conventional wisdom on its head, arguing that local financial resources are entirely adequate to most tasks of Localism development. The secret, Chapter 18 suggests, is recapturing our own money; taking back the funds now being sucked out of local pockets by the giant Shop-Vacs of Wall Street.

Chapter 19 continues the myth-busting of previous chapters, explaining why many conventional economic development programs have been such notorious flops. Community after community, region after region, state after state—all have tried to woo big transnational corporations to their areas, hoping to strike it rich with big tax revenues and good jobs. Localism abjures this "hey, sailor..." approach, preferring one that empowers local people and groups to plan permanent local enterprises of our own that will be free of the remote, unaccountable tentacles of big corporations.

In Chapter 20, we will look back to our old nemesis, inequality. We will seek to discover how Localism economic and social institutions and practices might relieve the widening economic/social/political chasms that have built up in America under Corporatism. Unlike Corporatism, which promotes elitism and hierarchy, Localism welcomes level, democratic organizations and widespread public participation. In fact, it literally *requires* them to thrive.

Finally, Part Three—and the book—will end with Chapter 21. Chapter 21 has a dual purpose; first, it will outline possibilities for local enterprises whose main purpose is to return carbon to safe storage in the ground. However, unlike corporatist proposals which claim to have the same objective through high technology and exotic powered machinery, the Localism-based "reverse carbon flow" efforts would make the maximum usage of natural processes: solar energy, photosynthesis, healthy soils and much lower-tech approaches akin to organic farming and forestry. The emerging research now clearly suggests heroic efforts to stop carbon from entering the dangerously warming atmosphere will be needed—probably within the next *10 or 12 years!* The first section of Chapter 21 will outline how such naturally-based efforts, organized under Localism, might work and succeed in large carbon capture where industrialized, high-tech gambles will almost certainly fall short.

The second and last section of Chapter 21 will summarize the distinctive ideas and features of the broad Localism concept. Much of the entirety of Part Three is an exercise in refuting reigning conventional wisdom and debunking the powerful implanted myths behind contemporary Corporatism. A major thrust of this mythmaking has been to discount and disparage any notions of returning to local life in America. Therefore It is only realistic to acknowledge that Localism will indeed have a tough "selling job" with many contemporary Americans.

The chapter and book concludes with some thoughts on how returning carbon to the soil with natural means is a metaphor for how Localism contrasts sharply with the conventional Corporatism now dominating our lives. The notion of returning to a "circular" existence—human life interacting symbiotically with natural life, and vice versa—instead of accepting the "linear" extractive system of the Industrial Age is the real allure of Localism. Getting Americans to understand and embrace this difference is the real challenge that will give Localism a chance.

CHAPTER 14

The Radical Nature of the Economics of Localism

As we move to the important practical questions of implementation—those of designing and incorporating Localism-based
economic processes and entities—it is critical to establish
the appropriate philosophical economic framework. As painful
as it might seem to loyal practitioners of the Dismal Science,
much of what we already believe will prove to be unhelpful,
or even downright wrong. We began developing this argument
at the start of the book through the "Trade Helps Everyone"
chapter. Clearly, economics in some form is not only helpful but
vital. However, the analytical framework appropriate for nurturing Localism has major differences from conventional wisdom.
Therefore, we pose an important starting question:

**How do the fundamental characteristics
of localist principles and institutions differ from those
within the conventional wisdom of
economic development?**

This is a crucial question to address because, in these days of
palpable economic stress, virtually every local, state and national
public official or decision-maker has come to emphasize the importance of creating jobs and improving the economy. Nowadays, even
a candidate for dog catcher is likely to stress that his or her main
campaign principle is "putting people back to work." (Clinton vs.
Trump—enough said...)

Cynicism aside, an entrenched conventional wisdom has developed as to how practically to approach the task of economic improvement at the local and regional level. Inevitably, this always seems to translate into the need to "promote growth." Any potential critic must necessarily proceed carefully here, since the questioning of growth per se and/or the generally accepted policies to achieve it can label that critic anti-community health, anti-progress, or even anti-American. Any novel approach can expect potential built-in opposition from the start. One would think, however, *if* that conventional wisdom were correct, that with such unanimity of support the results would be more favorable and effective than they have been. A closer look is needed to reveal some of the flaws in current economic thinking.

Where and how to begin? A simple table, devoid of much discussion, is a useful starting point. In espousing Localism, this book proposes a decidedly different philosophy toward basic productive enterprises as well as to the internal form of business organization. This work speaks to everyday people interested in strengthening their communities, and is not about macroeconomic policy at the national level. It is about local economic development, and you should note that the following table touches on both theory and practice. Some of the listed characteristics refer to the community's approach to the business, and others to the actual inner operations, goals and structure of the enterprise itself.

CORPORATISM	LOCALISM
Conventional Economic Wisdom	Local Community Capitalism
Produce a good for export	Produce a good for local consumption only
Seek exports to bring dollars back into the community or region	Produce a needed product that you now import—so dollars don't leave in first place

Seek to minimize labor costs	Seek to maximize labor as an input
Hold down wage rates to remain competitive	Increase wage rates whenever possible
Adopt the latest (large scale) production technologies to become "competitive in the global economy"	Produce on as small a scale as possible while still capturing "appropriate technology" efficiencies. Ignore the global economy
Seek outside investment capital, ideally from large or single sources. (Assume any significant project cannot be done without "big capital" help)	Fund with community resources, possibly from many small sources. Start community banking, credit unions, etc.
Control of the enterprise by (probably absentee) owner(s)	Control of the enterprise by solely local owners, including workers
Avoid union involvement, if possible	Encourage, even require, a union
Mount large advertising and marketing campaigns to promote products	Avoid expensive marketing by selling to workers, investors, friends, neighbors in the community
Invest in distribution and transportation networks	No transportation or distribution network needed (local streets will do)
Places the role of the owner/capitalist as the residual factor of production (i.e., the "risk taker")	Puts the "owner" in a fixed return position and places workers' wage rates (and prices) as the residual risk taker and "profiter."
Seek to grow and expand in the long run	Seek to produce sustainably at the appropriate level to meet community demand over time

Clearly, many other features could be identified, and more elaboration might provide helpful clarity. Some of this will occur organically in the remaining chapters focusing on specific economic sectors and targeted implementation suggestions. However, an examination of this list immediately uncovers some of the tensions and differences in the innate goals that exist (and historically always have existed) between the interests of the owners of a productive enterprise versus the interests of the community in which it is located. Historically, any writing, for instance on labor relations, has largely focused on innate tensions between **owners** and **workers**. We do not ignore this classic tension, but the focus here speaks even more to tensions between owners and **community** (in which the workers reside...). These tensions are very largely inherent within the very corporation and corporate structure itself. To oppress *workers* is to oppress *communities*.

Strikingly, note that very little, if any, economic analysis ever occurs from the point of view of the community. It is virtually always assumed that economic theory and practice adopts the point of view of the owner/manager/capitalist, and very seldom even from the self interest perspective of the *worker*, let alone the *community* itself. Expect the remainder of this section, indeed this book, to focus on what is best for the *community*—well-being of workers necessarily follows. It is well past time for economic theory to be assigned this task.

One prime example is that a business owner seeks to pay the lowest possible wages while the community wants the best paying jobs possible. A further corollary is that the "capitalist" seeks to minimize the necessary workforce, usually through technological change and innovation, while the community seeks to create as many jobs as possible. Thus, the community wants wages and number of jobs to go, over time, in one direction, while the typical owners of businesses want them to go in precisely the opposite direction. If "jobs" is our unanimously agreed-upon goal, how helpful can capitalist owners oriented in this manner be in the long run?

Need we say more? Is it any wonder that the reliance on growth as our method and on our traditional form—the (potentially) large corporation—for community economic health appears to be having such mixed success? Going no further, we can state with clarity our ultimate purpose for this work as we propose a strategy of Community Economics within the socio-cultural concept we and many others call Localism:

We seek to develop an economic strategy that harmoniously aligns the interests of the business enterprise with those of the community in which it is located, while effectively serving material human needs.

VALUE ADDED–THE CRITICAL CONCEPT

We promised in Chapter 1 to more fully define, discuss and apply the centrally important term value added. The time has come. A return to standard economic theory is necessary. Another way to state what we seek to create in a more sustainable locally controlled economy is an increase in value added per dollar of sale of a good or service. This is the portion of the value of a marketable product or service that is created by local resources as opposed to imported or foreign resources.

For example, a local automobile dealership, even a very well-run, profitable and community spirited enterprise, needs to spend perhaps 90% of the value of its final sale just to import the car from wherever it was built. Suppose, on a $30,000 sale, that the car cost the dealer $27,000; then only $3,000 of the sale is available to be re-spent and therefore multiplied in the local economy. The other $27,000 is immediately sent away.

Suppose, by comparison, a local blueberry farmer grows and sells $5,000 worth of berries, and that his total costs are $4,000, of which $1,000 is the purchase of inputs from outside the area (fertilizer, etc.). The other $3,000 is locally purchased labor and other locally exacted costs (taxes, caring for the tract, picking, etc.)

Application of the concept of value added allows a clear look at the real differences for the economy of the area between these two examples. First of all, total sales are 6 times higher for the car sale, and that will be the contribution to the GDP of the area. "Profits," although this is clearly a first cut at gross profits, also seem to favor the auto sale, $3,000 to $1,000. However, the value added available to be re-spent in the local area is $4,000 for the berry operation and $3,000 for the auto sale. Thus the total economic impact on the local economy itself is actually greater for the $5,000 farm sale than for the $30,000 auto sale. Examining how the $4,000 and the $3,000 are spent, and by whom, would add more nuance to the example, but that is not our point here. (What the heck—the blueberries could also be made into jam before they leave the area, and each berry becomes worth even more to the community...!)

IT'S ALL ABOUT MULTIPLIERS

The specific reason that value added plays such a vital role in the health of a local community is that the value-added portion of payments by producing firms to locally-owned factors of production, including labor, is that it is the portion available to be re-spent (and multiplied) in the community. To generalize the above example, the increased economic value of activities of all types will be re-spent by owners of those local resources, primarily labor, and is the source of local spending multipliers. Thus, simply stated: By focusing on value added, we seek a change in economic structure that increases local multipliers.

This is the economic "magic" that Localism offers: More jobs per dollar of consumer and business spending than we are now experiencing from goods provided by the corporatized and globalized world. This all-important point will be explained and exemplified more emphatically in Chapter 17, which addresses the creation of local manufacturing.

One prime goal, especially if an effective market economy is to be nurtured, is that the act of production must generate the wealth and value that supports the act of consumption. This is where the economic globalization frenzy has failed us. In short, the job of a global corporation is to extract and capture value added from a locality, not to add it. And globalization promises to fail us even more dramatically as we move into the future—especially a future marked by increasing resource supply shortages and acute environmental challenges.

The above example and conceptual conversations on value added in a real sense exemplify the purpose of this work. No economic conversion will ever be complete, but we seek to begin the process—not of "combating" globalization—but simply of going around it. Economic activity is an obvious and desirable necessity—people need material support. Thus an economy, however structured, must work. But it must work comprehensively for the participants (read that, "people") whom the economy serves.

This is not a new idea. Some forty years ago, E.F. Schumacher's revolutionary little classic, **Small is Beautiful**, had it right—as evidenced by its subtitle: *Economics as if People Mattered*. And over 100 years ago, Henry Ford also had it right. He wanted all his workers to be able to buy a Model T. Producers and consumers ideally are the same people. Ford Motor Company is alive and well today—if we can keep them from outsourcing jobs.

In summary, this chapter has set the stage for the ensuing action recommendations by underscoring the fundamentally radical nature of the economics we employ and the approach we propose. Furthermore, it becomes even more clear that the very nature of the corporate mechanism needs to be critically examined. In our view, this critical re-thinking provides an effective way to fight the most pressing economic issue facing our society today—the rampant growth of income and wealth inequality.

Expect the forthcoming examples of actions you can take to further drive home the idea that the necessary economic thinking will in many ways be a dramatic departure from much of what is now accepted as conventional wisdom. In short, whatever else the specific topic of the remaining chapters might be, the coverage will serve to indirectly elaborate the above list. At first glance, many of the dichotomies might appear intrinsically irreconcilable, but our view is that a single-minded approach to Localism might prove otherwise. This could be a bumpy ride, but it promises to be an exciting journey...

CHAPTER 15

Food and Localism

S tarting with the food sector as a cornerstone to a more self-reliant local sustainable economy is a no-brainer. Most places have already embarked on this journey. It is the most obvious "low-hanging fruit," so to speak. Further, increased food self-sufficiency fits squarely within the dominant rationale of this book, since it is clearly the most basic human need. This chapter makes specific suggestions for individual and community actions to further the cause of increased food self-reliance, and also details some of the advantages of doing so.

There is nothing really revolutionary here. As indicated, communities everywhere are moving in this direction, and with amazing results in many cases. Exemplary projects are easy to find, and we specifically identify a few in a specific section of our brief bibliography. Our emphasis, therefore, is on the broader picture: the integrative benefits of food production for local needs and the powerful potential of food for contributing to the entire framework of a more self-sufficient local economy. This emphasizes the *Think Holistically* element of our stated methodology.

FOOD-RELATED COMMUNITY MECHANISMS

Currently, data show that the average molecule of food we eat has traveled an average of over 2000 miles. And with some of those morsels, it's clearly been a long and tiring journey. Often, an item will be picked green and allowed to ripen en route, with flavor being left somewhere along the way (*probably detained at the border...*). Further, plant breeding characteristics for cultivars appropriate for such a system have gravitated toward favoring the ability to withstand such a trip. (Just what I've always wanted in winter—an indestructible tomato...) Obviously, we are getting ahead of the story by prematurely raising the issue of the *advantages* of a more locally-based food system. We first need to look at the *what* and *how*, and later in the chapter the *why* will become more apparent.

We list and discuss five different types of arrangements having potential to advance the local food movement: home gardening, community gardens, community supported agriculture, Saturday markets, and indoor agriculture. These are not the only possibilities, but even a cursory examination of this list effectively serves to make our case. The distinctions among these categories are not always clear, and the interconnections among them can (and should) be intricate.

Home gardening. Growing your own home garden has to rank at the top of the list, for those who know how and have the space. In truth, both the space and the know-how are probably more available than one might assume. A close examination of a typical building lot yields all kinds of spaces, perhaps now occupied by some pallid ornamental, where edible landscaping would thrive (and perhaps even double as an attractive ornamental to boot). Blueberries, for instance, in addition to being high in omega and great on cereal, have lovely blooms and fall foliage. As you probably realize, the general term for systematically converting where you live into a food production system is Permaculture. Google that, and you'll have an interesting and informative day.

As to the necessary know-how, it's not that tough. We've met few gardeners unwilling to share their expertise and talk to anyone who would listen (*and talk, and talk...*). Nothing beats a common gardening interest as a topic having the potential for building a healthy sense of community. Neighbors share produce, recipes and potlucks. The old teach the young. Master gardeners visit schools and conduct hands-on learning experiences. Then the kids return home, and the young teach the old... And they all clamor for more community gardens, and the life-enhancing activities that accompany them.

A popular phrase is "back yard gardening." We have an even better idea: *"front yard gardening."* If growing your own food is really to catch on as a movement, then make it visible to every passer-by. The conversations with people walking their dog can be truly rewarding, and if you give them a ripe tomato or a couple of juicy berries, you may have a friend for life. (Have a treat for the dog, as well—he may remember it longer than the person...) For instance, look closely at the average front yard. It's primarily just for others to look at, with little or no utilitarian benefit. Give it something to do rather than just look pretty. Chances are not only that it will make an important statement, but it may end up looking even prettier—especially to thoughtful citizens and impressionable neighbors.

One of us held a "favorite tomato" tasting contest at a neighborhood brunch on Labor Day this year. Neighbors, several of which garden, entered their own home-grown favorites for common tasting and voting (paper ballots provided). The spirited conversation as we voted on the more than 15 different varieties was the high point of the affair, which we resolved to institutionalize as an instant tradition; and several are harboring secret varieties with which they hope to dominate this coming year's event...

Community gardens. Vacant lots and unused spaces are being converted to community gardens all across the nation. These rank as a step up from home gardening, since they also stimulate food sharing—only more so. They also breed community interaction—only more so; and they make possible an even wider variety of fresh produce. An additional helpful feature is that they provide an opportunity for people who do not have space where they live, such as apartment dwellers, to enjoy the benefits of a home garden.

An excellent local non-profit with a mission of wiping out hunger in our area (Marion-Polk Foodshare), has sponsored and stimulated the creation of over 50 (and growing) community gardens in our city. They offer technical advice from experienced gardeners and even supply free seeds to anyone wishing to start one. Additionally, after gardeners use and share all that they wish, the organization assists in making the surplus available to hungry and/or homeless individuals and families.

Community supported agriculture (CSA). This increasingly popular mechanism has grown out of desires on the part of consumers to have an ongoing supply of fresh healthy produce, and on the part of the participating farmer/growers for increased local marketing and perhaps even to have a closer relationship with those who consume their products. Often, the arrangement involves organic, non-GMO or other specific desired characteristics. For the farmer, the extra work compared to a traditional (perhaps monoculture) crop is paid back in extra income—a straightforward creation of value added.

Normally, the arrangement involves a monthly or weekly fee, and the buyer picks up a weekly assortment of food at a designated spot. Requests for specific items are sometimes honored, and of course the composition of the package varies somewhat by the season. Backup greenhouse operations can allow more flexibility and range of choice, and the farmer can supply recommendations for other qualifying items that they do not grow (e.g., organically grown beef or chickens). It should be a simple matter for you to find out options for belonging to a CSA in your community.

It is worth pointing out the economic impact implications of such arrangements for the community and the sub-region as a whole. What is accomplished is an assurance that as many of the inputs and cost factors as possible remain contained in the area. In other words, it further minimizes *leakages* and increases value added, and thus local multipliers. Importantly, variations in price (or even a zero price in the case of freely given produce) of anything exchanged are irrelevant. It does not matter how the "surplus value" is distributed. The point is that it arises in and remains in the local area and expands the wealth that is to be multiplied. The "community" is richer.

Saturday markets. These popular community events are of course a distribution mechanism for locally produced food (and many other items) as opposed to a production entity. But they play an important role, since the existence of a Saturday market (*or any other day of the week, presumably*) is easily compatible with virtually any mechanism discussed or recommended in this final section of the book. They virtually cry out: *"Localism...!"* In most communities they function as entertainment and communication venues in addition to sales outlets. Commonly, they start out on a limited basis, and have seen popularity grow steadily as citizens (customers) and vendors alike look forward to being there for the social interaction, the ambience and information on events in the community as much as the purchasing opportunities. (*Olives? I didn't know Oregon produced olives. Yep. There's a booth at the Saturday market...*)

In the strict realm of food, a Saturday market of course distributes fresh local produce in season, and in that sense acts almost like a CSA. Also, there are normally food booths serving various menu items, or vendors selling crafts and processed items, such as jams, jellies, baked goods, etc. The food booths can therefore have essentially a local restaurant function. Along these lines, another value adding arrangement is a "farm to restaurant" business niche that channels fresh local foods to (generally upscale) restaurants and can fill particular roles in the local array of eating establishments—such as organic, vegetarian or gluten-free food. If local farmers and gardeners make such connections, and due to the high value-added contribution, steady production throughout the year can be assured through greenhouse production. And this leads to the next item on our list.

Indoor agriculture. This is a specialized function that has been yielding amazing results, both economically and nutritionally, in many cities across the U.S. Obviously, greenhouse production has long been with us, and as costs and climate allow, contributes substantially in selected areas with certain foods. That is a positive factor, especially in connection with alternate energy arrangements for the necessary power. However, the particular innovation we refer to here is slightly different: the re-use of old obsolete buildings and converting them to a virtual "food habitat."

Many of the buildings, prime targets for urban renewal, would be expensive to renovate to full urban code condition, and their ideal exact use is uncertain; but it seems like an unsustainable waste of resources simply to demolish them. Projects, with innovative employment of agronomic techniques such as hydroponics, have adapted such structures into virtually complete ecosystems. Some circulate nutrient-rich water, often through different floors of an old building, and grow a wide variety of crops as the particular "micro-climate" varies among rooms. Aquaponics are even involved, with the fish adding nutrients that are extracted and used by the plants.

Some of these buildings are quite large, and projects can have designs that anticipate offering a balanced diet to entire groups of people. Needless to say, many jobs are created, even as food is produced and out-of-date buildings are inexpensively restored and put to good use. Results from projects in such cities as Chicago, Detroit and St. Louis report dollar returns in excess of $200,000 per acre! It would be difficult to identify projects which more completely characterize the best of truly sustainable development, including jobs, positive sense of community, nutritional production of a basic need, alternate energy potential, environmental integrity and recycling of resources. (*And the hydroponic broccoli in Room 6 extracts just enough nutrients to nourish the strawberries when the water proceeds to Room 7, just before the virtually pure water returns to the fish tanks on the main floor....*) At last, a positive role for the Greenhouse Effect.

FOOD AND CARBON CAPTURE.

Presently, a major flaw of our globalized, industrial, corporatist food system is the enormous contribution it makes to climate-warming emissions, principally carbon dioxide and methane. A Localism-based food system of small, diversified farmers and citizen gardeners has great potential to make a huge dent in the climate-warming footprint of unsustainable globalized agriculture, now causing as much as 50 percent of atmospheric warming.

The particular crops grown and how they are produced will of course make substantial differences in greenhouse gas emissions. (For example, see the comments below regarding animal-based agriculture.) Community groups of citizens, academic institutions, local governments, and local finance could all be aligned to assist local farmers in developing and deploying carbon-capturing techniques that sequester carbon in the soil.

As climate threats mount in the immediate years ahead, carbon capturing and other such projects that cross boundaries to integrate energy, climate and environmental policies with food production will become vital ways to build local resiliency. Furthermore, carbon capturing could be closely tied to local climate mitigation initiatives such as local carbon taxes (a badly needed initiative, given the abject failure of carbon taxes at the national level). Chapter 21, as our final broadly integrative "general theory" of what Localism must seek to do, will provide further details in this critical, relatively unexplored area of using natural processes to capture carbon and prevent the overheating of the atmosphere.

In summary, local food self-sufficiency may rank as both the key climate mitigation element as well as the symbolic major factor in beginning to move communities toward Localism in general. Food is a basic need that can be provided in a variety of ways, which means that anyone has an incentive to actively participate in any emergent community efforts.

WHAT WE EAT: ALTERING AND IMPROVING OUR DIET IN ECOLOGICALLY POSITIVE WAYS

Staples and grains. A void that now exists in many local efforts developing organic and natural food systems involves staples such as grains. Most local farmers, often working with affiliated urban citizens, concentrate on produce: fresh fruits and vegetables. In some cases, processed foods such as jams, jellies, pickles, and freshly-prepared foods such as pies, cakes and bread also are bought and sold, especially at Saturday markets. More recently, animal-based products have become common; free-range chickens, grass fed beef, eggs from organically-raised hens, cheeses, etc., are becoming popular at farmers' markets or Saturday markets and from CSAs.

As communities seek to expand, diversify and strengthen their local food systems to ensure all essential food groups are provided locally, they will need to address basic carbohydrates and grains such as wheat, oats, rye, buckwheat and even rice. A promising way to do this would be to expand the CSA concept to form contractual agreements between citizens and small, close-by farmers to grow essential grains. These arrangements could lead to further enterprises—and job opportunities—such as cooperative mills which turn grains into flour. These enterprises could then feed other initiatives, such as local entrepreneurs producing baked goods and pasta.

Animal-based agriculture. No treatment of food production, whether based on present industrial/corporate models or Localism alternatives, would be complete without mention of one immense and troubling issue: animal-based agriculture. Eating animals and animal products is a fundamental part of most human cultures throughout history. However, it goes without saying that the consumption of animals by humans has come under fire from many fronts in recent years. Further, the ecological crisis drawing so much public debate during recent decades has added substantially to the urgency and often bitter rancor of that debate. Part Two has already mentioned that eating domesticated animals, seafood, and their byproducts consumes energy, water and land, and adds to climate warming emissions like CO_2 and methane.

While present organic food movements are often automatically linked to issues such as animal welfare and humane treatment, and other "green" concerns, there is nothing innate in Localism-based, self-sufficient food production that guarantees a rejection—or even sizable reduction—in mankind's present fixation with eating animals. The data from reputable research indicates that the full-system effects of animal-based agriculture probably has more climate impact than all other human-caused fossil fuel emissions together. This startling fact stems largely from the impacts of methane, (*darned cows, anyway...*) which is twenty to fifty times more potent as a greenhouse gas than its more widely discussed partner, carbon dioxide. Therefore, we feel it important to point out that, to realize savings in energy and warming emissions large enough to make a difference in our ecological crisis, Localism-based food systems are going to have to move away from eating animals.

Clearly, the manner in which the climate impacts of animal agriculture has been avoided by present political leaders indicates it is one of the most "radioactive" issues surrounding the topic of food. Certainly, the political and financial leverage of the various food industry powerhouses is a major factor explaining the deafening silence on the issue in the United States. However, given the way that eating animal products is embedded in the customs and everyday life of virtually all societies—rich or poor, "advanced" or "under-developed"—not all the blame can be laid at the feet of the various food industry trade groups or lobbyists.

Compounding the problem, the effects of excessive animal product consumption extends well beyond the direct measurements of fossil fuel and chemical use, or of carbon emitted. They overflow into areas such as land use, fresh water consumption and contamination, pollution of the oceans, cutting of remaining forests for grazing land, moral treatment of animals and species extinction. And we should not forget human nutrition and health concerns, such as obesity and cancer. Truly, the eating of animals and animal products is an issue that knows no boundaries. We can all appreciate (*as we head for the backyard grill...*) that agreeable solutions will be hard to come by, even in the somewhat more favorable framework of Localism. Exactly how this will play out, and what new social, political and economic decisions may evolve, remains an unsolved question.

FOOD AND VALUE ADDED

The direct economic impact of a Localism-based transition of food systems is quite clear. Purchasing the locally produced product creates net new jobs in the community. When we import some food item as opposed to locally growing or producing that same item, very little per dollar spent on those well-traveled molecules of food would be available for re-spending in our community. The grocery business is a notoriously low-markup/high volume business. The wholesale costs—those going to an outside "foreign" business—are quite close to the retail price the consumer pays. For the local grocery store, the imported item simply means that a large percentage of the retail price immediately leaves the community and is unavailable for further re-spending and increases in the multiplier.

Further, if the grocery store is a national chain, even the profits escape the community. We are left with some clerks' salaries to be multiplied. (Don't worry—growing your own tomatoes will not put Safeway out of business...) But this gets us to the potential indirect economic impacts. Most food items these days are processed in some way. Notwithstanding the personal health benefits of eating fresh as opposed to processed foods, what might this imply as a strategy for your community and the potential benefits of going local? Let's construct an example.

Suppose that a pound of fresh blueberries sells for $2.00 in local markets. Suppose also that a six-ounce jar of blueberry jam sells for $2.50, and that one pound of blueberries can yield three such jars. This means that the pound of berries is now generating $7.50, or almost four times the fresh price. Oh, sure, there are other costs, and the typical mainstream approach to this situation would be to scornfully look down our traditional noses at "all the labor costs" that would entail. But that's the point—There's no such thing as a cost—there's only a job opportunity...

Also, after sponsoring a contest among cooks in the community to choose the most mouth-wateringly delicious recipe for the jam, and seeing if the local community college has a glass-blowing capability to produce a re-usable "designer" jar (*shaped like a blueberry*...?), which offers a $.50 deposit against another purchase (*Hook that customer*...), the company can then start negotiating with local farmers to grow stevia for sweetener so that we won't have to import sugar to make the jam.

The example is whimsical, but it makes some important points. Refining some local products to an additional level of processing can not only magnify the economic impact of some local product (food or otherwise), it can offer consumers substitutes for other products which might otherwise be imported. Think ketchup. Think hazel nut butter.

As an aside, our county, Marion County, in Oregon, is the leading county in the nation for production of hazel nuts. An excellent value-added activity would be the production of hazel nut butter, both to saturate (polyunsaturate...?) the local market, and also for export. But we digress...

The job impacts multiply, and local sustainability inexorably increases one income at a time. No area economy is a closed system, and it makes no difference that you will, of course, never produce everything that you consume. Nor should you even want to—do what you can do. (*Greenhouse pineapples are still a bit in the future...*)

The general rule should be that any product under consideration automatically generates a series of questions about other complementary products and additional value-added possibilities. The example makes the point that there may be opportunities for expansion into the inputs necessary for these more refined products. Current economic development theory embraces the concept of input substitution, which operates on the premise that, once a major industry is established, distinct locational advantages may accrue to input suppliers for that industry—a comparative advantage due to lower transport costs, and perhaps excellent access to a technically trained labor force. This concept has been utilized by public and private economic development efforts in attracting satellite firms near large-scale industrial businesses, but our point is that it has equal validity with smaller local start-up operations. Localism can actually learn from corporatism.

SUMMARY: BUILDING ON WHAT WE HAVE TO START THE BALL ROLLING

We stand by our opening statement that there is nothing revolutionary here. However, as motivated food activists strive to energize Localism food movements in coming years, their jobs will be cut out for them. The "revolutionary" nature of the challenge will be institutional and organizational. While prolific technical information and ongoing research and pioneering efforts may offer a clear path for new Localist food systems, the comprehensive tasks facing communities and activists are imposing. Converting present industrial, corporatized food systems into local, self-sufficient and resilient, low-energy, low-environmental impact ones will be difficult in any comprehensive sense. It will demand more than agronomic skills.

We also stand by our statement made in the beginning of Part Three in Chapter 14. That is, the economics of Localism are truly *radical*. When viewed from the perspective of what must change from our current centralized systems, underestimating what it will take to transform key elements such as food production would be a grave mistake. Yet the vital nature of what is at stake—finding ways to feed ourselves in the years ahead—means the effort is critical. In concluding this section, remember one thing: Food production is a direct form of solar energy harvesting. And that is where we now turn—local options for producing our own energy.

CHAPTER 16

Energy and Localism

E nergy is clearly the beating heart of all economic activity. Further, its central role to virtually *all* human activity strongly indicates that producing our own energy must be a central element of Localism. Current energy thinking, however, is wrapped in the complex intricacies of centralism and global Corporatism. Whatever the other effects, this heightens dependency and robs small communities of control. The key question thus becomes: How can communities trying to transition to economic and social systems featuring increased local control hope to fight powerful and long-standing trends toward centralization, given the daunting technical, financial, organizational and distributive issues currently surrounding energy production?

With issues surrounding resource depletion and ecosystem collapse redefining the rules of the game, centralism, globalization and top-down control are rapidly losing their former luster in many sectors—not just the sphere of energy. A blatant case in point is the Great Recession that cratered the economy in 2008—2010. The allure of big solutions was clearly tarnished by the economic mismanagement and obviously self-serving policies of big corporate finance. Consistent with the thesis of this book, the well documented incompetence and blatant greed also markedly contributed to that other riveting social issue: the enormous problem of *inequality*. One upshot of this inability to comfortably rely on supplies traditionally offered by big business is likely to be simple contraction. We will experience supply constraints, undoubtedly accompanied by price increases.

Environmentally, the problems also multiply. The long supply and delivery lines of global fossil fuel systems, their innate hazards to life from synthetic organic chemicals, and the direct way they warm the atmosphere by hydrocarbon emissions make present energy systems dangerous to the planet. Despite the confusion sown by climate and "depletion" deniers, it is crystal clear that the current American and global energy systems are major culprits. In the near-term future, much fossil fuel usage—whatever the actual situation with "economically recoverable reserves"—will have to be severely curtailed if we are to save the planet—and ourselves.

On the positive side, local communities in America and elsewhere already are discovering there are many productive paths they can take toward increased local energy self-sufficiency. These paths combine a return to depending on the ultimate renewable resource—the sun—with innovative advanced forms of new technology. In an ideal world, the old meets the new.

LOCALISM ENERGY INITIATIVES

The following is a brief representative list of some of the ideas, projects and initiatives that Localism efforts mounted by local citizens can design and implement. First, it's vital to keep in mind that Localism-based energy production and delivery plans must be focused on the assessed critical **basic** needs of local societies. And secondly, Localism efforts should take maximum advantage of well-proven, available technologies such as solar and wind, as they seek to speed the transition toward renewables and away from fossil fuels as quickly as possible.

A. ENERGY USE AND CONSERVATION: WHAT YOU SAVE IS ENERGY YOU DON'T HAVE TO GENERATE

Energy conservation programs in one form or another have been commonplace in America since the "alternative lifestyles" decade of the 1970s. They have been a centerpiece of energy usage policies. This forty years of experience means that many businesses, communities and citizens have a healthy head start on how to cut our common and individual energy budgets. In the years ahead, serious energy conservation programs will be needed in virtually every locality. They will be crucial in combating energy/material depletion and climate/environmental damage, as well as preparing communities for an energy future of much lower overall levels of supply. It is both a technical challenge and a potential benefit that new future supplies will and must come predominantly in the form of electricity. Though much has been done—or at least learned—over the last forty years, the conservation programs of the immediate years ahead may well make these earlier (mild and voluntary) efforts look like child's play.

Following is a short list of general programs which hold great potential for energy savings. Keep in mind, the cuts they would make possible represent not just direct energy consumed (e.g., powering cars, or heating and lighting houses), but indirect energy that is embodied in the products, services and activities in which each of us is involved every day. The net energy notions presented in Part Two must remain a central policy feature in concert with the development of specific concrete steps and projects.

1. BUILDING ENERGY CONSERVATION

Existing homes, commercial, public and other buildings can be retrofitted to save enormous amounts of direct energy. Know-how in this area is very far advanced, with insulating materials and techniques currently available and at least some enterprises (probably not an adequate number) ready to accomplish the retrofitting. What is needed is broad education, public leadership and organization, financing and a heightened sense of urgency on the part of the public. This should become a top priority of Localism organizers, due to its tremendous potential for huge energy savings, its ability to shield citizens and families from disruptions and energy price spikes, and because it is a productive task that can be accomplished *now!* Oh, and did we mention? Lots of good local business and well-paying job opportunities are in the offing.

2. NEW CONSTRUCTION

Just as modifying existing buildings will save prodigious amounts of energy, so will building all new structures to much higher standards. So-called "zero energy" homes are now being built which, using passive solar and other advanced technology, require essentially no outside energy input. Similar standards should be applied to all construction. Presently, residential and commercial buildings account for approximately 40 percent of all US energy consumption. Aggressively attacking the unnecessary waste in that figure by conservation programs in both arenas—existing and new construction—is something Localism efforts can do with minimum political discord. And, because effective technology already exists, it can begin without delay.

3. LOCAL TRANSIT

As the decline of the fossil fuel age kicks into high gear, viable, comprehensive local transit will become a necessity if societies are to remain at all mobile. Localism-based efforts should immediately take the lead in calling for enhanced local public transit systems. As the personal automobile becomes a less viable option, transit systems will have to fill the void, including not just commuting, but in finding ways to fill the transit needs of people needing to shop, attend school, and fulfill their recreational and other needs. Hauling people around will be a big job; but better transit must also be ready to step in as current goods-hauling systems (e.g. private diesel trucks) decline. *Electrification* will be a keyword for better local transit; fossil fuels or alternatives in the form of, for instance, renewable liquids and gases, are liable to be rare and expensive commodities indeed. And finally, because hauling cargo is not normally addressed by current transit proposals, Localism energy planners should stand ready to tackle that crucial, difficult part of the transportation challenge.

4. MATERIALS, RECYCLING, REUSING AND WASTE

This catch-all area represents forty years of awareness of our need for "greener" practices regarding product materials, packaging, recycling, reuse, and, ultimately, throwing unwanted/unneeded stuff away. Unfortunately, it is an area in which only slight progress has been made.[19] Enormous energy waste, as well as environmental damage, marks today's practices in material handling and waste disposal. But, like retrofitting inefficient buildings, the possibilities are endless—and in most cases need not suffer long delays because of unavailable technology or organizational issues. Each community striving for Localism should consider a number of things in the materials arena:

1. Set up and encourage local businesses to recycle all materials for which practical, effective recycling now exists. At this point, recycling is just another industry that has gone global. Mountains of waste materials are being hauled daily to the four corners of the earth to be recycled; from which a small portion can then be hauled back in some reusable form—all so the whole process can be extolled as "green." As with all other aspects of the wasteful globalized economy, long distance is the unavoidable enemy of energy efficiency. Local materials handling enterprises immediately cut this transportation energy waste drastically.

2. Set up local composting stations (short distance from all neighborhoods and businesses) to compost all organic waste. Composting efforts obviously should be coordinated closely with Localism initiatives to grow and process food, as well as efforts to curtail the emissions of atmospheric warming gases (addressed in chapter 15).

---

19   And an area now in complete disarray and collapse, due to the Chinese decision to cut off the acceptance of most US recycling materials beginning in January, 2018.

3. In coordination with Localism efforts to recycle carbon back into the soil with better farming/ranching practices (mentioned above in Chapter 15 and more fully discussed in the final chapter), establish convenient, dispersed agricultural waste recycling/composting facilities.

4. Devise ways to encourage the formation of local businesses to, first, create packaging and other materials that are less energy intensive, less toxic, easier and safer to dispose of, and are made from local sustainable resources. Also, encourage new businesses that once again repair things. Durability used to be a hallmark of desirable consumer goods, with local small businesses repairing everything from television sets to furniture, small household appliances, shoes and even clothing. Our "throwaway" society has lessened this, with distinct environmental as well as cultural drawbacks.

5. Materials themselves. Finally, because recycling of all materials is not economically practical, not energy efficient, is often toxic, dangerous and difficult for other reasons, and because some materials do not lend themselves to repair, implement programs to regulate materials used in all product and service delivery. These programs could take a variety of forms; but in the extreme would consider banning the use of certain materials particularly hazardous to the environment—e.g., some forms of plastics and chemicals. Here again, some progress has been made in this area in recent years, such as selected cities banning plastic grocery bags or drinking straws. (But when a corporate fast food chain stamps "dispose of responsibly" on its mountains of Styrofoam and other throwaway, single use drink and food containers, that hardly qualifies as "progress.")

5. DEMAND MANAGEMENT

This final area of potential energy conservation, long ignored by a consumer society used to having energy instantly at its beck and call, attacks the energy problem from two directions. First, it seeks to lower overall energy use levels, even cutting out activities that are of lower priority or high demand. Secondly, "demand management" (perhaps the Mother of all Euphemisms) seeks to schedule energy use to better conform to the patterns of production...and to the patterns of nature. This rising-falling, irregular availability of energy is particularly important when it comes to solar and wind energy, the mainstays of America's future renewable energy systems.

Energy experts refer to the varying availability of solar and wind power as *intermittency,* a term made important by the simple fact that the sun doesn't always shine nor does the wind always blow, even though people demand a continuous flow of energy. Both the opponents and supporters of renewable solar and wind power usually propose dealing with intermittency by using complex, expensive and even environmentally harmful technologies. Many see keeping some fossil fuel generation plants around for filling in slack periods when solar and wind are not producing adequate electricity. Other proposals include pumped storage systems which would pump water up into reservoirs above hydro-electric generators at times of ample solar and/or wind power. Then, when high demand or low solar/wind production required it, the water would be released through the hydro generators to make up the temporary deficit.

More recently, battery storage facilities have become the vogue. Surplus solar and wind energy recharge the batteries during high production periods, then the battery power is to be drawn down during peak demand periods. With the exception of battery storage, which can be small enough for just a single site, proposed intermittency solutions are typically aimed at smoothing out the power fluctuations of large, centralized, connected electric grids. They not only assume these large grid systems will continue to be how power is generated and delivered, but that demand will remain high—in fact, continue to grow rapidly with the demise of fossil fuels. And finally, they assume power demand will continue its present inflexible profile. That is, whenever electricity consumers decide they want it, without regard to weather conditions, time of day, season of the year—or any other natural variation—that's when they will get it. This rather "hedonistic" set of characteristics assumes that dealing with renewable intermittency must not affect systems which must be designed for peaks and also must include sufficient additional capacity to handle outages and maintenance.

Instead of this "business as usual" scenario, we see a different picture ahead in this important area of demand management. Localities, which will inherit the bulk of future energy planning (sometimes willingly, sometimes reluctantly), will struggle to deal with forces constricting them from three directions. There will be short budgets for 1) energy, 2) money and 3) carbon. Squeezed from all three sides, local energy planners will naturally turn to demand management, which might involve imposing restrictions on many less necessary activities—but also learning to "ride the waves" of intermittent, varying renewable energy. A viable Localist economy would learn to use energy when it's available, and cut back when natural conditions dictate that it's not. A key part of our energy use policy will be learning how and when to *Just say no*. (Nancy Reagan would approve...)

B. ENERGY PRODUCTION: LOW-TECH IS BETTER THAN HIGH-TECH

The second dimension of a Localism-based energy future will be production. It's vital that renewable energy be the focus of whatever future energy systems America builds, Localism-based or not; but renewable sources by themselves are not enough to attain maximum efficiency, long system life and minimum impact on the climate and other ecosystems. As the old saying goes, the devil is in the details. To be truly "green," energy systems must be installed with the following three principles as primary objectives:

- **The lowest-tech possible.** Yes, that's right...low-tech is much better than the present mania for high-tech. Low-tech systems can be designed, constructed and maintained by local people with modest training and technical skills. Low-tech will be cheaper, and thus easier for local governments, credit unions, banks and private investors to fund. *"Get your money back from Wall Street,"* as you will hear in Chapter 18 ahead as we discuss local finance. (You're going to need it for all kinds of community-enhancing projects.)

- **The lowest-grade materials possible.** When it comes to essential materials, the object should be the same as with design and construction technology: keep things as low-grade and low-tech as possible. Ideally, materials should be available in abundance locally; and they should be as renewable as the energy source itself. They should also be easy and safe to handle, simple to fix and replace over a long system lifetime.

- **Systems that are located as close as possible to the final consumption of the energy they produce.** We have already noted the importance of cutting the vast, wasteful distances that drag down the efficiency of global economic systems— and may doom most of them in the Future of Scarcity. Renewable Localism-based energy systems should take this generalized advantage of dispersed, local, small-scale energy and press it to the maximum. Many residential, farm and small business energy sources need not be any farther than, for example, the solar heaters and photo-voltaic (PV) panels on the roof, or the wind turbines located throughout the city or, at most, on the outskirts of town.

The false efficiency of current energy systems—including renewable ones. Unfortunately, present-day energy production— including renewable systems like solar and wind—blatantly violate the above three principles. That is because they are in the thrall of corporatist institutions which assume (and demand) status quo globalization structures and centralized control. Rather than pursue maximum technical efficiencies, low costs, long system lifetimes, and minimum climate and other environmental damage, corporatist centralism dictates sacrifice these crucial goals to maintain their central control and maximum (at least in the short run) profits.

The following three potential Localism-based energy initiatives combine the general requirements of renewable energy sources with low climate change impacts. They then add the three specific objectives of sustainable low-tech approaches and materials, and close proximity of energy production and consumption. Notably, while centralist planning normally pays homage to the first set of requirements, they studiously ignore even any mention of the latter.

1. SOLAR PRODUCTION

Current solar energy attention has shifted to producing electricity with photo-voltaic panels (PV); or building large high-temperature solar electrical power plants which are connected to grids and serve large geographical areas. Though PV solar electricity certainly holds huge promise, this tends to overlook the valuable contribution lower-temperature, lower-tech solar systems can add when energy production becomes part of the Localism movement. Thus, solar energy planning logically separates into two directions:

a. **Solar thermal.** Localism organizers should aggressively encourage the installation of solar thermal systems for space and water heating. Low-temperature systems could retrofit both residential and commercial buildings, as well as become the standard for virtually all new construction. These relatively low-cost systems work effectively in the majority of climatic zones in the US, and have been proven to be useful and reliable worldwide since they first gathered attention in the 1970s. Though somewhat "un-glamorous" and too low-tech for some technophiles, solar thermal technology is yet another example of a well-proven, affordable way to go fully within the capabilities of local firms, governments, finance and citizen groups. In the past, we may simply have not done it because we haven't had to. Countries like Japan and Israel have thought otherwise.

b. **Solar electrical (PV).** Similarly, Localism activists should press for rapid expansion of solar PV, aiming at rooftop installations on as many local homes, businesses and farms as possible. In addition to accelerating and focusing the currently direction-less, non-integrated grab bag assortment of PV programs, there would be one significant difference: These Localism-based PV programs would employ the three above principles of low-tech/low-grade materials/close-proximity. Presently, under the guiding mantra of centralism and corporate control, these principles are being ignored, meaning among other things a diminishing amount of equipment is even US-made, let alone manufactured within communities striving to implement Localism. With the technology increasingly coming from China, and the constantly rising use of higher- and higher-tech materials and processes, most solar PV technology becomes obsolete in as little as a few months. Current solar PV efforts, while well meaning, are stumbling without coherent guidance. While for a time Localism projects may have to buy solar PV equipment off the global economy from large, controlling corporations monopolizing its availability, the goal should be to develop local materials, local manufacture, local installation and maintenance—and thus *local control*—as soon as possible. Keep this in the back of your mind while reading Chapter 17 on Local Manufacturing just ahead.

2. WIND PRODUCTION

In general, generating electricity from wind currently is struggling under the same lack of coordinated guidance afflicting solar
energy. Presently, the direction and priorities established thus far
are pushing wind into the familiar centralism/Corporatism model
used for solar. Localism planners need to move quickly to cut the
umbilical cord tying communities to destructive outside control.
And, here too, a rigorous adherence to the efficiency principles of
low-tech/low-grade materials/close-proximity are needed to wring
the most energy output from wind turbines at the lowest cost in
both environmental and dollar terms. While it's true that larger
wind turbines with longer blades offer some efficiencies in capturing more energy from the wind—and it's also true exotic materials used in the permanent magnets of wind generators also offer
minor efficiency advantages—these high-tech approaches come at
a cost. They require more expensive, technically-demanding infrastructure for both the construction and maintenance phases of
wind turbine operation, plus they demand higher-tech, less widely
available materials which will soar in price as globalization falters.

Specifically, effective Localism-based wind systems would look
like this:

a. **Smaller scale.** Instead of the giant wind turbines with
   blades up to 75 meters in length now becoming common
   on remote, corporately-controlled wind farms, most local
   wind turbines would be much smaller. Though slightly
   less efficient, the lower costs and increased reliability
   would more than compensate. Small scale horizontal and
   vertical axes wind turbines can be placed in many locations
   impossible to install the giant turbines used on remote wind
   farms. Further, wind can be used for both electrical power
   generation and for pumping water. (This of course was once
   common on early Great Plains ranches and farms...but was
   "put out to pasture," so to speak, by cheap fossil fuels and
   fossil fuel-generated electricity in the 20th century).

b. **Both grid-connected and off the grid.** Where viable, smaller wind turbines can be installed on farms, businesses and even home sites as "standalone" generators, not connected to the electrical grid. They can be usefully deployed as supplements and complements to solar PV systems, lessening intermittency by charging batteries at night (if the wind's blowing) while solar panels charge them during the day. In grid-connected applications, wind turbines would feed surplus electricity back onto public grids. (Localism organizers should consider pressing to change applicable state and local laws to allow small-scale solar and wind generators to be compensated by utilities for power these generators supply to local grids. At present, many state "net metering" laws prevent such compensation, along with the fact that the pattern of state laws is a confusing mish-mash that synchronization would distinctly help. Officials and utilities should recognize this possibility for what it is: a positive chance to supply substantial power to the public grids, reducing the tremendous expense of building and operating traditional central power plants.)

c. **Designed around the "low-tech/low-grade materials/ close-proximity" principles.** Yet again, Localism wind energy planners should scrupulously apply the "keep it simple and close by" standards already described above. Though many will find this axiom non-intuitive in an age worshiping at the Temple of the Highest-Possible Tech, it will pay long-range dividends in sustainable financial and energetic low cost, maintainability, and especially in facilitating local control.

3. BIO-FUELS; OTHER RENEWABLE POSSIBILITIES

Solar and wind rate top billing as the probable mainstay renewable energy resources of the near future in this country. That is simply because they are widely available possibilities for virtually all-American regions, small microclimates and communities. After solar and wind, potentially viable local renewable sources become distinctly different, depending on climate, local vegetation, land and water supplies, proximity to seacoasts, overall population and size of urban areas. For that reason, it is imperative that Localism planners conduct comprehensive surveys of renewable resources available to them in their own areas. Until complete inventories of possible renewable resources are available for each locale, local decision makers cannot know which of their actual choices will best answer the crucial benefit/cost question: how to produce the most net energy for the least monetary and environmental costs. Furthermore, they won't know what consumption decisions—products and services, homes and other buildings, transit, food production, and so forth—will actually match up with their real ability to produce clean energy.

Liquids and gas. Special attention must be paid to possible renewable resources capable of producing liquid and gaseous fuels. According to current studies, approximately 80 percent of foreseeable renewable energy production will come in the form of electricity. Richard Heinberg and David Fridley, in their indispensable book ***Our Renewable Energy,***[20] emphasize the electric character of most renewable energy systems, and the large task of converting American infrastructure to electricity. Currently, the United States consumes only approximately 25 percent of its end-use energy in the form of electricity; the remaining 75 percent represents direct and indirect burning of oil, gas and coal. Clearly, economic and social patterns so addicted to liquid and gaseous hydrocarbons must undergo massive overhauls in a very short timeframe if crippling disruptions are to be averted.

Two vital industries have a special dependence on liquid and gaseous fuels: agriculture and transportation. With that in mind, Localism planners, especially in the early years as Localism transitions are getting underway, must make special efforts to (1) reduce the liquid/gaseous needs of these two areas; and, where this is not

---

20   Richard Heinberg and David Fridley, ***Our Renewable Energy: laying the Path for One Hundred Percent Clean Energy,*** Island Press, 2016

totally possible, (2) reserve precious supplies of remaining fossil fuels for agricultural and transportation purposes.

For those reasons, Localism planners will be eagerly seeking fossil fuel substitutes that can be produced locally, will not draw down precious remaining (and imported) supplies of oil, coal and gas needed to build necessary new infrastructure, and that will not add unacceptably to climate warming or local pollution. To state the obvious, this will be an extremely tall order!

Bio-fuels. Bio-fuel systems offer perhaps the best potential for most localities to find liquid and gaseous fuel substitutes for natural hydrocarbons. Because the history of current bio-fuel systems is not good, Localism bio-fuel efforts should concentrate on these factors to avoid the same pitfalls:

- **Locally growing, naturally occurring grasses and other plants**

- **Forest residues and byproducts of forest or agricultural industries**

- **Ocean organic growth/products (for seacoast communities)**

- **Waste organic materials, such as sewage, landfill garbage, feed lot residues or output from certain local businesses**

Avoiding the pitfalls and pratfalls. Special care must be taken for Localism planners to avoid falling into the trap that has captured current bio-fuel development in the United States. The present poster child of bio-fuel production in the US is corn-based ethanol. In the absence of a strong, unbiased "systems-approach" analyses which would have identified many flaws, America's highly politicized corn-based ethanol system is an ecological "loser" on at least two fronts. It neither produces significant *net energy* (the residual energy available for consumption after all system input energy has been accounted for), nor does it lower the overall system emission of climate-warming gases.

Again, the centralized, corporately-run ethanol system is the real culprit inflicting this "loser" system on American drivers and taxpayers—who must pay more for the privilege of also polluting more under a system that actually increases fossil fuel dependence rather than reduces it!

SUMMARY: LOCALISM OPPORTUNITIES, DESPITE TECHNICAL COMPLEXITY AND CORPORATIST OBSTRUCTION

Along with producing our own food and beginning to build Localism-based manufacturing of other necessary products, producing our own local energy will be an early, essential task facing Localism. Gaining widespread public understanding and support may appear difficult, given the aura of almost mind-numbing technical complexity, complex economics, and long history of dominance by giant energy companies and other powerful elements of corporate centralism. (*Even owning oil stocks in one's pension plan has been known to cause reluctance for change...*)

The centralists have a strong head start, having already moved to corner many of the technologies of renewable solar and wind energy to add to their remaining stash of fossil fuels. But Localism organizers who remain determined to resist the alluring carrot-and-stick appeals of centralism, and who remember a few valuable rules, can make great strides in furthering their independence and local control in a surprisingly few short years. In conclusion we summarize sequential steps that can be initiated and coordinated by Localism energy planners within their individual communities:

- **Start with conservation, the truly low-hanging energy fruit.** No immediate actions will yield more positive results than comprehensive, community-wide programs to save energy. Energy saved is energy you do not have to produce.

- **Solar and wind: it's what's happening now in renewable production.** For many communities, renewable sources of energy like bio-fuels, small-scale hydro power, and ocean tide/wave-related systems will ultimately prove very beneficial. But for now, almost every area of the United States will find great payoffs in the proven areas of solar and wind power. Thus, harnessing the sun and wind is the place where we should start. In maximizing solar potential, we must not forget the value of lower-grade energy from solar thermal systems that provide space and water heating. As nations like Israel, Cyprus, Japan and China have shown, these systems can be easily installed on buildings using inexpensive off-the-shelf proven technology and provide much of the one-sixth of US total energy that now goes to heating and cooling buildings and supplying hot water.

- **Public transportation.** Comprehensive public transportation, not just for hauling people but also for hauling goods, will be vital to communities which emerge as resilient, prosperous and stable. Therefore, transit as a means of not just conserving mountains of energy, but as a means of preserving a vital service now dangerously dependent on fossil fuels, deserves every community's attention.

- **Planning: pulling it all together.** To sum up, the success of Localism-based energy production efforts only can make full sense if they are carefully, tirelessly integrated with thorough energy consumption analyses, and with planning for how communities are going to provide for producing food and other essential goods and services in the energy-short future.

As we now move forward into chapters 17 and 18, and begin addressing related subject areas such as local manufacturing and providing adequate local finance for a Localism transition, it's crucial to keep in mind this need for constantly integrating our ideas, plans and programs. While many of our best-laid plans will and must change as we plod into what can only be a somewhat uncertain future, Localism can only succeed if local citizens continually communicate with each other and share ideas about where we want to go.

CHAPTER 17

Local Manufacturing

Introduction

The previous two chapters have made the case that food and energy are two areas where citizens can effectively begin to craft a sustainable and productive locally-controlled economy. Every locality has outstanding opportunities in these two spheres. However, progress will be only partial and modest until inroads are made into production of a wider range of the vitally important "stuff" that we need and use daily. This key chapter addresses the seemingly daunting challenge of extending *Localism* into the mainstream producing sector. (*And wresting it away from the global economy...?!*)

To begin, let's review where we stand, and in so doing, retrace the logical thread of the argument for this entire book. Cutting through the detail, we summarize below the several main points we have attempted to make. If you wish, call it a **rant**:

1. Capitalism as it is currently structured throughout the world, and especially in the United States, is a virtual blueprint for creating inequality in the system

2. Growing inequality over time, more than any other strictly economic factor, is the most certain guarantor of the ultimate failure of our economic system

3. The first decade of the 21st century, piggy-backing with globalization and following the disastrous policies of political administrations for quite a while, has put this tendency on steroids

4. These policies insured the creation of the housing bubble and its subsequent collapse into an unprecedented breakdown of the wider economy with the 2008 "Great Recession"

5. Climate change and energy constraints promise to compound the economic problems and forestall effective long-term recovery

6. The behavior of multinationals exacerbates many of these problems, since corporations are impersonal, give us shoddy products, pollute the world environment, promote poor income distribution, buy off our politicians, export jobs, overpay their chief executives, and in general just rip us off for the personal gain of the already wealthy elite.

If all of this—or even some of this—is true, how should we seek to redirect the mainstream core of our economy? Barring major structural adjustments, we are on a disastrous and tragic course. (It may not be clearly or widely recognizable as yet, and it may take some time to unfold, but assuredly it is coming.)

The often-heard beginning recommendation is that we should work toward a more sustainable smaller scale locally-owned economy. Oh, dear. Sound familiar? For almost 50 years now, since Earth Day of 1970, Rachael Carson's Silent Spring, the Limits to Growth debates, or Oil Shock and the original energy crisis, versions of this have been the refrain of most of the environmental and "counter-culture" movements dissatisfied in some way with the "system." Do you have some sort of problem with the status quo business-as-usual world? The bottom line answer is to work for a sustainable local economy. The talk is familiar, to the point of becoming trite. But that doesn't mean it's wrong... In this chapter, we propose doing something about it.

The quest for a vibrant local economy has become pigeon-holed, in the minds of the mainstream corporate and "consumerist" belief systems, into the realm of the Birkenstock and sandals crowd, knee-jerk environmentalists, or perhaps the "harmless" back-to-the-land dropout crowd, selling their homemade crafts at the local Saturday market. Picture the type of quasi-religious testimonial article routinely appearing in the Mother Earth News:

> *"Maude and I were highly paid advertising executives, deeply involved in the daily Madison Avenue rat race, until one day we couldn't take it anymore. Since buying our rundown farmhouse and 10 acres outside Hendersonville, North Carolina, we've never been happier. I love my chickens, organic rutabagas, and let me tell you about the best way we've found to stake tomatoes..."*

We're sure they really are happier, and we certainly wish Maude and her husband all the best, but there are problems with this fervent endorsement of the alternative lifestyle—at least if it is to be viewed as a general model offering comprehensive solutions to the current economic dilemma. At least four problems immediately come to mind. First, few have the financial ability to do it. Second, few have the skills to do it. Third, not everyone even wants to do it. And finally, there are nowhere near enough rural spaces and places to accommodate movement of our current urban populations in any sort of a mass "anti-yuppie" back to the land migration. In other words, it has no chance of becoming the profile of the mainstream economy.

Nonetheless, even though this is a totally unrealistic solution for all but a few, the "new rural" couple may be well on their way to having their heads screwed on correctly with their understanding of the problems of the world and the directions in which our over consuming under investing culture may be headed. However, before we leave Maude to tend her organic raised beds, the question we seek to address is how to learn from such examples and their accompanying value base, and how to generalize in structuring realistic and workable models for our entire culture.

Some useful points become apparent if we extract the salient principles from this admittedly tongue-in-cheek example. One point is that they embody experiences in creating a more self-sufficient lifestyle where everything from jobs held to the goods produced and consumed are not dependent on multinational corporations or national chains. Clearly, such experiences are generally motivated by the type of sustainability-based values and attitudes that might well prove appropriate for the future we are facing. Unfortunately, efforts to create a more sustainable locally-based economy have been seen by mainstream economic thinking as isolated "toy" experiments of the hyper-committed environmental elite.

So the refrain is familiar, but two things have been missing. First is the notion that such experiences are anything more than optional isolated lifestyle choices on the part of virtual "dropouts" with both overdeveloped environmental values and the financial capability—either in the form of enough money or the willingness to live with much less. Missing is the notion that some version of the experience, along with the accompanying attitudes and values, is an imperative, rather than an almost whimsical lifestyle choice for a lucky and committed few.

Second, and a vitally important point, is that they are individual examples and were never intended to create jobs for many others. There is no practical plan or roadmap for incorporating the essence of the experience into mainstream economic solutions for the broader society at large. Putting these two points together in clear stark terms:

Why is a sustainability-based locally controlled economy a necessity, and how to get there?

Addressing these crucial points is the focus of this section. Many have described what such a culture might look like—at least some of the forms it might take. Further, some have even begun to experience it. However, prior to the recent virtual collapse of the financial and economic system, there has been little apparent need to generalize or mandate a broad transition.

Our view is that all that has changed. Given the structural flaws in the existing system, we can no longer expect that it is even possible to return to a healthy middle-class society with a broadly shared reasonable standard of living and enough jobs to go around—*if we rely on the corporate world that caused the problem in the first place to get us there*. This has probably been true for quite some time now, but the impending economic crisis alone (let alone climate change issues) underscores the problem, accelerates the need, and perhaps even creates more of the necessary willingness to change.

As usual, the "crisis" nature of the American psyche comes into play. When things are going well, there is little impetus to change the status quo—especially on the part of leadership. However, when current arrangements break down, you have peoples' attention, and the broad-based realization of impending stress tends to cause it to become a political issue—finally...

In light of the current economic challenges, whether these challenges are widely acknowledged or not, this chapter makes the case for Localism as a potential creator of good paying permanent jobs; and it offers practical suggestions as to how to promote them. As you will see, much of this is done largely through an extended example of a local shoe production company. As an additional bonus, however, we develop the economic theory justification for the superiority of such a strategy.

Let us be clear as well as practical. In no way do we seek to impose a "counter culture" lifestyle on the populace at large. Put another way, some selective attitudes and behaviors now seen as "counter culture" need to become more reputably mainstream. Status quo "corporatist" thinking might criticize such an effort as economic reversion to more Spartan times, and thus forsaking the hope of broad prosperity—"giving up," as it were.

Quite the contrary, our objective is to facilitate the broadest possible prosperity and economic stability for communities and for the system in general. This should be the predominant economic goal at any level, from community to region to national and even international. However, the world as it is currently working cannot achieve that within the globalized corporatist consumerist paradigm, and that paradigm must therefore either be changed, or viable alternatives created. We choose to create alternatives. We can only hope that paradigm shift may follow.

THE ECONOMIC NEED AND THE STRATEGY

Revising the economic world as we know it is a big job—a massive understatement at best. Given the daunting nature of the task, this calls for the simplest possible approach. Remember, the strictly economic problem is to begin to replace the current domination of our economy by multinational corporations with locally controlled enterprise. There are secondary social and environmental benefits as well, but those are not the concern for the moment.

Many who have railed at the impact of corporations on our everyday lives seek to fight them, regulate them, tax them, boycott them, remove their corporate "personhood," or in some way impose our will on them. These are good ideas if they could be accomplished—and more power to efforts to do so—but to our minds, this direction is likely to prove to be a fruitless waste of time and energy—and take longer than we have. There is a much better way. Our chosen strategy can best be described as "Go around them." Build an alternative economy from the bottom up. Start producing our own basic needs. Ignore the big corporations. Positive steps yielding tangible benefits can then begin immediately.

Let us be clear. Without a massive movement, attempting to confront, boycott, or in any direct way negate a major corporation is likely to be a monumental fool's errand. Don Quixote would look like a practical functionary by comparison. Moreover, they currently supply our wants and our needs, and will continue to do so even as we gradually build alternative local productive mechanisms that offer viable paths around them. We will need them until we don't need them any more....

Possibly the best way to approach the organization of the rest of this section is to begin with the commonly heard objections to such a strategy. Admit it, they're probably already on your mind as well. Here are a few of the reservations that have arisen to this admittedly utopian-sounding concept:

- **How to compete with a big, powerful corporation?**

- **How to match the cheap (foreign) labor they can employ?**

- **We can't make complicated products (e.g., cars, computers, etc.) ourselves, can we?**

- **How can you market your products against the familiarity of known brand names?**

- **How can we possibly produce everything we need?**

- **Where can we get the raw materials we need for complex modern products?**

- **We've got what we need now—why bother?**

As we have tested our ideas for what we now term Local Manufacturing, we have repeatedly heard versions of these same questions—by supporters and critics, liberals and conservatives, anyone who would listen. As a result, we conclude that the most effective way of addressing these practical and legitimate reservations is in the context of examples. Moreover, this allows some additional real-life challenges and potential advantages to be uncovered. First, however, we need some baseline practical guidelines for business in general.

THE BUSINESS ENVIRONMENT

The first step is a simple one. If the goal is to create successful alternative business structures, ask the question: "What comprises a successful business? There are universal common denominators for commercial success, regardless of the dominant motivations.

This is not rocket science, and after making lists and even consulting conservative friends (who are convinced they know best in this hard-headed "commercial" realm) we conclude that a successful business has at least the following:

- **A necessary product or service**

- **Good management and business skills**

- **Access to necessary technology**

- **An adequate labor force, in both numbers and skills**

- **Access to necessary productive inputs or resources, including energy**

- **A stable market for its products**

- **A favorable regulatory environment**

- **FINANCING**

Any business that has the above features can be profitable and successful in a market economy. This section of the book speaks to these issues as well as the questions previously raised. We work largely through the example of a shoe manufacturing company, but the core objective is to extract the principles supporting a comprehensive and workable plan that might apply to any basic need industry.

Our target audience for these observations is not professionals, but everyday citizens who share the unease about our current economic situation and seek to enjoy a secure and comfortable lifestyle in a typical community. There are important points to be made about each of the above necessary features of a successful business. Indeed, most of the necessary human and managerial inputs are surprisingly available in many communities. We are convinced that the top need will turn out to be finance, which is why this topic comprises the next chapter in this book. (We would be surprised if you don't already sense that much will depend upon how to *find the money* to create the alternative economy....)

AN EXAMPLE–SHOE PRODUCTION: LOCALFEET, INC.

There are two effective ways to construct a viable example depicting how the construction of a new economy could work. First, we could somehow identify the principles that must be met, and then hypothesize a particular product in order to examine how the production of that product would fit those principles. Alternatively, we could start with a hypothetical product, determine what would have to happen to successfully start such a business, and then extract the principles that were met in achieving this. These two methods are the "inside out" of each other. Either should lead to the same conclusions.

We choose the second approach, since the overriding goal of an effective strategy or policy is the establishment of clear and inviolate principles; and those should not be hypothesized out of thin air. Rather, it is much preferable to have them become self-evident through an example. Then the comprehensive local sustainable economic development strategy would evolve into applying those principles product by product, industry by industry, in constructing a new economy. Plus, it makes sense to start with a list of products and services for which there is a clear, known need, and work from that back to principles. After all, the reason for considering a Localism alternative in the first place is to provide viable alternatives for securing basic needs given the many overt problems with globalization, corporatism and centralism.

Our hypothetical business is shoe manufacturing, which we choose to call LOCALFEET. Shoes are a basic need, and therefore a local market, supported by current purchasing power, certainly exists. Assume they will be semi hand-made and purposely of very high quality. The necessary technology for producing shoes has existed for centuries, although there are certainly different methods employed around in the world.

In beginning to understand what might be involved, someone from the local area could contact shoe companies in New England, which is the historic heart of shoe manufacturing in the United States. In all likelihood, the ones that have survived are struggling in niche "high quality" markets, finding it difficult to compete with cheap mass-produced imports. Indeed, some talented but discouraged managerial and technical employees might be willing to temporarily relocate to help provide the acumen for structuring and starting LOCALFEET. It might make a good break from a cold New England winter, recently plagued by the Polar Vortex, resulting from climate change... Minimally, such people would be delighted to offer consulting assistance. Whimsy aside, in any case the necessary technical know-how, both for effectively starting up and for the ongoing operation, can be easily assembled.

The choice of technologies for the manufacturing process is absolutely key. The tendency, especially in light of recent trends in world markets, would be to ask: "How can we structure an assembly line so that we can efficiently mass produce and compete in the world markets?" This is the ruinously wrong question. Alternatively, the approach for building a local sustainable enterprise must be: *"How few can we sell and still be efficient enough to make a profit by selling into the local market?"* Instead of "How big can we get?" the question is: "What is the appropriately small *optimum* size?"

Instead of producing for export and entering a losing race to offer minimal quality products and compete in global markets against similar operations with much lower labor costs, we seek to offer local consumers a high-quality product produced by people who are friends and neighbors. We are producing for ourselves. Given that we also visibly become the lifeblood of a local job-creation mechanism, an effective and easily protectable local monopoly gradually emerges. If you or your friends and neighbors work for LOCALFEET, and it's a great product, where else are you going to buy your shoes—even at a slightly higher price than Walmart...? (As an aside, make a mold of a customer's foot—and the shoe will be so comfortable you'll have a client for life...!)

Could it be done, and can LOCALFEET compete with the national and international chains? For two reasons, the labor costs would be higher. First, paying a reasonable wage is a necessity. In fact, that's the point. Conventional thinking is again reversed, since the goal of the entire enterprise would be to pay workers as high a wage as possible rather than access the cheapest labor force on the planet. Second, as mentioned earlier, the higher quality implies more hand labor.

However, the business dynamics are entirely different. In analyzing any presumably local business, a necessary and useful question is: *For every dollar of sales revenue that comes in, what percentage of that dollar goes to any of the various productive inputs or factors of production?* Asking and answering this question has long been central to standard economic theory, but we are now seeking different answers. Primarily, the percentage of revenue going to labor will be much higher for LOCALFEET than for a typical large multinational or chain shoe producer. What a novel concept—capitalism that is designed to help the workers!

Given the current tendency of large corporations to avoid or minimize labor costs in every way possible, this would be seen, if recent conventional thinking is applied, as the death knell for our local startup shoe company. Poor LOCALFEET—it would not be deemed to be "competitive." However, that is not necessarily the case.

A radical sounding idea would be that the operation, applying this type of logic, should seek to maximize, not minimize, the wage rates and thus the labor cost. The reason is clear: In the local shoe market place, labor costs are the wherewithal to buy the product. As Henry Ford realized over a century ago with the original Model T Ford, paying workers to produce a product creates the income and demand to buy the product.

The global economy seems to have completely forgotten this, even though economics textbooks still refer admiringly to a model called the "Circular Flow Economy." This simple introductory concept, which we invoked in Chapter 8 in a critique of the growth ethic, demonstrates to beginning economics students the inherent interdependencies between consumers and producers, or alternatively, demanders and suppliers. Businesses pay workers and other factors of production to make products, and then rely on the recipients of that purchasing power to purchase the goods that are produced. Money circulates around in the system—in the opposite direction of goods and services.

Given the dynamics of the global economy, where goods are produced in the corners of the world with the cheapest labor costs and then hopefully sold in the world's highest priced consumer markets, who are we kidding with this model?! A world where workers cannot afford to buy the product they produce and where consumers earn too much to allow them to be hired to produce the products they consume is an irrational system doomed to fail. This is exactly what we have built in this era of globalization. And, as we indicated earlier in Chapter 2, this simple truth has been disguised under the old adage that Trade Helps Everybody. Let us dig further into how Localism deals with this.

LOCALFEET ECONOMIC IMPACT–HONING IN

A few years ago, it was revealed that the production of a pair of Air Jordan basketball shoes by Nike contained approximately $6 worth of labor (outsourced to China or Indonesia) for each pair of shoes. Since the shoes sold for $120 to $140, this would mean that no more than 5% of each revenue dollar went to the direct productive labor force.

The remainder would be packaging, distribution, transportation, retailing, energy costs, advertising and marketing, profit, and so on—plus expensive upper level management to tie all this together. Michael Jordan himself earned more per pair than the workers who produced them! Many of these costs would be much lower for LOCALFEET, and some of them would not even exist, so from the outset it would be free to pay a larger percentage of each revenue dollar to labor.

Suppose, for instance, that the cost of producing a pair of shoes was $40 for all other non-labor factors of production. If the shoes (any shoes, not necessarily athletic shoes) sold for $80, this would leave $40 for the workers who produced them. If the price were $100, this would leave $60 for the workers, and so on. Applying this hypothetical math, the local workers could receive 6 to 10 times the wage rate for a (similarly priced) imported competitor, and still offer an equivalent or better product at the same or lower price.

To finish the Nike example, consider the fact that at that time it would have taken the (largely female) workers in the shoe manufacturing plant about two month's work to earn enough to buy a pair of Air Jordans. This would be equivalent to an average wage earner in the U.S paying about $4,000 for a pair of shoes—it isn't going to happen.

A viable local economy seeks to overcome this irrationality of being unable to consume what you produce or produce what you consume. A coldly logical strategy for doing that is to cut out payments to all or most of the factors of production that must necessarily accompany a global operation (transportation, distribution and advertising, for example). Those returns can then be redirected to higher wages and business profits to local ownership, and the operation can pay considerably higher wages and still price its product competitively.

We must get over thinking of the global production model as cheaper or more efficient. Additionally, it is certainly more stressful environmentally. The tunnel vision analysis lionizing that false assumption of efficiency usually concentrates only on labor costs, and the full picture goes much beyond that. Of course, such corporations are eager to have the debate focus only on labor costs, since they are in a desperate search to justify their ruinous and predatory labor policies and outsourcing activities. What better way than to make domestic workers feel guilty about their high wages?

Furthermore, any such locally based firm will only become more competitive over the years as, for instance, energy costs rise. This increased competitiveness over time is insured by the fact that such non-labor costs would be a much smaller percentage of the cost of each pair of shoes than for a global corporation. Probability of success is all about designing and planning the cost structure of the firm to minimize the percentage of each sales dollar for the kinds of costs borne by large corporations. This will, of course, maximize the percentage of each revenue dollar that is re-spent for inputs that are supplied or produced locally. The primary input is labor, or in the case of LOCALFEET, perhaps ultimately of locally produced shoe leather.

MULTIPLIERS–AND VALUE ADDED REVISITED

The reason for seeking such a structure is that, as discussed in Chapter 14, only locally produced and purchased inputs comprise value added contributions to the local economy, and thus become available for a multiplied impact on that economy. Indeed, the role of multipliers is intrinsic to the most powerful argument for working toward a locally owned more self-sufficient economy.

As dollars are spent to purchase a product in a given locality, those sales receipts are re-spent by the business to hire workers and purchase other needed inputs owned or produced by local people and businesses. This then leads to a secondary re-spending by the owners of those inputs. For example, assume you work for a firm and draw a salary. You then take your income and purchase groceries, furniture, clothing, entertainment, whatever, or even savings. In fact, those recipients of your expenditures then do the same, and so on. The calculation of the cumulative effect of this hand-to-hand process leads to a multiplier, which is the sum of the direct and indirect effects of any new expenditure or newly created job in a locality—as the economic impacts of that original dollar injection reverberate through the community.

Significantly, multipliers are higher to the extent that these secondary and tertiary recipients in the hand-to-hand- process spend a larger percentage of anything they receive. Ironically, multipliers are larger to the extent that people are living on the edge and must spend virtually their entire income to survive. In other words, new spending goes further in a poor community than in a wealthy one! (Exploring all the implications of this intriguing conclusion is another book in itself...)

This process continues over time until all expenditures go either to savings or to purchase of inputs or goods supplied from outside the area. These are termed "leakages" from the local economy. At that point no further expenditures or economic benefit can occur, since the dollars have left that system and are not available to be re-spent and multiplied. Clearly, multipliers are higher to the degree that the economy under study is large and/ or a self-sufficient closed system, and lower for a small or highly specialized economy that meets very few of its own needs.

Quantitatively, the exact estimation of a multiplier effect, which can be applied either to incomes or jobs, is a somewhat inexact science. It depends in large part on expenditure patterns of people and businesses in the area. A multiplier is the sum of the direct plus the indirect effects. The numbers below are representative of historic empirical economic research, and are admittedly not exact or up to date. There is little current research. In fact, it is entirely possible that the globalization movement may slightly serve to lessen multipliers. (*After all, if all your "stuff" comes from China, your dollars could get out of town rather quickly...!*)

Currently, for a diverse state or region, income multipliers are in the range of 3 to 3.5, which means that the direct effect is one dollar and the indirect is between $2.00 and $2.50. For a large city, the range might be 2.5 to 3, and for a moderately sized city a typical result would be 1.8 to 2. For a medium sized town, estimates would be in the 1.4 to 1.6 range. To cement this concept, imagine a small hamlet with no business establishments whatsoever. Any dollars received by residents of that hamlet would immediately need to be spent outside the town. If a new job came to a resident of that town, the multiplier of new income would be 1, which means there is a direct effect (of that one job) but no indirect "re-spending" effects in that community. There is nowhere to shop...

Extending our example will help demonstrate the importance of these ideas. Suppose LOCALFEET is competing with a chain shoe store (Kinney, Thom McCann, Payless, etc.). Assume that the chain store, because it is basically just importing shoes, marking them up, and re-selling them, expends 75% of each revenue dollar on their shoe purchases. This money is an immediate leakage, and therefore only $.25 of each dollar is value added to the locality, and thus available to be re-spent and multiplied.

Conversely (no pun intended) assume that LOCALFEET spends only 25% of its receipts on imported productive inputs and 75% are purchased locally. This means that a dollar spent with the local store results in $.75 to be multiplied, while a dollar spent with the chain store contributes $.25, or only a third of the local contribution. Therefore, the local area gains not only the new jobs (which it did not have before) producing the shoes, but more jobs from the secondary spending that occurs (compared to the national chain) as a result of the sale. Depending on the size of the area, and thus of the multiplier, this is a striking difference in total economic impact.

Further, the jobs for the chain are mostly lower salaried sales people. Profits for the chain, as well as higher-paid management positions, are all outside the area. For the local store, all management salaries as well as profits remain to be spent in the local/ regional economic system as value added, and thus will also contribute to a greatly enhanced multiplier. And this gain in jobs and incomes occurs without the community spending any more on shoes than it was before!

A moment's reflection allows some important conclusions. The effect of an economy dominated by large national and international chains is essentially to reduce local value added as a percentage of any revenue dollar. Although they would not be caught dead stating it this way, that is in effect their role in life—to capture and keep as big a percentage as possible of every sales dollar—that is, to lower the local jobs and income multipliers and extract the maximum dollars from the community. Suddenly it becomes apparent why entry of a new Walmart on balance tends to depress rather than enhance any given local economy. That is why large corporations incessantly squeeze their workforce. For the locality, this means that such an economic structure will create the fewest possible jobs per dollar of local expenditure.

It is little short of criminal to hear Walmart crow about being the largest private sector employer in the country. By actual measurements they have destroyed about one million more jobs than they have created in gaining that market share. It is no wonder that, emerging from the 2008 downturn, there appear to be very few jobs outside the low-paying service sector. People must scramble for the slim margins available by re-selling the output of major corporations. We can do much better.

EXTRACTING THE GENERAL PRINCIPLES

Our example of shoe manufacturing might seem a special case that could be difficult to generalize for major sectors of the economy. We acknowledge that important reservation. However, recall that our purpose was to create an example from which we could extract the general principles that could direct the process of beginning to create a more diversified new local sustainable economy. Therefore, let us turn to that task, and see where that leaves us.

Some of the identifiable principles for beginning to build a sustainable local economy include at least the following:

- **To insure a permanent market, start with mainstream products that everyone needs**

- **Seek to employ the local labor force**

- **Seek, for additional value added, to use local natural resources when applicable**

- **Even in initial planning, begin to identify a local market in advance**

- **Scale the operation technologically to produce for the local market, and if efficiencies develop, export first to the immediate region**

- **Identify local capital sources in advance**

- Insist on local ownership and decision-making

- Use local entrepreneurial talent—you have more than you think

- Use local educational institutions (e.g., high schools and community colleges) to develop managerial and technological skills that you don't have, or seek to improve, or foresee as necessary in the future

- Employ local imagination and participation to identify new opportunities

- Be willing and eager to learn from other communities, and to share your own experiences with them. It will get easier over time.

APPLYING THE PRINCIPLES

In summary, it all doesn't have to happen at once. Products and services can be introduced one at a time, and should ideally be chosen with broad community participation. To insure the best possible chance of success, start with the proverbial low hanging fruit: Food and Energy. We have already documented that these products are excellent first choices because they are uncontestably vital needs, and in part because they offer valuable secondary health and environmental benefits.

Efforts to produce green energy are encouraged everywhere, from national down to state and local areas. To be sure, there is to date a lot of talk and little viable progress on workable strategies. We submit that the problems in settling on workable energy solutions stem in large part from the fact that we have continued to think about large scale solutions. Further, the "technological fix" mindset results in asking how to get the big companies to bail us out. Small scale solutions are overlooked. Community helplessness is still assumed. Applying the principles developed here could rapidly change that dynamic.

How to begin to expand one successful effort to other products or economic sectors? What a wonderfully exciting and dynamic question to begin with at a community workshop:

What products and services can you think of that we could produce locally that you would be willing to buy, and even invest in with your own savings?

Such an effort should be structured so that the workshop itself both starts to create a market and also to raise the necessary start-up capital. Obviously, jobs would be created—that is a given. With each product that is begun, and that works—in terms of commanding a local market, creating local jobs, and offering a profitable investment opportunity—the next one gets easier. There are talented local business people in every community, and many of them would be eager to apply their skills to a new enterprise. How refreshing it would be for many of these people to be accepted finally as a vital driving force behind the local economy as opposed to some sort of predator destroying our quality of life for a quick buck.

And the model can be instantly generalized. If it works for a small city in Oregon, it can be easily reproduced in Kansas, Pennsylvania or Alabama. Remember, the goal is to serve a local market, so there is no question of a competitive turf war. Information will be freely shared. Unlike normal startups, they would not, from the outset, have designs on being another Microsoft. (Of course, Bill Gates and Paul Allen probably didn't have a world-wide monopoly in mind either—initially....) Similar businesses all across the country can only help the viability of the movement. The learning that occurs in one town can be replicated, and small mistakes that were made can be easily avoided as similar enterprises spring up all over the country. Whoops. Sell your Nike stock....

Indeed, a new "export-based" opportunity might develop for people in communities that have successfully introduced one product or another. Someone from Oregon could happily go to Peoria, business plan in hand, and show them how to do it. One can imagine that the key people in that successful startup, facilitated by the communication capability of the Internet, would be in tremendous demand as consultants for communities all across the nation seeking to replicate their experience. And there is no reason this could not happen quite readily anywhere, given the economic crisis which we are facing, and the widespread hunger to reclaim our economic future from the forces that have so obviously taken it from us. It may be our best hope for a salvation from the ongoing "jobless recovery," which is the only possible outcome from Corporate America.

THE ENHANCED ROLE OF LABOR

Be prepared. The features recommended here not only disagree with conventional economic thinking, as we foresaw in Chapter 14, but in some ways are exactly opposite what most business leaders—bolstered by standard economic theory—have apparently come to believe. Perhaps this should not be surprising, since the rapid globalization of the economy basically caused the problem, and, ala Einstein, you can't solve a problem with the same mindset that caused it.

This section somewhat reiterates what was said earlier, but we intend it to offer clarifying detail on the specific advantages of promoting local manufacturing. Some repetition is by design, since the arguments presented here in making the case are the absolute core of what we are proposing in this book. In short, it bears a bit of repeating.

First, a newly established business entity operating within Localism can consciously and easily eliminate many costs associated with operating as a multinational. (*As long as it is clear what it seeks to be, and it purposely does not seek to be or emulate a multinational...!*) These savings include, but are not limited to, such functions as distribution, transportation, warehousing, marketing, advertising and endorsements. Furthermore, such typical features of business profit and loss statements involve additional energy expenditures, along with the accompanying environmental and resource-based costs. Along with many technical middle management expenditures, these would be greatly reduced or eliminated.

This has the tremendous benefit of allowing a much higher percentage of total sales receipts to be re-allocated to labor costs. This is the whole point—to *support workers and thus local purchasing power*. But, viewing this as a desirable goal is akin to economic heresy within the current paradigm. It will, on the surface sound strange to a typical business person, since the entire rhetoric of economic success has become growth, expansion and aggressively holding down labor costs. Targeting efforts toward a limited and localized market simply doesn't compute. However, labor is the life blood of value added for the local economy. Incidentally, this is the very feature that allows the local labor force to not be in competition with the Chinese (or any other "low wage haven") work force. This form of global labor competition is disastrous and un-winnable. The pay differentials are too great, while the skill differentials (thanks to the modern technology) are too little.

By eliminating such costs, the local firm is avoiding the types of expenditures that currently never come close to benefiting a local economy. These costs are usually simply a transfer from the product-producing corporation to another related multinational. (*McDonald's buying little packages of ketchup from Heinz rather than a local source...*) For example, suppose a bicycle produced in China for Walmart is shipped back to the U.S. for national distribution. The expenditures to the shipping companies, energy companies, national advertising companies, distribution warehouses, etc., have no economic impact on the locality where the bicycle is purchased. By definition, when you buy the bike, a large portion of the price is necessarily allocated to these functions. This insures that your dollars are immediately drained off to other corporations upfront, and the local area gets to keep only a small increment, perhaps due only to sales efforts.

Localism doesn't just pull these costs back into the community and thus make them somehow available to local interests. It does better than that—it eliminates them altogether, and those completely "avoided payments" become available to pay workers more. This is why a local manufacturer, who does not seek to export, can pay workers (perhaps several times) more than a global competitor pays its workers, and still sell the product for less. This is a powerful feature, since it is immediately apparent that it completely counters the conventional wisdom that locally (or domestically) produced goods must cost more because wage rates are higher. Significantly, their elimination also has substantial *ecological* benefits, freeing up energy, resources and carbon "budgets" for more crucial activities.

No—those products can cost the same or less because the non-labor costs are much less and some even non-existent. The labor costs (including the attendant wage rates) are free to be more, which is exactly what you want if you're seriously interested in the health of the local economy—and in people instead of profits. National or multinational corporations essentially subsidize each other and join in a chorus to squeeze workers and their salaries down or even out of the picture. (*And can you say "robotics"...?*) The rhetoric supporting this anti-worker process has become so finely crafted and strident that the general public and even workers themselves are inclined to believe and accept it.

We cannot help throwing in a little wistful "side comment" before concluding this chapter. As you read this section have you noticed or acknowledged what would be necessary to pull all this off successfully to the benefit of your community and its long-term economic health? We have a suggestion: The planning and economic development processes, even to the point of structuring new businesses, should ideally (and *purposely*) be for the benefit of the *community as a whole*, as opposed to *private profitability*. In other words, the dominant purpose should be the Common Good. Private profit will follow—it isn't either/or. (*Side comment or dominant principle*...? You decide.)

There is another powerful conventional assumption at work here, and that is that larger scale operations are always more efficient. This argument is normally made by invoking scale economies that enable businesses to serve larger markets. If the local firm is careful to judiciously employ similar technologies—adjusted of course to their smaller scale, then the reverse is true. By avoiding certain types of expenditures altogether, they can have per unit costs permanently lower than can the large corporation, and simultaneously pay much higher wages. *Now, what other useful products can we think of...?*

ASSESSING THE RESULTS

The practical bottom line Big Question looms: Is LOCALISM better? How would it improve what we have? Overall, we see two broad necessary outcomes if Localism is to be a socially and economically superior strategy to corporatism. For any economy, local or national, we suggest this simple twofold standard: 1) Creating more jobs (and thus Value Added) *per unit of economic activity*; and 2) Increasing economic equality. In other words, the approach must *lower unemployment* and *reduce inequality*. Simple enough? If these two goals can be reached, this would be a powerful result. The brief concluding section of this chapter identified the striking advantages for employment and salaries within a Localism framework. The other all-important issue of inequality is afforded its separate treatment in Chapter 20, following discussion of the vital element of finance in Chapter 18 and a new look at local economic development in Chapter 19.

CHAPTER 18

Generating Local Finance

Bypassing Wall Street

To review basic principles, our stated goal is to effectively create a locally and regionally based economy that seeks to meet real human needs and build in resiliency by providing stable permanent jobs. Such an economy would not result in the massive concentrations of wealth and power that we now see under the current system of monopoly capitalism, but it would create many adequately paying jobs, a more equitable distribution of wealth through work, and would allow a more democratic political structure to thrive.

Locally, if economic structural change in this optimistic direction were to evolve, most communities certainly appear to have, or can easily develop, the necessary management skills, labor force, technological know-how, markets, and political environment. That's a great start. Nonetheless, one more vitally needed feature looms: And of course, that is the Big Enchilada: FINANCE. Without appropriate access to the necessary capital, a revitalized sustainable local economy is little more than a counter culture pipe dream. In this chapter, we develop and discuss both some conceptually important ideas as well as some details of sample specific plans for achieving the necessary financial wherewithal to fund effectively the transition that we seek.

There is an old saying about banks and bankers: They will be pleased to loan you money if you don't **need it.** In short, their ballyhooed fiscal "prudence" dictates that they look for a proven track record of success involving familiar types of projects yielding reliable rates of return. Clearly, this does not describe innovative community activist efforts to reform communities, battle inequality and promote effective climate change mitigation efforts. *After all, what's that got to do with profit...?* How do we seek to change this? Clearly, the order of the day must involve innovation, perhaps bordering on radicalism, as we imagine financial thinking and institutions appropriate for a Localism-based future.

At a minimum, any newly proposed financial arrangements must first speak directly to the perceived difficulties with our current state of affairs. In light of that, a useful starting point is to identify clearly what an ideal financial system is *not*, or more specifically what it cannot be if it is to work properly. There are three points to be made.

First and foremost, it cannot depend on Wall Street. Much is made of the tendency of large producing industrial corporations to export jobs and control mass markets as they re-import cheap goods and sell them to the general public. Concentrations of power and abuses due to monopolistic control are palpable. But, it is important to note that these types of problems occur within the *real*, or manufacturing and goods-producing sectors. Our task at this point is to turn attention to the *financial* sector.

Whatever might be said about these obviously troublesome features with production-based corporations, let us be clear: The financial sector is probably the *most* monopolistically structured of any economic sector in our society. It is the easiest to move the resources involved nationally and internationally, since there are no physical inputs or products to transport over long distances with high energy costs. There are few troublesome environmental or labor regulations—it can all be done electronically. The ruinous economic equivalent of manufacturing outsourcing can, with a computer, be accomplished instantly by the financial sector.

Furthermore, the de facto monopolization of finance serves to concentrate wealth even more quickly and effectively than can any big producing corporations—even oil companies. Inequality can expand unfettered by the troublesome "stodginess" introduced by the ownership and geographic immobility of physical assets.

After the 2008 collapse, how long did it take the big financial monopolies on Wall Street to grab their huge Federal subsidies because they supposedly were on the brink of causing total system failure? (You recall the mantra: *"Too big to fail..."*) In one year they experienced one of the most profitable years in history and even started paying executive bonuses bigger than ever before—***and all without creating any new jobs***.

Indeed, bonuses were paid to people who, given their earlier shenanigans, almost certainly should have *lost* their jobs. In return, the banks are even now visibly applying much tighter credit than before. Let's see—we shoveled billions of dollars to save the financial system, and as a result enabled them to develop an effective bottleneck on the job-creating mechanisms in our economy. *What's wrong with this picture....?*

While we're at it, there is probably no better metaphor for explaining the inequality in our system than these Wall Street bonuses. The procedure is to take it from the general public, who, along with their children and grandchildren, must pay it back over time, and give it to the already rich to have right now. It is a grotesque "reverse Robin Hood" effect of the worst order—and furthermore it has a negative intergenerational time dimension impact that Robin Hood (with or without his merry men) couldn't begin to understand.

We conclude that, given the inextricable corporate connections between the major multinational "producing" corporations and the largest banks, if future finance remains centered on Wall Street, the bulk of the rest of the economy will remain dominated by transnational corporations. We do not attempt here to prove this debatable point—we must move on to solutions—but it would be very difficult to *disprove*.

Second, a new financial strategy cannot depend fundamentally on the Federal Government. Unlike Wall Street, the Feds could play a positive role; but it would be largely as a passive enabler insuring that it stays out of the way and protects the vital local efforts somewhat from other negative forces (*like Wall Street...*) that could interfere.

Make no mistake, new federal regulations for Wall Street would be a good thing, and are absolutely necessary for the continuing health of our macro economy, but there is no way that alone can or will return control of finance to local/regional interests. Indeed, even the existing and proposed regulations in place (e.g., Dodd-Frank) are clearly not designed to bolster financial control of communities. At best, they would stabilize Wall Street so that it could continue its present monopolization of our collective financial future, and thus play right into the hands of corporate/global hegemony.

Third, and as a direct corollary of the first two, the core vitality of the movement must be from the grassroots upward; it cannot be top-down. In perhaps our only plaintive plea for action from the federal government, we ask it to recognize and bless what is going on in communities and stay out of the way. And do anything in its power to see that other "monopolizing" influences stay out of the way as well. Even this passive "enabling" role for the Feds implies that a measure of healthy populist thinking be present in Washington, and with the current Beltway Bandit culture, awash in big special interest money, that situation is hard to imagine.

UNDERSTANDING THE CHALLENGE OF LOCAL FINANCE

First, it is necessary to frame the problem correctly. Perhaps you have noticed, we do not always view the perspective of traditional economics as overly helpful or appropriate. However, in the case of responding to the challenge of local finance, economic theory is of some help. Specifically, straightforward supply and demand analysis gives us a good start.

Problems with imagining ways to negotiate the challenge to secure more local control of our own money and of the local economy in general can take two forms. First, an individual family can lament that they would like to invest their savings in their own local economy, but do not know how. Buying a business outright works for very few. Having exactly the right amount without involving others is tricky. Information about what is available and assessing its profitability and safety are overriding concerns. These are problems with the **supply** of capital. Financial wherewithal might be available, but there are barriers to the smooth supply of it. People don't know where and how to put their money to use.

On the other side of the coin, potentially effective and profitable uses of funds and/or small businesses could productively contribute to the local economy, but the potential "venturists" cannot attract or assemble the capital. Banks consider them too risky. Individual investors do not know of the opportunities or cannot get together with other like-minded people. Risk and reward are difficult to assess. These are problems with the **demand** for capital. There are willing and profitable uses, but because of various barriers, the demand for capital cannot be met. The challenge for this chapter is putting these two together; the smooth intersection of supply and demand makes a *market*. The need is to create a *functioning local financial market*.

The problem of creating a viable local financial "market" is analogous to the evolution of the issue of organic foods. Initially, growers were small family farmers who produced organically due to their strongly held resource/environmental/health values commitments. As the movement caught on, sensing a market opportunity, many business food providers (e.g., Safeway) would like to respond, but could not be assured of a steady supply in the volume needed.

As a result, the small producers/suppliers sense the buyers/demanders are unwilling to deal with them, and the buyers/demanders sense the producers/suppliers cannot adequately meet their needs. Thus, the market fails to clear (or even to develop), not because of insufficient supply or demand, but simply because each side fails to meet the other's exact needs.

It should be noted, before leaving the organic food analogy, that this is changing. Larger mid-sized agricultural operations, motivated on the supply side by economic opportunity, are beginning to fill the demand of the larger suppliers. Clearly, we all note a growing "organic food section" in our local supermarkets.

Thus, the "market" is clearing. We are pleased; though we might (cynically) wonder if the march toward monopoly hasn't merely started in a new arena. We can only hope that the small growers continue to thrive with more values-based participants in venues like Saturday markets on both the supply and demand sides...!

TAKE OUR MONEY BACK–
LET'S GET PRACTICAL

So Wall Street currently has most of our money. How did they get it? The answer is clear: ***We gave it to them***. And we need to take it back. Of course, that is easier said than done, and understandably will make common people nervous for their financial future when they imagine "cutting the ties" to the smart establishment— no matter how much they might object to their reputation and actions. Thus, a prescription for how to do that is an absolutely key feature of any workable financial plan for creating the New Economy. Let's review some key features of our current financial system as it applies to everyday people.

Home ownership has long been considered a desirable component of American culture. As a family commits its future wealth and income earning ability by taking out a mortgage, it creates a financial security that, as we have seen, has been manipulated to enrich large financial interests. Again, it is the abuse of that trust which was centrally responsible for the Great Recession of 2008-9, the sluggish recovery and the evolution of that crisis into the growing inequality that we continue to experience. Therefore, it would be desirable to devise more mechanisms for approving and making home loans at a local level. We speak to that later. That is not the key element, however, in a functioning local financial system. The key rests with managing the remainder of our savings in the creation of new enterprises.

If as citizens we secure a reasonable job and manage some savings, we normally turn those savings over to Wall Street, directly or indirectly. Clearly, buying traded securities or some mutual fund shares does the job of transferring money and control to Wall

Street in one step. Charles Schwab or E-trade is all too happy to help. If we participate in a pension plan or have a 401K, the management of those funds will almost invariably end up channeling through large Wall Street players.

How do we change that? Admittedly, it seems difficult, since many of these transfers are made without our knowledge, participation, or even our permission. And, primarily, we think we have no options. Indeed, as we deal with our trusted and competent local financial advisors, we often don't even think to question it. We have been conditioned to accept and approve this phenomenon through the repetition of such concepts as "diversification into the global economy" and "access to capital markets." We are invited to assume that the closer you are to Wall Street, the smarter you are, and smartness equals wealth. And, you wouldn't want someone "dumb and local" to manage your wealth, would you? Well, perhaps we would. And, in fact, *how has Wall Street been doing for you lately*?

Obviously, we haven't talked at all about mechanisms or strategies for accomplishing this, but it should be made clear that we do not play the role of investment advisors. The purpose here is not to propose an alternative investment strategy that will be more profitable and/or less risky for the investor than what currently exists—if we accomplish this as well it would be a bonus—but it is to address the questions: "*What is your money doing or accomplishing?*" and "*How can we best arrange finances to serve the goal of achieving a local sustainable economy?*"

Think about it. When you invest money by giving it to a local broker or investment manager, what sense of purpose do you have for that money? With most people, we expect that the likely answer is none, other than making more money. The goal is simply to protect capital and possibly to expand it by investing wisely in some vibrant, safe, but probably unknown venture. Surely, we more or less "glorify" that nest egg by allocating it mentally to college for the kids or a comfortable retirement—but that is the "higher purpose" of the ultimate future use for it, and not the current use by the entity holding and operating with that money now. It is how you ultimately *use* the money, not how you initially *get* it.

In fact, a moment's thought reveals the unsettling fact that your mutual fund, pension plan or 401K undoubtedly supports the purchase of shares of companies whose goals you might staunchly oppose. (You believe we need an alternative energy transformation away from fossil fuels, and you're financing your future by owning Exxon shares in your pension fund. Hmmm...) So, in all likelihood, current investment habits for most of us involve not just "making money" in an amoral sense, but actually getting in bed with the enemy in order to secure the future for ourselves and our children—and then looking the other way...

As alternative local options are considered, the criteria for financial decision-making is thrust (perhaps a bit uncomfortably at first) into the arena of the values of the citizen/investor. In other words, social and moral purposes are invited to the party. People begin to care about what their money is accomplishing, and the role played in the community of the enterprise itself. What it is doing and how it's behaving become important—in addition to merely capitalizing the operation. If the enterprise is sound, profitability for the supplier of the capital (i.e., the local investor) will follow. Almost as important, personal satisfaction for that investor will also follow. Your values and your money will be on the same page.

Specific mechanisms and institutions that begin to answer the all-important questions raised in this section depend in large part on the structure and the features of the local economy that we have to work with. The task before us is to surgically extract some of the desirable features of that local economy—and learn how to support them. Remember—as the previous chapter asserts, one primary overall goal among many possible others, is to facilitate *small scale manufacturing operations producing locally needed products*.

There are two possible directions to take in doing this, and they are completely supportive of each other. First is to concentrate on building local institutions whose primary mission is to provide such finance (e.g., credit unions, locally-owned private banks and local public banks). The second is to start up appropriate businesses producing carefully selected basic goods, and finance them directly from the people. In other words, put money directly into appropriate businesses, and put money into local financial institutions which specialize in supporting those businesses.

These strategies are not mutually exclusive, and would often merge, since the financial institutions could participate with additional capital once the businesses are started by private individuals. An example will help immeasurably in understanding how this might work and in drawing out the essential features. The following discussion, including some quantitative "injections," is not intended to develop one targeted example that proposes an exact formula. That is not necessary. Rather, it seeks to stimulate thinking and generate some helpful practical tips for citizen action in any community.

CREATING A LOCAL FINANCIAL INSTITUTION– SNARING OUR HIDDEN ASSET

Starting a bank? It sounds like a daunting task that only the existing well-to-do movers and shakers in a community would even think about. But that doesn't have to be the case. Let us introduce a key term: *Community Development Financial Institution*, or CDFI for short. This term is one actually in use in the literature of local development, and has a particular sanction within the federal government. We will expand on this mechanism more at the end of this section.

For now, assume we choose to start a credit union, which is a bit more user-friendly form than a straight commercial bank. Call it LCU, for Local Credit Union. Credit unions often have a different structure and operating purpose than traditional banks, and usually operate within a somewhat more lenient regulatory structure, especially if they apply only to specified uses. They, as well as other less common forms of specific-purpose financial entities, often have specific areas or geographic limitations within which they serve. They can be non-profits, or depositor-owned.

For our suggested example here, for reasons that will soon become apparent, it is **essential that the entity contains the payment mechanism capability**. That is, depositors can pay their bills with it, write checks on it, borrow from it, and in general carry on basic banking activities. Indeed, the LCU need not even be a credit union, and may in effect be little more than an investment club. The important question is: *How to attract capital to it?*

Here is where the rubber meets the road for the necessary capital transfer from Wall Street to Main Street. We call your attention to an asset that we all have, but don't think much about. Specifically, that asset is: **The Average Balance in your Checking Account**.

Think about it. Everyone is an economic entity. We have income coming in—from current employment, pension plans, Social Security or past savings, etc. We also have bills to pay monthly or continually for normal living expenses. We all dread and assiduously avoid writing a bad check and getting a non-sufficient funds overdraft notice from our existing bank. This impairs our credit rating, embarrasses us and causes all kinds of bad things. Therefore, as we consciously process the business end of our lives, we keep an average balance. Most people probably think of it as a minimum balance, although it of course fluctuates. That fluctuation will be at different levels for each of us.

The question we ask of you is: *How much of a return do you expect on your particular ownership of this fluctuating account?* Indeed, most checking accounts are rather disarmingly advertised as "interest-bearing accounts." Most people of whom we've asked this question simply laugh and say something along the lines of "Forget it." Rates of interest-bearing checking accounts, in this very low interest rate environment, are largely just symbolic. Though they fluctuate monthly, they have recently been in the range of less than one-tenth of one percent. People commonly earn a few cents per month. One person allowed that just to demonstrate the ridiculousness of it all, she saved a bank statement that showed her earning a strapping two cents on her account the previous month! (Are we making much headway on that retirement nest egg...?)

SOME NUMBERS AND AN EXAMPLE

Let us explore some hypothetical calculations (along with some sample implementation tactics) that underscore the possibilities with LCU, and demonstrate the substantial economic power that could be marshaled quite easily and in a short period of time. The first need is a core group of people (not more than six to eight—call them "PIONEERS") who understand and are committed to both the concept and the chosen strategies for the local finance project. These could comprise most of the original board of directors for LCU.

Informal "surveys" we have conducted with random groups of citizens indicate that the average balance in a typical checking account is almost certainly at least $5,000. At the low end are people who just barely meet their bills each month. They may have as much as $4,000 to $5,000 after a paycheck, pension or Social Security check comes in, and draw it down to as little as $1,000 or less after all bills are paid. This person's account still will average in the $2,500 to $3,000 range.

In the slightly higher range, many report that they don't feel comfortable letting the account drop below a certain figure. $5,000 is typical, and amounts upward of $10,000 have been reported to us as common. And these figures are for strictly middle-class people, including retirees—not even upper middle class—and certainly not the 1%...!

And now, for the all-important added incentive. The new LCU should pay perhaps 1.5% to 2% on **unrestricted checking accounts**. This rate makes them competitive with money market instruments such as certificates of deposit (CDs). In fact, that is a higher rate than many CDs currently pay, and even with those there are restrictions on removal. The higher rate paid by the LCU should readily attract additional "near cash" balances.

For example, some middle-income retirees who have a moderate savings nest egg in less liquid pension plans, IRAs, 401Ks, mutual funds, etc., might have as their current operating strategy transferring an amount (say, $50,000) each year to a CD for meeting their liquidity needs for the year. Then they systematically draw it down for living expenses, being careful to comply with the omnipresent withdrawal restrictions of the CD. Citizens who employ a strategy anything like this would be easily attracted to the unrestricted checking account paying the same or higher rate—*PLUS* more awareness of what your money is supporting, *AND* the satisfaction of knowing that it is helping your community thrive. Again, welcome psychic benefits arise when values and finances get on the same page.

Suppose that the LCU attracts 100 depositors at the outset. There should easily be that many people that the PIONEERS group could contact (friends, neighbors, acquaintances) who share a values-based commitment to taking financial control back from Wall Street and/or making *more money than they're making now* on an asset that they each currently own. Understand—all they need to do, and are asked to do, is start banking there. They are not asked for any new investment capital above what they already have.

If these 100 depositors average the minimum $5,000 per account, that is $500,000 in capital. If, as is possible, the added incentive of the 2% rate increases that average to $10,000, then $1 million is the figure for total deposits from just the 100 people. One recently retired friend, when casually asked the average deposit question, surprised us by answering: "*Well, it currently has $85,000 in it, and I'm looking for a CD since I don't trust the stock market as far as I can throw it and don't want to tie it up long term, since I'm going to need it to live on. And I can't find a CD paying over 1%.*" This amount probably makes that person an "outlier," but it doesn't take many special little surprises such as this to draw the average account to $10,000 or more. When it becomes apparent that such a mechanism is a preferable option for any needed short-term liquidity, including a simple bank savings account, interest could grow (*pun intended...*) considerably.

And the word spreads. The 100 could become "deputy PIONEERS," and it might not take long to have 500 or more depositors supporting $5 million or more in deposit assets. A small bonus could be paid to current depositors for sponsoring and attracting new customers, and, well—you get the idea. Then if the depositors all buy shoes at LOCALFEET, which the credit union helped finance, people can begin to see and feel what a viable local economy can look like. The LCU in effect ends up a catalyst for building community—now there's a novel concept: *Make your investments safer and your local economy healthier by buying shoes...*

Some details that deserve to be addressed are not dealt with here. Obviously, careful banking practices, especially at first when the capitalized value is small, should be employed. As financial strength grows, the LCU can more actively serve stated social or geographic needs in the community. (favorable policies for lower income neighborhoods, funding for affordable housing, specific worthwhile sustainable business projects, initiatives to combat homelessness, etc.)

A pertinent question is how the LCU can afford to pay much higher rates. The answer, analogous to how LOCALFEET competes with multinational shoe companies, is that they hold down or avoid costs that are borne by their competitors. With easily available software, the LCU can offer an excellent range of services and effectively act as a "virtual" bank. Other traditional banks invest in large buildings, oak-paneled meeting rooms and marble counter-tops, (That solid established aura of safety and dependability is important, don't you know...?). LCU gives the money that would otherwise finance such niceties to its depositors. It barely needs an office—possibly operating completely on-line, or perhaps an ATM machine and a booth at a locally-owned coffee shop. (which will be a depositor, of course, given the additional business their active participation brings in...) Innovations on this core hypothetical strategy should readily spring from the imaginations of motivated people in any particular community. Then share them with others.

On a final conceptual note, and connecting with our earlier economic framing concepts, we have uncovered both a *supply* and a *demand* element underlying the motivation for proceeding with an LCU. It could stem from a desire to have a locally-controlled entity with which to **supply** one's capital. On this score, it would be stimulated by a thought such as: "*I wish to have a place to put* *my liquid cash balances and earn a little higher return than is possible from my current bank."*

When we get to the **demand** side of this, all we need to do is to simply add to the above statement: *"...and which is controlled locally for the good of my own community."* And even better, the social criteria are built in by adding another phrase that virtually summarizes a comprehensive vision for the whole effort: *"...and provides funding for low- and moderate-income projects that combat inequality and poverty in my own community."*

Thus, you will have accomplished three things: 1) Take your money back from Wall Street; 2) Put it to work in your community meeting the needs of both demanders and suppliers of capital; and 3) Begin achieving social equity goals—all while earning a bit more than you were earning before on the same pool of wealth. What's not to like...? Ideally, such a comprehensive image would permeate the thinking of the PIONEERS for your community.

MEANWHILE, BACK AT THE CDFI

Earlier, we mentioned Community Development Financial Institutions (CDFIs). There is a branch of the U.S. Treasury called the Community Development Financial Institutions Fund, which has a stated vision to: "...economically empower America's underserved and distressed communities." The extensive and enlightening website is easily accessed by simply entering CDFI; and our purpose is not to summarize it here. The important point is that it makes it clear there are sources for direct financial help for community-based financial efforts, **when their social criteria are clearly and appropriately identified**.

This federal office has several different types of programs that it administers. Particularly applicable for the types of suggestions made here is the ability to offer start-up capital for CDFI certified banks or credit unions **as a grant** for up to $2 million dollars. Grants and loans for specific projects can be for more. Certification, which the website spells out, and for which training programs are available, amounts to appropriate stipulation of the sociocultural criteria (fighting poverty, inequality, improving a blighted neighborhood, etc.) for the financial mechanism contemplated. It does *not* mean that the recipient organization must be an actual chartered bank or credit union. Various kinds of loan funds and community development funds have qualified—the key point is that their stated purpose for existing must be related to fighting poverty and inequality—preferably in a defined geographic area. Bingo.

CDFI certification can be a complex process, but many have done it. The website lists recipient organizations by state. (There are approximately 90 projects in our home state of Oregon.) This is an opportunity that clearly deserves exploration by interested community activists. There are many successful projects in all states that would make additional practical information easy to obtain—including sample by-laws and descriptions of successful projects. Perhaps the Federal Government could be helpful after all...

A FINAL NOTE TO MAIN STREET FOLKS

It is tempting to feel financially powerless when well-meaning citizens contemplate attractive and needed projects. Conventional wisdom is that Wall Street has all the wealth, and their representative banks in our communities must be entreated for the money. But this is not true—Wall Street has little of the real wealth. We in communities throughout the nation have the real wealth—Wall Street merely has claims on it. They expand the impression of massive capital by constructing claims on our wealth and even by pyramiding claims on claims in the form of derivatives, credit default swaps, options, mortgage-backed securities, and the like. They even create financial instruments betting against the success of you, their client.

Regardless of how it is done, and what institutional mechanisms are used, it doesn't have to be that way. We have tried in this chapter to describe some options for reclaiming substantial control of our own financial strength. That control will never be complete, but it doesn't have to be. It merely has to be sufficient so that groups of well-meaning citizens, inspired by ideas for improving and stabilizing their local economic fate, have the resources to act. Their sense of community and local sense of purpose, as well as their economy, will all be the beneficiaries.

CHAPTER 19

A Closer Look at Economic Development

What it Has Been and What it Could Be

No set of recommendations designed to assist citizens in communities everywhere in taking positive steps toward building a vibrant and sustainable local economy would be complete without speaking to the process of economic development. What are some current typical local policies designed to improve the economy? It is our belief that a mindset consistent with corporatism and globalization has unerringly permeated local economic development efforts in most communities. Further, this strategy has been ineffective and even occasionally worked to the detriment of those communities in the past, and that will only get worse in the future. This chapter critiques the current models, and is designed to unearth alternative strategies that promise to serve the goals of the community much more effectively as we move into the future we are facing.

Get the economy moving again! *Create jobs*! Everywhere you turn these days, this is the strident call. Politicians, pundits, experts, the media—anyone even close to (or seeking to be near) a position of influence sounds the siren signaling the need to promote higher levels of economic activity. But if you ask them exactly *how* they intend to do that, the details suddenly get *verrry fuzzy*... In fact, some fall strangely silent.

Nobody seems to have a clear and specific idea of how to promote this holy grail of a vibrant full employment economy. Or if they do, they're not talking. Conservatives promote lower taxes and less regulation, but there is evidence that this is what caused all the problems in the first place. Progressives advocate more public investment and stimulus spending, and they're attacked as over-regulating "socialists." Maybe that's why they all fall strangely silent...

We need to examine the historically typical process of local economic development as it has evolved, then compare it with how it might take place under a philosophy of Localism. Clearly, strategic details will differ among localities and parts of the country, but we identify what appear to be strong similarities and common assumptions. For convenience, let's bundle some characteristics that lead to a handy acronym: Strategy for Having Economic Benefits and New Growth (**SHEBANG**).

And what does the conventional wisdom for having and enjoying the whole *SHEBANG* amount to? For beginners, some of the frequently observed principles can be enumerated in simple bullet point format:

- **Bring in jobs by attracting a major corporation to locate in your state or community**

- **Employ the local (ostensibly very hard working and talented) labor force**

- **Concentrate on export-based products you can sell to other regions (or ideally even to world-wide foreign markets)**

- **Make substantial tracts of serviced "shovel-ready" land available**

- **Pre-approve the appropriate industrial zoning and infrastructure for those lands**

- **Promote property tax breaks (e.g., often 5 years) on such industrial lands**

- **Consider free or inexpensive "below market" deals on these lands**

- **Consider direct financial incentive grants to prospective companies**

- **Offer to develop training programs in local educational institutions for appropriate labor force development**

- **Undertake trade missions to any and all corners of the developed world to promote all of the above.**

Sound familiar? In essence, the construct of *SHEBANG* is meant to describe the typical practical face of the overall marching orders to: (Drum roll...) *Become competitive with the Global Economy!* (That one should sound familiar as well...)

And what's not to like with the whole picture? In recent years, as rampant globalization has proceeded apace, the efficacy of this overall development strategy for states and communities has been increasingly questioned, in line with critiques of observed behaviors of major corporations. (Mildly, because one doesn't want to be accused of being "anti-growth" or not being "community spirited").

In this chapter we address specifically the implications of the above (ten, but there could be others) points of *SHEBANG* for the economic well-being of communities. Parallel to that, we compare implications of a Corporatist approach versus one within a philosophy of Localism.

In our experience, something as deeply ingrained in so-called "conventional wisdom" as *SHEBANG* will remain pretty much invulnerable to attacks and outside criticism unless those criticisms are accompanied up front with a proposed better alternative. It is in that spirit that we proceed—within the structure of the ten points enumerated above.

1. ATTRACT A MAJOR CORPORATION

First, there are perhaps 10,000 other communities also trying to get a "branch plant" of any company willing to expand—but none of that will probably work, since the company itself wants to go to China! And forget attracting the "head office," it's not moving— unless it's to the Bahamas or Dubai for tax purposes. Anything a community does attract will be the absolute lowest-paying jobs in the corporation, and your community in effect becomes an economic colony. The decision-making remains elsewhere.

With Localism, new startups are the goal—we are not interested in "branch plants"—so no need to woo big corporations. This has its own challenges, but read on.

2. EMPLOY THE LOCAL LABOR FORCE

To be sure, if a community succeeds in getting a major company to open a facility, they employ some local workers—doing whatever the *company* wants and needs them to do. Data show that, despite talk you always hear about "future expansion," the major company often employs the most workers it will ever have at the outset of business in that locality. Frequently, it quickly evolves into perpetual "cutback mode," since these days that is commonly the operating mode for the whole corporation. After all, virtually all major corporations, domestic or international, have been routinely shedding workers for decades. This keeps their stock price up, and allows the CEO a big raise. Avoiding labor costs is their favorite sport, which is the driving force behind all the outsourcing.

With Localism, startups employ a certain number of workers at first, and unerringly expand employment over time if they are successful. Further, a range of all types of jobs—whatever the company has to offer—will be available. The average salary per employee is likely to be higher, since the entire operation, including the CEO, is located in the community. Growth of the employment base and rising average salaries over time are much more likely under Localism as opposed to *SHEBANG* strategies.

3. PRODUCE PRODUCTS FOR EXPORT

Invariably, traditional economic development efforts are strictly targeted at firms that produce goods for export—out of that locality if not out of the country. After all, you can't just "take in each other's laundry." Economic base analysis is clear: No city, state or region is a closed system. There are always goods that you do not produce yourself that you need to import from other areas. (Automobiles or televisions, etc.) Such purchases send your dollars outside the area; and goods that you produce and send outside to others are needed to reverse the flow and bring dollars back in for recirculation.

Facilitating production of export-based goods is the historic role for large corporations. We do not need more corporations to come in and simply help recirculate our local dollars to each other—Walmart does enough of that for all of them combined. Of course, this puts a local labor force in direct competition with labor markets all over the world, since a good produced for export can, by definition, conceivably be produced anywhere.

Here is where a strategy of Localism differs starkly from Corporatism. Under Localism, the target is strictly the local market. There is no goal of producing for export—if the business should thrive and its output begin to exceed local demand, the market should be expanded in concentric circles around the point of production. Send stuff to the next community... Keep the consumer base as close to home as possible.

It is reasonable to ask how this helps the local economy, compared to some company that produces for export and thus relies on the income of other areas to support a healthy level of sales. The answer is simple. *SHEBANG* seeks to bring back dollars spent in purchasing goods that we don't now produce ourselves. Localism seeks to produce those goods locally, so the dollars never leave in the first place. The impact on the local economy (for a locally produced good that supplants an import) is exactly the same as for an export-based product, and consumers still get what they need of the goods in question.

There is no more important point about Localism than this one, and many of the other potentially beneficial side effects—such as product quality, business cycle stability, environmental sustainability, etc.,—spin off this one reality.

4. HAVE INDUSTRIAL LANDS AVAILABLE

Most communities desperately seek to have as large as possible tracts of land available for industrial location—as if just having space will make them come. In recent decades, as industrial land became scarce and prohibitively expensive in the burgeoning Silicon Valley of the San Francisco Bay area, the watchword in the Pacific Northwest among communities desperately seeking a branch plant expansion of the proverbial "good clean hi-tech electronics" nature, was that they would not consider a site of less than 100 acres.

There are not many qualifying parcels (and it must be flat—sort of like farmland...) in most communities. Further, the siren song to the locality was enhanced by the information that they wouldn't use all that acreage at first, but the future would bring expansion (and even more jobs). The data show that most firms never used more than about 15 acres, and the rest was held, not for expansion, but for speculation. One thing that "glamour" firms do understand is that the very announcement of their impending arrival will drive up industrial land prices in the area—a phenomenon made even more lucrative if a low-priced "sweetheart" deal can be made in the first place.

None of these shell games need occur under Localism. In the first place, a startup may not need much land. Second, the entrepreneurs are already local citizens, and presumably aware of the entire range of alternatives in the local real estate market. They are very likely to be able to find just the right location at a reasonable market price. If later expansion is appropriate, that will probably be accommodated readily, and the whole process will put much less strain on infrastructure and finances of local municipalities.

5. ZONING AND INFRASTRUCTURE

Along with the amount of land, the *SHEBANG* approach demands considerable effort in the area of quality of land. If the average large corporation is to be attracted, the industrial zoning must be exact, and must protect the firm not only from incompatible commercial or residential uses, but from more intense and potentially polluting heavy industry uses. (Of course, if a "heavy industry" activity unexpectedly shows interest, the municipality has often scrambled to change the zoning—any old smokestack in a storm...)

Further, the nature of needed services to the site can be quite exacting. Electronics firms, for example, often have extremely high-water requirements—both for quantity and quality. A local area can essentially be asked to sell its best natural resources in exchange for some jobs. A full range of services (police, fire, water, utilities, etc.) is expensive to provide—especially in advance of a definite location commitment on the part of a company when no property taxes are yet available to support the expenditures.

Needs of this type should be dramatically lower under Localism. A startup firm is in no position to force unreasonable bargains or subsidies, and whatever services that might be needed can presumably be negotiated among existing members of the community. Indeed, required land may already be owned, since existing business interests may well be (and ideally are) involved in any new venture.

6. PROPERTY TAX BREAKS

Property tax breaks are one of the most common incentives for business location. Since there are literally thousands of communities willing to offer such incentives, for many firms it qualifies simply as a necessary condition. Often, as with so-called "enterprise zones," these are for a five-year period. Common among corporations seeking to establish a branch operation (somewhere) is the premise that, unless they can foresee a complete return on their investment in five years or less, it will not be deemed feasible.

Then, as current corporate conventional thinking goes, having recouped their initial investment, they will need to make a decision whether to stay or leave. Especially with "hi-tech" types of firms, technology changes so rapidly nowadays that it often proves feasible to simply abandon the old facility rather than upgrade it—especially with another community somewhere else waiting to start the five-year tax-free clock running all over again!

These games will not be played under Localism. All their options, by definition, are properties in the local area. The apparent bargaining power is considerably less, and that may not even be considered as a variable with the local interests that are involved. Ironically, tax breaks are actually a better idea than with the large corporation, since if a tax break is offered, the increase in wealth that results will accrue to someone in the community itself, as opposed to having the benefits magically disappear to the head office of some national or multinational corporation. It will definitely serve in some way to benefit the local economy. The subsidy stays in town.

7. FREE OR INEXPENSIVE LAND

Here, the dynamics are similar to those for property tax breaks. Any such "sweetheart deal" goes to the bottom line of a balance sheet that is not kept locally. The benefits sought in exchange for the local area must be strictly in terms of the jobs created, since the economic impact of the subsidy itself disappears into the books of the corporation. Further, if any land appreciation or capital gains result later, those gains will not benefit anyone in the local area.

Similarly, an entrepreneurial team under Localism is less likely to seek such a subsidy, although their need for it and potential productive use of it are probably greater. All gains and wealth enhancement, including taxable incomes, remain permanently in the local area.

8. DIRECT FINANCIAL GRANTS

In recent years, it has become common to make direct financial grants (often administered through the state in question) to firms that agree to locate in the area. Normally, only large corporations can qualify, since only they are assumed to employ enough workers to really "make a difference." This is little more than legalized bribery, even though it may be in lieu of offering some public service or infrastructure. Rest assured that if some service is forsaken, it is either not needed by that firm, or it can be provided by the firm itself inexpensively. Again, this goes to the bottom line of the overall corporation.

Any direct financial grants under a Localism strategy end up enhancing incomes, profits or wealth in the local area, and will in all likelihood be handled with much more transparency. For instance, the funds could go to salaries, training programs, or purchases of capital equipment, all of which have manifest long term benefits for the area. Further, they represent expenditures subject to local spending multipliers, and may even increase the tax base and thus represent a measurable return on investment for the granting entity.

9. EDUCATION AND TRAINING PROGRAMS

Frequently, cooperative partnerships between, for instance, economic development agencies and local community colleges are forged for the purpose of assuring any potentially interested business firm that sufficient labor force skills are present or can be quickly developed. Mind you, this is a good idea under any strategy. The problem with Corporatism and SHEBANG is twofold. First, they wish to hit the ground running and be at full production in as little time as possible, and any needed training program is probably not up and operating.

Second, as mentioned earlier, most corporate expansions seek to offer jobs at the very bottom end of their salary range and with little needed technical skills. You do not need to attend a local college to work in a communications industry call center, as many English-speaking people in India already realize. Often, if key technically trained people are needed by a newly locating firm, they are normally brought into the area from other branches in the corporation. Any time a job is created that also requires a new person to move into the area, the net job creation benefits of the new business are lessened.

With Localism, the opportunities for effective educational and training programs should be greater. The firms may start small, and predictable labor force expansion can be smoothly served over time. Indeed, the startup entrepreneurs may even have already attended the local educational institutions, and the close cooperation needed to develop effective training programs will be much easier given that the business firm is comprised of local people to start with. Further, the range of skills that can be usefully provided through local institutions will be broader—including business management skills as well as any needed technical skills. Indeed, the successful startup manager may even end up teaching a course at the local community college. Who knows…?

10. TRADE MISSIONS

Ah, yes, trade missions. Some of them occur to "open up markets" and thus sell more of the products a state or region already produces. Others are to talk to corporations that are potentially willing to locate in the area. The more far-flung the trip, the better. An envoy to California might not attract much attention, but go to China or the European Union, now we're getting somewhere.

There's something a bit pathetic about the whole premise. It says, "We can't stimulate our own economy—we don't have the money or the skills—*Come save us…*" In effect, it's an invitation to offer all the features just discussed above in the first nine points, and ask to have your pocket picked. If the goal is to attract new firms, rest assured those companies are playing one community against another, and all the resources expended to land them represent a particularly cynical form of a zero-sum game.

To be sure, regions have occasionally succeeded in generating more sales of certain products, where the area is particularly good at or suited for something. (Oregon and Washington apples are popular in China.) Even then, in this era of strident globalization, often some place in the world is very quick to ramp up production and seek, especially with much lower labor costs, to undersell whatever products the trade mission addressed. And on the general issue of "opening up markets," (e.g., China's 1.3 billion people), it is telling that after all the trade liberalization efforts of the last two or three decades, we still import many times more goods from China than we export to them. How's that working out for you...?

Clearly, none of this is an issue with Localism. There is no need to induce firms to locate. The firm is a startup, and its key managerial people and its labor force are already local residents and committed to the economic health of the local area. Further, they're already invested in and supportive of local institutions, such as schools, service organizations, churches, local government, etc.

Finally, there's no need to undertake trade missions to sell the product, since the target market is local residents. In fact, the target market is even the workers themselves. (Let's hear it for Henry Ford...) Also included are the owners, the investors and the whole network of family, friends, acquaintances of all of the above. And they all come to realize that their purchases keep the local economy healthy, let alone support the people they know and love. Realizing all this, many comprising the local market wouldn't consider purchasing that good anywhere else—the firm has a de facto monopoly! And it will only expand—organically.

SUMMARY

In conclusion, we contend that virtually all of the ten points of *SHE-BANG* discussed above would be more effective if pursed within a world view of Localism. Others become irrelevant under Localism and can be discarded. In fact, new criteria applicable to the revised goal of a sustainable local economy will emerge as specific projects involving food, energy or manufactured good are proposed. For example, longer term goals, such as technical training in local high schools and community colleges will look increasingly attractive. Proactive planning will become more viable.

The action item for citizens is to use these guidelines to become active in setting the criteria within which the current local "movers and shakers" seek economic improvement. Your access to such leaders may be direct or indirect, (Or, hopefully, you may *already* be one of those leaders...!) but some avenue for input can probably be found, most likely within the arena of local politics. A bottom line benefit of such involvement is that people become more aware of their local economy—how it works and the role they play in it. This can serve as an excellent long-term community-building and conflict reducing element in the community. Environmental activists and Chamber of Commerce members might even end up on the same page.

Finally, once some Localist economic development results are achieved, this leads to what may be the most important point of all. Due to the fact that there is no need for the extensive transportation, distribution, storage, advertising and marketing expenditures (all out of the area) that are necessary for a national or transnational corporation, **the local entity has a cost-based comparative advantage that cannot be competed away**. This is the dream of all commercial operations. Certainly, the goals of such firms will evolve more toward stability as opposed to growth. Ironically, a major question that must be answered at the onset of operations is: *Can we produce efficiently on a **small enough** scale to make it happen*? Now there's one that you don't see anywhere in the textbooks.

CHAPTER 20

Inequality Revisited—Empowering Labor

The Need for Radical Change

Throughout this work, we have held that income and wealth disparity is the most serious economic problem, and furthermore is increasing at crisis level proportions. Unless the inequality issue is effectively treated, nothing else can be permanently improved. Indeed, we have emphatically made the case that malaise in the economic sector will inevitably engulf the other major challenge we have identified: Climate Change. True to our adopted "everything is connected to everything else" methodological mindset, it is worth repeating that a continuing cultural drift into an increasingly rich/poor world, whether at the local, regional, national or international level—or all of the above—will usher in an even more brutal economic competition for power and resources that will inevitably take down the environment with it. That would be the ultimate tragedy. Again, it is both or neither in the search for solutions to our joint crises of economics and ecology.

Much of which we have already proposed will indirectly help the inequality problem. Nonetheless, it cries out for a bold approach that attacks the issue directly. As we have indicated, we are sympathetic with the many "progressive" proposals that have emerged over the years, such as a higher minimum wage, increasing union membership, more progressive taxation, and the like. We certainly support these, but helpful as they might be, (and however politically difficult they might be to enact) they are not enough—and essentially treat symptoms.

We need solutions that also speak to root causes. You have by now had it hammered into you that our primary premise is that the very presence and economic importance of major national and multinational corporations is at the root of most of our societal ills. We have made this case in many ways—while also acknowledging their advantages. What, therefore, might an effective equality-promoting initiative or institution look like? It is neither possible nor completely desirable simply to do away with those corporations, so what hope is there? We made the point at the very outset that the larger the firm, the more acutely it de facto creates inequality. Additional economic tools will help build on this notion and lead this chapter to suggest a mechanism that could prove uniquely powerful in speaking to the inequality problem.

SOME BASIC ECONOMICS

It is fundamental neoclassical economic theory that a business firm hires productive resources, produces and sells a product, and then pays out the sales receipts back to the various factors of production employed to create the product. As we said earlier, it is a "redistributor" of national income. Those productive inputs are "rewarded" according to the marginal product, or incremental value, they produce in the operation. This is basic marginal productivity theory, and leads to returns called factor shares. Land receive shares called rent, labor receives wages, capital interest, and entrepreneurship, or ownership, receives profits. This is elegant if basic theory, capable of concrete mathematical formulations.

But as any business entrepreneur knows, it is clearly difficult to measure in practice exactly how much "value" the land, or the lending banker, or certainly the workers, contributed to the actual dollar receipts of the sold product, and should therefore be paid. This measurement uncertainty becomes important, since more statistical clarity would be needed in order to determine in practice if some factor is being paid fairly, and/or if one factor is exploiting others. And another even more important element of uncertainly must also be addressed.

During the act of production, it is often unclear whether the product will even sell or if so, what price it will bring. Thus, in addition to the statistical uncertainty of how returns are to be proportionately shared among the various factors of production, the total amount of money available to repay productive factors is unclear. Since many factors must be paid a fixed amount (overhead and land rent, interest on bank loans, payroll, etc.), there needs to be a "residual" factor of production that gets what's left over—even if it is a loss. This is where owners come in, and it is a bedrock principle of both economic theory and practice that: *Entrepreneurship is the **residual factor of production**.* This important and widely agreed-upon principle is why the capitalist/owner is seen as the innovative risk taker, and in the more hairy-chested macho versions of laissez-faire market capitalism, needs to be handsomely rewarded (and accorded the widely celebrated reverence of Fortune Magazine—incidentally, Jeff Bezos has passed Bill Gates...!).

Thus the successful business person reaps the residual profits. And "success" means growth... And "growth" means market power... And "market power" **necessarily** eliminates competitors and therefore **necessarily** leads to monopoly and accumulation of wealth in the hands of a few. Thus, growth, market power, monopoly, and wealth accumulation unerringly lead to: **Inequality**...!

And it all happens because of the simple fact that the capitalist owner is the residual factor of production. But, you might ask, "How about the risk taker who *doesn't* produce efficiently, or who *doesn't* guess the whims of the market correctly, and goes out of business or even loses everything? There is much risk—doesn't the successful one deserves a big reward?" It's true that many if not most small business start-ups fail and are never heard from again. Or, as the recent presidential election demonstrated, one can declare bankruptcy, stiff creditors, start up again and hit the jackpot the second, third, or ?th time around...

CHANGING ALL THIS

The important central fact of all this is that the gradual accumulation of power that has resulted in the current profile of our corporate-controlled globalized economy is a direct manifestation of a long series of accumulated *residual returns*. The "winners," over the decades, have gradually employed and expanded wealth and power, both economically and politically, in an absolutely predictable manner. We may not know who is going to win, but we know for certain that someone will. The phenomenon of modern globalization is exactly what conventional economic theory and practice, followed to its logical conclusion, would predict. Why is anyone surprised?

But there may be a light at the end of the gloomy tunnel of inevitability with a simple premise: If this has all resulted from the fact that entrepreneurship is the residual factor of production, then <u>change it</u>. If it could be done, this would provide a powerful lever. Is this something easier said than done? Maybe yes, and maybe no. We need to explore some of the ramifications, as well as the central question of how to do that.

Our proposal is straightforward: ***Make labor the residual factor of production***. It sounds disarmingly simple. How would it work? Existing forms of business organization can serve the purpose just fine—even (ironically) the corporate structure itself. Corporations have long been able to issue preferred stock, which provides ownership, but a fixed return with no common stock voting rights. It is virtually an interest-bearing bond. Currently operating major corporations would be beyond hope of converting voluntarily to this structure, but any new locally owned and operating businesses could qualify, and in fact might find it the easiest way to raise needed capital.

Suppose Initial investors were paid a fixed return, perhaps in the 6% to 8% range, which would be very attractive in these times of low interest rates. The common stock could be owned and controlled by workers, or perhaps by a union, with all proceeds automatically allocated to salary increases. Investment by local citizens in any enterprise structured this way would carry a moral advantage over the typical process of contacting a friendly stock broker, financial planner or investment advisor of some type, notwithstanding that the two of you enjoy the occasional golf game. This normally amounts merely to a user-friendly form of giving your money to Wall Street.

Alternatively, you can know what and who your investment supports, recommend it to anyone you see, maybe even participate in its success through your consumption decisions, and have the satisfaction of knowing that you are supporting both economic and environmental benefits for your community. We suspect that there are more good people than one might think willing to accept this sort of satisfaction in exchange for a potential stock market killing. *(And how has Wall Street been treating you lately, anyway...? How's that 401-K doing?)*

Let us be clear. This is not a new idea, and efforts to create such dynamics have long been with us. Cooperatives, worker-owned entities, Profit-sharing, ESOPs, etc., whatever their full agenda might be, all contain the feature of underscoring the economic health of workers and common people. Certainly, these are admirable efforts to be supported, and even learned from. They are seen, however, as isolated, sometimes quirky economic experiments. We simply suggest that mainstream producing entities be established with inequality-fighting features that purposely move the entire economy in the same direction.

THE REVOLUTIONARY COUP–HARNESSING THE CORPORATION IN THE SERVICE OF EQUALITY

The advantages and attractive characteristics are many. For one, incentives are finally placed where they should be. Workers know that if they become good at their job and increase their productivity, their salaries will go up quickly, and perhaps quite substantially. *(And under their own control for a change—just like a CEO...!)* In fact, a very successful firm might lower prices to attract further market share for that product, displacing additional imported items in their community. At last—monopoly power and the specter of growth helps the worker...!

What about the issue of recession-proofing the economy? Cyclical variation of capitalist market-based systems has been a concern since the birth of economics as a discipline. The State of Oregon suffered a sharp recession in the 1980s primarily because very high interest rates squeezed out housing starts nationally and plunged the important lumber and wood products industry into a depression. Think about the essence of this: Demand declined *elsewhere* and caused a recession *here* when our basic sector (export based) industry suffered a derived downturn in demand. An important basic economic sector had no control over its own fate. To the degree that we localize our economy, we are our own market, and the productive health and the consuming health depend symbiotically on the same people. Our economic health would depend more substantively on our own consumption, supported by our own productivity, and nourishing and nourished by our own investment capital. What a thought...!

These straightforward organizational "tweaks," upon thought and examination, offer very simple and powerful levers for converting growth, sales and business success into a tool for enriching common working people and creating **more equality** as opposed to **more inequality**. As increments of production for basic needs are gradually pulled back into the local sphere, there will be continual extra job creation resulting from higher spending multipliers. Also, the fact that the economic success of a business automatically results in higher wages for the workers will become visibly apparent in your community. Expansion of market share will happen without any expensive marketing campaigns—simple word of mouth over time will do the job.

Finally, the demonstrated effect that one business sector can thus transform itself will offer compelling evidence that it can be done with others. The "model" will become more and more proven, the innovative managerial talent in town will increase and become more confident, the supply of locally-based financing will grow (prosperous workers might even become investors...!), educational institutions will respond appropriately and the entire paradigm shift will become easier to replicate with each new business sector that is taken up.

New venture choices should ideally be fueled by the imagination of local people. The economy will become more of a participatory activity contributing to community spirit and cohesion. Opportunities arise by virtue of groups of citizens getting together and asking: *What do we need and what do we now consume*? It's pretty simple—people can begin a process of taking over their own economy and directing their own fate. Compare this to begging some multinational firm to "come save us" by locating a branch plant and gracing us with some bottom-level jobs, in exchange for which we give away local taxes, land, valuable natural resources and worst of all, future control of our own fate. Energy and transportation costs diminish, providing a bonus of sensible climate mitigation policy support.

The relationship most of us have now with corporations is decidedly love/hate, but many seem to feel that the negatives have visibly expanded in recent years. We love the products they offer, but end up with opposing interests in many other ways. They oppose tax increases, clean-up efforts, ballot measures and any suggestions that a class war exists. We object to their outsourcing, their ubiquitous and misleading advertising, and their contention that it is for the good of the economy that they eliminate the jobs of thousands of workers. The problematic worker/owner relationship has a long and often sordid history as evidenced by any targeted study of the American labor movement. It doesn't have to be that way. We could make the basic producing entity in our economy automatically be an instrument for creating equality.

In conclusion, these suggestions are in full compatibility with the previous chapters discussing food, energy, local manufacturing, finance and economic development. How something is done is as important as what or why. Specifically, such mechanisms would strike at the institutional heart of the reasons for our inequality by directly converting the business firm itself into a powerful tool for fighting inequality and an actual ally of workers, other citizens and community cohesion. Who knows—such features, applied broadly across the United States, could even comprise big steps in helping to restore the disappearing middle class and restore its currently receding efforts to achieve the American Dream.

CHAPTER 21

Localism and Reestablishing
Nature's 2-Way Carbon Flow

Summing things up: It's all about carbon

The overriding first premise of this book is that our culture faces two monumental challenges: First, an economic crisis that largely takes the form of a ruinous acceleration of wealth and income inequality. Second is an environmental crisis ominously and comprehensively represented by global climate change. Either could irreparably damage our current way of life, to the point of complete environmental, economic and social collapse.

A corollary of this premise is that the two are inextricably related—perhaps even destined to occur simultaneously—though the connection may not be clear on the surface to the average citizen. Further, we argue that neither can be solved independently of the other—it is both or neither. Two brief scenarios, incorporating simple logic, underscore this assumption. First, if the economy were to falter, which ironically would be most likely to happen due to physical (read, *environmental*) resource scarcity and degradation factors, our growth-obsessed world view would likely deem the problem to be a form of underproduction, and pressures on the resource base (again, read *environment*) would re-double. Heightened efforts to feed, clothe and house threatened human populations would drive the environment into deeper levels of stress in a tragic positively reinforcing feedback loop.

Conversely, if the environment were first to demonstrate extreme stress, (which can be argued is already the case) the effects are immediately extended to the economy. This occurs in three ways. First, for some time increased expenditures on cleanup and environmental control technology have become part of both regular governmental and private sector budgets. This is the "business as usual" model, has already increased costs, and is often characterized as resulting from needless regulation. The antipathy to paying for cleanup and prevention is one feature of the dominant "economics versus environment" mindset, wherein the environment is essentially seen as an enemy of economic health.

Putting lipstick on the pig, the development of new cleanup technology is often billed as healthy innovation for the economy and a source of new jobs. This seemingly positive take on mainstream environmental protection is little more than evidence of the classic American attitude, fueled by the ingrained technological optimism of standard economic theory, that new technology will invariably come along, and we will be bailed out of the problem. Certainly, environmental control technology should be encouraged, but total reliance is dangerous, since it delays addressing problems that basically have no technological solution, and also insures that the crisis will be worse when it finally matures.

Second, the increased frequency and severity of weather events stretches and even exhausts public budgets from the local to the federal level. The climate is already exacting a huge cost, and this will only get worse. Expenditures here are for unpredictable events outside business as usual, and serve to rupture budgets in even more random and dangerous ways. Will we really be able to afford to re-locate Miami, or New York City, or to completely replace towns engulfed by fire or flood? The small city of Paradise, in California, has been virtually annihilated in flames this week even as we write this.

Third, as increasing costs of remediation and mitigation are borne over time, the drain on the needed resources will further stretch the resource base and recursively impair the ability of the environment to yield the needed economic means. In other words, the increasing need for resources, and the accelerated environmental pressures that entails, will itself shrink the very supply of those resources—an impending tragedy if there ever was one.

Everyone seeks "first principles" that yield cohesion and meaning. So it is with this book. We have put forth many ideas for reforms in a variety of areas: food, energy, manufacturing, finance and economic development, to name a few. How to find a common denominator that ties it all together, and perhaps even allows typical citizens in any community some clear and straightforward criteria against which to measure any action being contemplated? In short: It's all about carbon.

How so? Carbon would appear to be a topic for environmental, but not necessarily economic debate. The biosphere of Planet Earth has, over billions of years, evolved into a balanced carbon cycle that created a habitable equilibrium condition. Humans have intervened, through industrialization, capitalism and the supporting growth ethic, and released millions of years of prehistorically stored sunlight. This strictly economic intervention must be understood and intelligently mitigated if we are to expect the kind of future we would like.

That is the task of this book. Achieving tangible results will admittedly be a challenge given our massive and increasing numbers along with our world-wide institutional reliance on the unsustainable growth ethic. This chapter focuses on the ubiquitous basic element of carbon in hopes of creating some universal insights that nudge people a bit further down a path toward restoration. Our quality of life at least, and possibly our very survival, depend on it.

BACKGROUND: PUTTING THE CARBON CHALLENGE INTO A PROACTIVE, LOCALISM PERSPECTIVE

In Part Two, we floated the possibility of restoring comprehensive "2-way" regenerative carbon flows to extract atmospheric carbon and return it to safe storage in the ground. Pre-industrial agrarian societies routinely used this ancient practice to replenish soil nutrition. It is distinctly possible this can be reintroduced—bolstered with the benefits of modern scientific knowledge and technological capabilities. It would buy much needed time and carbon budget space. This "reverse direction" movement of carbon can greatly reduce carbon already either in the atmosphere or on a fast track to enter it. An innovative recent book, *Drawdown*[21], serves as a guide to many practical individual landowners, farmers, foresters and allied activist groups can work with local authorities to implement regenerative carbon flows

What Localism-based storage of carbon would be about… and not. An immediate caveat is in order. There are two camps that advocate extracting dangerous excess carbon from the atmosphere and safely storing it away where it cannot contribute to climate warming. The high-tech camp, loyal members of the corporatist coalition supporting fossil fuels, continued industrial growth and centralized control, has been peddling their version for some time. It is usually given the formal name ***Carbon Capture and Sequestration* (CCS)**; although a more recent trend is to refer to these technologies as Carbon Dioxide Removal (CDR) or Negative Carbon Emissions (NCE). Whatever the terminology and the favored acronym, it is important to understand these mechanically powered/technological methodologies are not what this chapter is about, though we refer to it for comparison. Rather, we focus on the approach of the second camp: advocates of lowering existing carbon levels through natural, essentially non-mechanical, non-powered techniques. This *non*-high-tech alternative uses the power of nature—principally photosynthesis—to suck CO_2 from the atmosphere and store it in soils and living systems. For convenience, and want of a better term, we will call this natural alternative ***Regenerative Carbon Flow* (RCF).**

While CCS is promoted by the technologists who dominate powerful energy corporations, federal agencies and many technical university departments (and even some in the climate activist scientific community), it does not lend itself to development or operation by Localism activists and their communities. Mostly, CCS is a "point source" effort aimed at cleaning up the carbon emitted from large power plants and other industrial facilities. Basically,

----

21   *Drawdown*: the Most Comprehensive Plan Ever Proposed to Reverse Global Warming. Edited by Paul Hawken, Penguin Books, New York (2017)

it represents a way of keeping these plants and their institutional owners alive and operating.

RCF, on the other hand, is ideally suited for use by interested climate and energy activists who are part of broader Localism movements. Its main activities are small in scale, involve a variety of "low-tech" agricultural, forestry, geology and related skills, require modest financial infusion, and in essence fit the pattern of possible Localism initiatives. However, we do not emphasize RCF solely because it opens Localism opportunities and discourages central, corporatist control. We lean to RCF and away from CCS for the same reasons we have advocated local food raising, manufacturing, and other similar Localist-related efforts. Centralized and globalized approaches relying on high technology, complex central control, long distance transport of materials and goods and huge inputs of capital will be vulnerable to failure in the near future. RCF piggybacks on nature, using natural flows of solar energy and the processes of living systems to do the work of removing carbon which otherwise will dangerously warm the already overheated atmosphere.

Presently, many small-scale experiments are being conducted around the world to find the most effective ways to augment this reverse carbon flow while complementing current farming, land use and land ownership patterns. These efforts are also uncovering valuable new enterprises that will form business opportunities, jobs and produce valuable products during the coming transition years. In short, this amounts to an approach which is as positive and productive as one might imagine, since it asks: How can "business as usual" be tailored to be as productive as possible?

For many thoroughly indoctrinated with Industrial Age thinking, just how regenerative carbon flow might work and fit in with current American lifestyles may at first be unclear. The remainder of this chapter attempts to outline just a few of the possible approaches that *Drawdown* describes, weaving them into the larger picture of changes the transition will bring as America tightens its belt and "goes local" to deal with ecological scarcity. As you assess the following measures, keep in mind our central message: We must solve both the economic and environmental challenges if we are to solve either.

REGENERATIVE FLOW POSSIBILITIES–THE PICK OF THE LITTER

The researchers and authors of *Drawdown* identify 80 promising proposals for rapidly expanding reverse carbon flows, largely by revising the land use practices of in both industrialized and less developed societies. In America, these examples apply primarily to food raising and other conventional and non-conventional agricultural and forestry practices. Substantial results could be achieved in many other areas. The following eight examples merely provide an illustrative selection as having some of the highest potential savings of carbon over the next three critical decades of transition. Further, they have practical, proven potential for rapid implementation in the United States and North America. Taken together, and pursued worldwide, just these eight represent a potential savings of almost 100 gigatons of atmospheric carbon before the year 2050.

Below is a simple listing of the eight selected proposals, followed by a brief thumbnail description of some features of each. The remainder of the chapter applies a few of these features as it identifies practical considerations in starting and supporting actual projects in communities where we live.

Selected food and forestry related land-use ideas to store carbon

1. Perennial bio-mass

2. Regenerative farming

3. Peat lands

4. Bamboo

5. Bio-char

6. Compost

7. **Temperate forests**

8. **Afforestation**

Some features of each—what they do:

1. PERENNIAL BIO-MASS

The growing of perennial plants and shrubs to restore degraded, unused or marginal land has been going on for many years, though admittedly in a piecemeal manner. Harvesting these crops for energy, which would require more systematic planning, would allow large amounts of current hydrocarbons—coal, oil and natural gas—to remain in the ground, thus reducing global warming. Certainly, burning grown bio-mass emits carbon, but the overall carbon balance is neutral due to the manner in which the bio-mass removed CO_2 from the air while it was growing. Proposals being made would produce bio-mass energy in two forms: direct burning for use in thermal electric power plants; and liquid and gaseous fuels which could substitute for gasoline, diesel, natural gas and other currently used fossil fuels producing much higher total emissions.

The net results for this as well as others in the following examples would represent an energy system based more on cycles and permanent income flows than upon linear drawdown and depleting of capital—a vital feature of most successful and sustainable economic processes.

2. REGENERATIVE FARMING

Modern American agriculture often resembles extractive industries like mining or oil and gas drilling more than it resembles actual farming. Regenerative farming employs techniques such as no-till planting, minimum use of synthetic chemicals and outside soil amendments, nutrient-restoring cover crops, and restoration of soil organic matter to reduce water demands. The aim is first to restore and protect soil nutrition, which has been the objective of the growing organic/natural food movement for decades. But beyond nutritional soil improvement, regenerative farming also seeks to restore carbon, using photosynthesis as the primary agent for moving atmospheric carbon into the soil and living plants for safe storage.

The benefits of growing perennial bio-mass for tangible energy products are primarily to replace more polluting hydrocarbons. By comparison, regenerative farming uses many of the same horticultural techniques with a compatible but somewhat different goal of reducing overall atmospheric carbon. Certainly, neither is a new approach, having been used by non-traditional farmers even during the recent heyday of industrial, mono-crop, synthetic chemical agriculture. Of course, the classic example is wood heat, the fuel of choice for all of human history before the Industrial Revolution.

3. PEAT LANDS

Peat bogs, those mucky mixtures of both dead and live plants that cover some three percent of the Earth's surface, are rich storehouses of carbon. Humans have long known this, and therefore have for many centuries derived valuable energy for heating and industrial uses by burning blocks of peat. The potential for carbon saving thus lies in stopping its extraction, and moving to protect and even enlarge existing peat lands. Peat bogs are over 50 percent carbon, which makes them not only a valuable commodity in the global economy, but a potent source of warming if their carbon is released. (*Drawdown* lists peat lands as second only to the oceans in the amount of total carbon they store—and keep out of the atmosphere.)

Climate change, which brings higher temperatures and often droughts, threatens the survival of current peat lands, which rely on adequate supplies of fresh water. The challenge for the limited locales in which peat lands exist will be to safeguard them from further exploitation and extinction, not unlike the efforts to save other endangered living species such as elephants, rhinos, whales and redwood trees.

4. BAMBOO

The growing of bamboo as a regenerative carbon flow crop may sound improbable for many North American locales. Often thought of as a tropical plant, certain strains of bamboo nonetheless grow well in temperate climates. The advantages of bamboo are many: it sequesters more carbon in the soil and in its own internal structures than almost any other plant. It can grow on virtually any degraded land, on steep slopes and where other crops are impossible. And, a very important attribute for localities attempting to start other viable local industries, the fiber itself can be made into all sorts of valuable products.

Growing bamboo would fit well with similar efforts to raise plants for bio-mass, and to convert to nutrient and carbon-restoring farming practices that reject present industrial/extractive methods of agriculture and forestry. It could offer local farmers and land owners, whether they have big or small plots, an opportunity to plant carbon-extracting bamboo that will need little irrigation or care, and little mechanical cultivation or expensive chemicals. Finally, it can put marginal acreage now thought of as valueless to sound environmental use while providing valuable raw material inputs to new sustainable local small businesses.

5. BIO-CHAR

The practice of adding bio-char as a soil amendment involves "baking" or cooking organic material in the absence of oxygen— a process called *pyrolysis*. The resultant carbon-rich charcoal material is then mixed in with soils. The carbon-enriched soils not only safely sequester huge amounts of carbon from the original organic wastes and residues, but retain water, essential nutrients and organic matter which increases their ability to grow most crops. Fertility is greatly enhanced. The most notable example of the use of bio-char comes from the Amazon, where ancient peoples learned to dispose of their organic wastes by covering them with a layer of soil then burning other organic matter on top. This "cooked" the buried material in the almost total absence of oxygen, greatly enriching the otherwise thin, acidic and nutrient-poor soil leached by the heavy rains. Today, the practice continues, being used on an estimated 10 percent of Amazonian jungle land.

More modern bio-char projects usually use large gas-fired ovens or kilns, fed with wastes such as peanut shells, rice hulls and wood wastes. The process produces both carbon-rich solid materials (much like charcoal briquettes we buy for our backyard barbeques) and flammable gas and oils. The latter can be used for fuel, while the solid bio-char becomes a soil amendment. Soil treated with bio-char has great porosity, thus providing a hospitable habitat for microorganisms, direct nutrients and water. It also acts to reduce industrial farming problems such as excess runoff, groundwater contamination and soil salinity. In short, farmers employing bio-char could reap triple benefits: new clean liquid and gaseous fuels; enriched and more productive soils; and the safe sequestration of large amounts of carbon otherwise headed straight into the atmosphere.

6. COMPOST

As with growing bamboo and burying bio-char, composting is a familiar process that may hardly seem like a dramatic venture that will save the world. (The Mother Earth News has promoted it for years...) Thousands of American cities and towns have had public composting programs for some years, and millions of Americans have a compost bin in the back yard. As *Drawdown* indicates, some 38 percent of American food waste is now composted.

But that leaves an immense amount of wasted food, grass clippings, agricultural waste and other organic matter not composted, but usually just thrown in landfills where its benefits are lost—or, worse yet, become dangerous pollutants such as methane. An aggressive and systematic expansion of composting would accomplish three things: first, enrich the soil and avoid the use of a great deal of energy-intensive, non-renewable chemical fertilizer; secondly, prevent careless disposal of organic wastes that generate methane, a gas much more lethal than CO2 in its climate-warming effects; and third, ensure that compost stations would be located close at hand for all communities, ending the wasteful long distance hauling of compost that now often occurs given the few, scattered facilities that are available.

Communities, working closely with surrounding farmers and with neighborhoods, could move to establish universal composting stations conveniently placed for all to use. Pickup would be a standard, regular service, just like the collection of garbage and recyclable materials. Further, this universal composting service should ideally be "full cycle," marrying the pickup activities to the processing, and finally to the distribution and use of the final compost products by farmers, gardeners and others in the local area. All of this could be carefully coordinated with bio-char, regenerative farming, urban gardening, bio-fuel and other ongoing projects, so that the materials produced would go to the best uses while minimizing the wastes and sequestering the most carbon. Clearly, many communities already have services along these lines, but few fully integrate all these activities to the point where the common perception rises to awareness of the material as a valuable **resource** that provides jobs and isolates carbon rather than a **waste** somehow to be disposed of.

7. TEMPERATE FORESTS

Considerable media attention has been devoted to the preservation of tropical forests as a means of slowing the climate crisis. But temperate forests that lie outside 30 degrees latitude (mostly in the Northern Hemisphere) also offer considerable potential for returning carbon from the atmosphere to the ground. On the positive side, much of the current 1.9 billion acres of global temperate forest land is in a state of slow recovery, following the devastating exploitation and general abuse of the 19th and 20th centuries.[22] However, future predictable economic crises could bring political pressure to accelerate development in any way possible.

Nonetheless, much former temperate forest land remains degraded and un-restored. And, it is now being threatened by a new problem: the warming temperatures caused by climate change. Increasing droughts, wildfires and invasions of new pests and diseases are replacing the chainsaw as the biggest threats to forests in many temperate zones. Single dramatic disasters such as a huge wildfire (like the ones raging in California even as we write this...) can pump massive amounts of carbon into the atmosphere and totally negate positive carbon sequestering over many years.

Despite these obstacles—including the complex ownership and current usage patterns of rural lands that might be adapted to reforestation projects—the potential amount of capturable carbon make reforestation an attractive target for Localism efforts. Like bio-mass, bio-char and other possibilities already mentioned, it dovetails ideally with activities designed to protect soil and water quality, provide wildlife habitat, and begin reversing the flow of carbon now moving relentlessly into the atmosphere. Plus, (as we continue to note...) they all offer intriguing opportunities to supply potentially valuable resources for locally owned start-up small businesses.

8. AFFORESTATION

This vague-sounding term refers to attempts to grow forests either where they have never grown before or have been missing from the landscape for at least fifty years. The previous topic addresses

---

22   In a definite twist of irony, some of this recovery has been made possible by the vagaries of globalization. The US and other nations have begun importing more of their lumber and wood products, thus reducing domestic logging. In the eastern US and other areas, slower economic growth and the abandonment of farmland have made possible the regrowth and repair of badly damaged forest areas. But of course, where is the lumber now coming from? There is no global free lunch.

the renewal of existing temperate forest lands that have been severely cut over, degraded or otherwise damaged. Afforestation targets lands now under cultivation, or that have been abandoned for industrial use, or are in any use *other* than a forest. Afforestation efforts seek to plant trees and other perennial plant life that mimic the living elements of a natural forest.

The goals of both temperate forest restoration and afforestation are identical: first, create a regenerative carbon flow that reduces ambient CO_2; and secondly, improve the health of soil, animal and plant diversity and watersheds, thus reducing erosion and miscellaneous other land use problems. Examining the above list, afforestation most closely resembles #1, bio-mass planting. The distinctions are that afforestation emphasizes tree plantings for semi-permanent sequestration, while bio-mass concentrates more on perennial shrubs and grasses, often with the goal of direct production of harvestable food or organic material to turn into energy resources. Afforestation doesn't seek direct energy production, but instead concentrates on creating regenerative carbon sinks and improving general micro-environmental health.

Presently the most successful afforestation projects plant native species of trees. Plots range from large acreage—abandoned grazing land, for example—to tiny plots such as urban lots and highway median strips. Any unused land, or land now devoted to less valuable usage, is a potential candidate for afforestation. And, significantly, afforestation projects can and should involve both public lands and privately-owned parcels.

Even a simple list like the above eight suggestions, incomplete as it is, can inspire many creative ideas for effective RCF projects. Importantly, RCF can act quickly, in keeping with the sobering deadlines imposed by worsening climate change. Even casual examination of RCF clearly reveals that the various ways carbon can be extracted, secured, processed into usable energy and enhance soils and living systems all have a great deal in common. They are based on similar natural processes revolving around plant growth, photosynthesis, natural decay and chemical processes within the soils supporting the plant life. And the bottom line is that the energy source is daily incoming sunlight—not long-gone prehistoric plants and animals.

PROSPECTS, PROJECTS AND POLITICS

Most RCF projects are so tightly woven around these natural biological processes that it would be an administrative mistake to separate them artificially. This is where community organization, including local political support, becomes critical. In short, all regenerative carbon flow (RCF) initiatives can and should be integrated organizationally when being considered by individuals and groups promoting Localism. The output of one RCF project may well be the input of another. One project's waste may be a valuable fuel upon which another depends. To get one promising RCF activity off the ground, Localism planners should actively seek to initiate the development of other businesses, economically linked both as suppliers and end users. In this culture (*we contend with only a hint of cynicism!*) anything smacking of economic development will normally be afforded a running start... (*See Chapter 19...*)

Further, RCF ventures will always have a considerable amount of overlap. Whether growing plant life for food, fodder, as a feedstock for energy production, or as a basis for cooking bio-char, many of the natural—as well as industrial—processes are the same. Many valuable products and results are possible, depending on local conditions of climate, soils, water and other indigenous resources, not to mention other initiatives with a wide variety of characteristics that may already have been set in motion by Localism activists.

Given this obvious need for connection and close integration, our point is that Localism proponents can productively consider all the possible RCF ideas as part and parcel of one big idea: the natural, living system-based regeneration of carbon. Accordingly, we feel a need to lay out some hypothetical specifics that might prove helpful. Following is a small number of suggestions as to how local RCF activities might be organized and set in motion for quick results. We concentrate on ideas and projects that will

produce the quickest results with the least amount of technological development, investment—and political haggling. We borrow
shamelessly from our earlier list of eight to focus on three with
definite "low-hanging fruit" potential: composting, afforestation
and regenerative farming.

Composting. A prompt start can be made in all communities,
whatever the size, by establishing distributed composting stations. The logical political jurisdiction for carrying this out would
be counties, which would establish the composting stations at
convenient places throughout the entire urban and sub-regional
area. In some cases, larger cities may take the lead and set up
urban composting yards—but whatever the final arrangement,
counties and the towns/cities within them should closely coordi-
nate the final composting system set up. It should be funded and
operated so that all citizens, farmers, and other businesses will
have close, easily-accessible composting.

If adequate composting already exists, and is well coordinated
with local waste haulers, etc., and the distribution of finished
compost is also being handled well, the task may be relatively
easy. But many areas will start from an inadequate system where
all waste is simply collected together and this mixed "garbage" is
then hauled to a single landfill or other disposal site. (Some rural
areas may still be totally without formal garbage or waste pickup of
any kind.) Still other areas may be collecting compostable organic
material, but are then hauling it long distances because they lack
their own nearby composing processors. In all likelihood, even in
the most progressive communities already committed to universal
composting, there will be things to do to make composting a more
convenient, low-energy activity that produces a widely-available
final product.

The composting lead can be taken by community activists,
who will engage with county and municipal government officials
to organize the needed effort, and perhaps even to lay out how it
can be funded and operated. In our minds, government ownership
of the major activities—hauling, the actual compost processing
yards/sites—should ideally be public, since the final produced

product really represents energy. This is in keeping with our conviction that all energy to be made available publicly should be owned and controlled by public bodies and/or groups of citizens such as cooperatives and non-profit organizations. However, in some communities, decisions have been made that privately owned enterprises provide some or all of the composting services. If these are adequately controlled by community oversight, a mixture of public and private activities can function well.

Afforestation. Afforestation is another area in which projects can be rapidly jumpstarted in many communities. In fact, many cities now have such projects already in operation, replanting common public areas for beautification and recreational reasons, if not expressly to capture carbon. These programs are straightforward to do, and can be rapidly expanded and duplicated elsewhere. Citizens and neighborhoods can be recruited to plant vacant lots and their own yards with plants that effectively absorb carbon. Farmers and owners of open land can also be organized and encouraged to plant bamboo and other similar fast-growing species. Cities and towns can speed up the planting of park areas, right-of-ways and other public land, again favoring maximum carbon capture rather than traditional "cosmetic" landscaping.

New regulations for approving residential, commercial and industrial building permits could require that substantial carbon-storing plantings be included on the building site. Plus, should mass transit be expanded and future private automobile use shrink, current parking lot space for commercial sites can be relaxed. Then, instead of giant parking lots for customers, a smaller (locally-owned) retail store could replace that paved space with carbon-storing shrubs and trees.

Regenerative farming. Ideas raised in this section purposely integrate with and extend, as we prefaced there, the local food production discussion of Chapter 15. Obviously, the focus there was on the central human task of feeding people while minimizing the problematic effects of importing the major share of what we eat. The coverage here in this final chapter merely expands the consideration of food production to the big topic of intersection with the all-encompassing carbon flow issue. *Everything is connected to everything else...*

Regenerative farming possibilities with strong potential for immediate action receive a powerful boost from the many years of pioneering efforts in the organic farming/gardening movements that have proliferated in many communities throughout the United States. These continue to expand and thrive as methods of distributing and marketing become more sophisticated. (Though, as Chapter 15 indicated earlier, the local Saturday Market may still be more pure **fun** than the expanding organic foods section at the local Safeway...!) Activists involved in the organic movement or other aspects of "green" agriculture, such as the fight against GMO (genetically engineered) foods are naturals to lead this movement.

Historic export-based crops produced locally are often cherished and strong creators of value added and traditional local employment. They even contribute to local culture through annual festivals and the like, while extracting wealth by employing a superior indigenous resource (e.g., prime farmland). While supporting these valuable activities, it would nonetheless be of great help if local governments could be convinced to curtail their outright support of industrial agriculture—or in some slightly better cases, their fence-straddling indecision—and endorse a rapid commitment to environmentally sustainable agriculture. This is admittedly a tall order in the current political environment.

With or without solid governmental support, citizens can use the nucleus of local organic food raising to begin building interest in regenerative farming techniques in expanded ways. One very useful task for this fledgling effort would be to contact farmers and foresters in the local area. Many will be at least somewhat familiar with and involved in regenerative techniques; but Localism advocates can begin the arduous work of making them aware of the need for and advantages of farming/forestry approaches that can reduce the current one-way flow of carbon straight to the atmosphere. Integrating such information with tangible sales opportunities (e.g., restaurants or community supported agriculture clients) can certainly enhance the attractiveness of the appeal to farmers—who sometimes tend to be set in their ways...!

Admittedly, those organizing carbon regeneration-related activities initially will be feeling their way, trying to find the best avenues for productive activities that might grow into permanent enterprises and movements. Whether they concentrate on expanding local organic farming and gardening, planting trees and shrubs along every city street and vacant lot, or working with local officials to build a network of composting stations, the exact details of the directions chosen will be unique. Incredible networking help through social media, etc., will ideally become increasingly available from communities everywhere. Nonetheless, tangible measurable progress ultimately relies on local skills responding to local conditions. A national and even international movement is necessary, but individual communities must supply the basic building blocks—and are probably the best hope for getting things started.

ORGANIZATIONAL CONSIDERATIONS:

The initial information campaign must involve carefully nurtured partnerships and coordination. One objective, in addition to building essential lines of communication, should be to develop detailed data on every pertinent aspect of how land is used in the local area. This storehouse of information will prove invaluable in making decisions about high potential carbon capturing projects. It will enable organizers to put together those producing useful organic materials with those needing them. And, very importantly, it will provide the information necessary to attract financing for new businesses that might ultimately become a part of the whole RCF effort.

Here, few radically new wheels need to be reinvented. County extension offices are a wealth of information on current farming and farm practices, as are state departments of agriculture. Both are closely tied to state university agriculture departments and their research capabilities. Further, farmers and their existing farm organizations—even if they are currently an integral part of present industrial agriculture relying on chemicals, monoculture, fossil fuels, exports, etc.—are also excellent data resources. However it is done, the building of a local agricultural data base is vital to making smart future decisions on integrated RCF activities. The differences in each locality will make it an indispensable "bible" as RCF movements proceed. In fact, the act of sharing information and experiences with other (perhaps quite different) localities should prove helpful in assisting any given community in discovering and developing its own uniqueness. A good idea might be to establish a Director of Research position in the Localism entity. Who knows? He or she might uncover an available grant...

Opposition? You Bet! As harmless and obviously positive as RCF Localism may seem, activists must be prepared for both subtle and direct counterattacks. First, and perhaps the most predictable, will be the established farm and forestry interests. Those that are now (at least temporarily) successful in the globalized, energy-intensive food and wood products markets are comfortably embedded in their industrialized, highly technical approaches. They often have very large investments in land, machinery and other inputs, and are tied in with rigid networks of finance, marketing, product research, and sales of final products. Necessary change will not come easily, especially if they do not acknowledge that impending world conditions will soon *force* such changes. Hopefully, the supply of "climate deniers" will steadily shrink.

Similar arguments apply to a myriad of support institutions such as equipment manufacturers, finance/banking, and of course elaborate university agriculture and forestry departments and private researchers. Further, there are institutions that make chemicals, grow and market seed, do GMO research, and support the industrial food system in many other ways. And, who could forget the huge food processors and the supermarket chains engaged in moving the final industrialized food products along the complicated assembly line to "we the people?" To many of these players, big changes in the way land is cultivated, what is grown, and where it ends up in the food, fodder and fiber chains will likely be seen as unwelcome and disruptive—and thus to be resisted. In short, the economy is a complicated organism, and the many current subtle input-output relationships offer almost endless possibilities for entities coming out of the woodwork in opposition—minor or major—to the agenda of RCF Localism.

As long as the targets for RCF-style land-related practices are the low-hanging fruit, this resistance will probably remain muted. Because minimal legislative and regulatory rule changes are needed for composting, afforestation plantings and other similar efforts to proceed, establishment industrial interests likely will remain relatively silent—even supportive to some degree. They do not yet feel threatened. This "lull before the storm" will present a definite opportunity to Localism RCF organizers, who should seize it by concentrating on accomplishing two early objectives. First, they should work hard to make certain early projects are well designed, organized and run. They should also take care to meticulously document their achievement, carefully showing that the early projects are showcases of well-conceived, skillfully-run, successful carbon saving projects. Their case must be a strong one in preparation for pitched "World View" debates that may lie ahead.

The second key objective flows naturally from the first: win the public over to your side. Partner with existing sympathetic groups (Sierra Club, 350.org, etc.). Clear citizen support will be vital, because that provides the springboard for winning the necessary support of local public officials. With county commissioners, city councils, mayors and local bureaucrats supporting RCF activists, any next steps will be much easier. Of course, climate change lobbying has been occurring for some time, and the current great hope of climate change activists nation-wide is that state and local governments appreciate the effects of collective action, and sweepingly sign on to ecology-based, self-sustaining, resilient socioeconomic policies that just happen to be at the heart of the overall Localism movement. Such a "movement" would allow compelling responses to the plaintive question asked by skeptical local (and even state) officials: "The problem is global. What effect can we have here in our own little _____?" (Fill in the blank...)

Even though support for Localism by the public and local government leadership is essential for the long-term movement, it will almost certainly raise red flags with wary land-related establishment interests. Only if public opinion is firmly established (including bolstering the political courage of local officials) will it be possible to move forward with a larger RCF agenda. This could involve more radical changes to farm and forestry practices, modified zoning and land use, different crops, products, customers and so forth. Deeper public sector commitment might include quick facilitation of citizen cooperatives to grow and distribute organically-raised food or products like bio-fuels and bio-char. And, even more significantly, they could establish public banks to provide low-cost funding for attractive projects. You, the astute reader, will no doubt notice the strong congruencies with the earlier chapters of this third and final section.

COMPETING OVERALL PHILOSOPHIES: LINEAR VS. CIRCULAR?

There are two competing conceptual images of the modern economy appropriate to mention as we conclude this book. First is the traditional linear "throughput" model, dominant since the Industrial Revolution. Economic activity is seen as a process of extracting resources, production of intermediate inputs and then final products, distributing and selling to consumers, final consumption and then disposal of wastes. Characterizing the process at all stages is ubiquitous transportation, along with the injection of energy and the creation of wastes at all points. Thus, the endowment of raw materials, including energy, is incessantly transformed into waste, with production and human satisfaction somehow involved along the way. A common thumbnail characterization within environmental literature is *"Sources to Sinks,"* and hence the linear designation.

Contrasting with Throughput is the "Spaceship Earth" concept, a term coined about 50 years ago by the legendary futurist Buckminster Fuller. More recently, the equivalent term Circular Economy has emerged. It acknowledges that we occupy a finite planet and implies that we humans will ultimately run into intractable difficulties with a linear growth model that does not recognize the concept of finitude and the need for ultimate recyclability and/or renewability of all resources in a permanent and sustainable world. Sinks become Sources, if you will. The environmental movement and the Limits to Growth studies, along with often-pitched debates that ensued began in earnest in the early 1970s. Not surprisingly, those promoting greater ecological awareness readily developed a preference for Spaceship Earth over Throughput whenever the structure of our economy arose in conceptual debates. It is an understatement to say that critiques of the mainstay of industrial society were met with stout resistance.

The discussion we have injected here, comparing CCS with RCF approaches, is comfortably analogous to these competing images of the modern economy. The push to adopt RCF over CCS is tantamount to opting for Spaceship Earth over Throughput. The elements of 2-way carbon regeneration systems fly in the face of most modernist practices and modes of thought. It admittedly appears to be a throwback to simple technologies used by earlier man who lacked the concentrated non-renewable energy and powered devices to do otherwise. Now, as those temporary artificial supplements of the Industrial Age decline, and become too hazardous to use at the promiscuous recent levels, modern man is forced to re-employ his brain, along with the power of nature and natural processes

Not everyone will be pleased by this change, which they will depict as an unnecessary regression (to the Stone Age...?) and a certain sentence to rapid economic/social decline for America. Instead, we can expect a clarion call for the use of yet more technology as our savior. Unfortunately for the plans of these CCS technophiles, there remain giant questions blocking the path of powered CCS.

Presently, only small prototype-level CCS systems have been demonstrated. Fully operational models installed on the thousands of coal and gas power plants remains a distant dream.

And where would all the carbon captured from the smokestacks be stored? Ironic possibilities raised include old coal mines, or exhausted oil and gas wells—as well as natural underground caverns. Unfortunately, simple logistics preclude large scale workable arrangements, since most candidates are nowhere near existing power plants. An important recently released report underscores the challenge:

> *(October, 2018 update: A just-released report by the IPCC indicates that, to keep climate warming below the 1.5-degree Celsius level now deemed to be the safe limit, radical reformation of world economies and social practices must occur. Among the steps mentioned is the wide-scale use of CCS: i.e., a worldwide deployment of machines to extract atmospheric carbon dioxide directly. CCS technology, previously mentioned as a possible way to mitigate carbon levels, is now widely being seen as an absolute requirement if the more stringent 1.5 C level of warming is not to be exceeded. Further, to be successful, the CCS machines would have to be in operation by 2030.)*

Though careful examination reveals that technological CCS is a totally flawed idea even a schoolchild could see through, it continues to draw support—even, as indicated above, from some IPCC scientists in closest touch with the grim reality of climate numbers. The reason should not perplex us. CCS is the anointed "business-as-usual" answer for slashing atmospheric carbon to safe levels, and the accompanying analytical "box" is assumed to be inescapable—even by many scientists who should know better. CCS would allow present industrial production to continue, with fossil fuels supporting increased resource extraction, consumption, growth... and growing waste. Essentially, the linear process of Industrial Age economies could proceed uninterrupted by the dangers of growing atmospheric carbon. The straight-line linear movement of physical materials through the industrial chain—extraction, processing, manufacturing, distribution, consumption, waste—would carry on in familiar fashion.

Standing squarely in contrast to this technological approach are all the various flavors of regenerating carbon through natural, non-mechanical means. The linear one-way system of the industrial technologist is replaced by the circular, self-contained system of the ecologist. RCF, in all its forms, rejects the exploitive practices of industrial-era systems for a circular and holistic system in which one component's wastes are another component's vital inputs. Inevitable depletion and collapse are replaced by a system which is the very definition of ecology: renewable, interconnected and self-sustaining. Finally, it is an alternative that favors local control, rejecting centralized corporate organization, money, and technology as just so much wasted baggage. This offers further powerful incentives for us to get on with local RCF projects as soon as possible.

IN CONCLUSION...

This is where we choose to end this book. Our final point is that the "General Theory" of what the human species has done to itself, and the economic and environmental predicament it has created, can be accurately interpreted as an interjection in, and abuse of, the carbon cycle of the biosphere. This has occurred within the last three centuries—a mere fly-speck in the overall life of the planet. There is an inherent great irony as well as a sober warning. Clearly, the references here are to developments since the Industrial Revolution—the fossil fuel era, if you will. Further, as intellectual history teaches, it is synchronous with the Enlightenment.

The Industrial Revolution is celebrated for having freed mankind from the shackles of hand labor with rudimentary tools and reliance upon beasts of burden and the like. (Ah, our savior—the machine...!) Scientific doors were opened that steadily created pathways to previously unimaginable wealth and technological achievements. Similarly, the Enlightenment supposedly allowed the human spirit to usher in the institutional changes appropriate for accompanying these physical and technological advances. Gone was the Divine Right of Kings and hegemony of the Church, and in came the reliance on representative government, scientific method and individual inspiration and ingenuity. It is understandable that the common world view considers the modern era as superior to ways of the past in almost every way. The irony is that these hallowed features, vital and revered components of our "Western Tradition," have currently, in their mature forms, led directly to many of the difficulties that we chronical in this work. The cure may have become the problem.

Compounding this irony is a sober warning. Although societal problems may fundamentally stem from hallowed beliefs and traditions, this will not be generally realized or accepted. Therefore, the first instinct of any society in crisis is to look to its favored traditions for solutions. Rely on what has always worked. Technology will be aggressively sought for answers to problems that the unintended effects of earlier technologies have caused. Economic failures and maldistribution caused by semi-religious reliance on market systems and the growth ethic will result in calls for freer markets and more growth. Inequality will likely proceed unabated. Resource and environmental scarcities will be ignored or minimized in assuming that substitutes and technological breakthroughs will bail us out. And so on. In short, we not only are faced with a need to find new and innovative (often "low-tech") actions and approaches, we are swimming upstream against the powerful mores and behaviors of the dominant culture. Success will demand that social change becomes at least as important as economic change.

Thus the task of survival rests not just on innovative ideas that help craft new ways of doing things and helpful "happy face" adjustments to existing institutions and within communities, but it faces a cultural world view that **simply doesn't want to change**. Does this sound daunting—even virtually impossible? Perhaps. But supporting efforts to reform is the increasing realization both that we are facing seriously deepening problems, and that what we are doing now is not working. Tell people that federal government reform is the key, and they may turn away in apathy—these days even in anger. Show them positive changes available for their own lives in their own communities, and you may have created an enthusiastic ally.

This is why we place our faith in what we and others call **Localism**. We stand more convinced than when we started that it is the most compelling and positive hope for a vibrant, prosperous and humane future. Finally, in what can look increasingly like a bleak world with forbidding prospects, it is the greatest source of that vitally needed commodity: human optimism. Let's get to work.

Bibliography

BOOKS

Brown, Ellen and Hazel Henderson. *The Public Bank Solution: From Austerity to Prosperity.* Baton Rouge: Third Millennium Press, 2013.

Daly, Herman. *Beyond Growth: The Economics of Sustainable Development.* Boston: Beacon Press, 1996.

Daly, Herman and John Cobb. *For The Common Good: Redirecting The Economy Towards Community, The Environment And A Sustainable Future.* Boston: Beacon Press, 1989.

Deffeyes, Kenneth. *Hubbert's Peak: The Impending World Oil Shortage— Revised and Updated Edition.* Princeton, N.J.: Princeton University Press, 2001

Douthwaite, Richard. *The Growth Illusion: How Economic Growth Has Enriched The Few, Impoverished The Many, And Endangered The Planet.* Tulsa: Council Oak Books, 1992.

Gilens, Martin, and Benjamin Page. *Democracy in America? What Has Gone Wrong and What We Can Do About It.* Chicago: University of Chicago Press, 2018.

Greer, John Michael. *Dark Age America: Climate Change, Cultural Collapse, and the Hard Future Ahead.* Gabriola Island: New Society Publishers, 2016.

Greer, John Michael. *The Long Descent: A User's Guide to the End of the Industrial Age.* Gabriola Island: New Society Publishers, 2008.

Greer, John Michael. *The Wealth of Nature: Economics as if Survival Mattered.* Gabriola Island: New Society Publishers, 2011.

Hansen, James. *Storms of My Grandchildren: The Truth about the Coming Climate Catastrophe and Our Last Chance to Save Humanity.* New York: Bloomsbury USA, 2009.

Hawken, Paul (editor and author). *Drawdown: The Most Comprehensive Plan Ever Proposed to Reverse Global Warming.* New York: Penguin Books, 2017.

Hall, Charles. *Energy Return on Investment: A Unifying Principle for Biology, Economics, and Sustainability.* Cham: Springer International Publishing, AG, 2017

Hedges, Chris. *America: the Farewell Tour.* New York: Simon & Schuster, 2018.

Hedges, Chris. *Death of the Liberal Class.* New York: Bold Type Books, 2010.

Hedges, Chris. *Wars of Rebellion: the Moral Imperative of Revolt.* New York: Bold Type Books, 2015.

Heinberg, Richard. *The End of Growth: Adapting to Our New Economic Reality.* Gabriola Island: New Society Publishers, 2011.

Heinberg, Richard. *The Party's Over: Oil, War and the Fate of Industrial Societies. Second edition.* Gabriola Island: New Society Publishers, 2005.

Heinberg, Richard. *Snake Oil: How Fracking's False Promise of Plenty Imperils Our Future.* Santa Rosa: Post Carbon Institute, 2013

Heinberg, Richard, and David Fridley. *Our Renewable Future: Laying the Path for One Hundred Percent Clean Energy.* Washington: Island Press, 2016

Hopkins, Rob. *The Transition Handbook: From Oil Dependency to Local Resilience.* Foxhole, Dartington, Totnes, Devon: Green Books Lmt., 2008.

Hudson, Michael. *J Is For Junk Economics: A Guide To Reality In An Age Of Deception.* (Germany): ISLET—Verlag, 2017

Hudson, Michael. *Killing the Host: How Financial Parasites and Debt Bondage Destroy the Global Economy.* Petrolia: Counterpunch Books, 2015

Klare, Michael. *The Race for What's Left: The Global Scramble for the World's Last Resources.* New York: Metropolitan Books, 2012.

Klare, Michael. *Rising Powers, Shrinking Planet: the New Geopolitics of Energy.* New York: Metropolitan Books, 2008.

Klare, Michael. *Blood and Oil: The Dangers and Consequences of America's Growing Dependency on Imported Petroleum.* New York: Metropolitan Books, 2007.

Klein, Naomi. *No Is Not Enough: Resisting Trump's Shock Politics and Winning the World We Need.* Chicago: Haymarket Books, 2017

Klein, Naomi. *This Changes Everything: Capitalism vs. The Climate.* New York: Simon & Schuster, 2014.

Korten, David. *When Corporations Rule the World.* Oxford: Earthscan Publications, 1996

Korten, David. *Agenda For a New Economy: From Phantom Wealth to Real Wealth—paperback edition.* San Francisco: Berrett-Koehler Publishers; Second edition, 2010.

Krugman, Paul. *The Return of Depression Economics and the Crisis of 2008.* New York: W.W. Norton, 2008.

Kuttner, Robert. *Can Democracy Survive Global Capitalism?* New York: W.W. Norton, 2018.

Leopold, Les. *Runaway Inequality: An Activist's Guide to Economic Justice.* 2nd edition. New York: Labor Institute Press, 2015.

Mackay, Kevin. *Radical Transformation: Oligarchy, Collapse and the Crisis of Civilization.* Toronto: Between the Lines, 2017

Meadows, Donella and Dennis Meadows, Jorgen Randers, William Behrens. *The Limits to Growth; A Report for the Club of Rome's Project on the Predicament of Mankind. 2nd edition.* New York: Universe Publishing, 1972.

Meadows, Donella and Dennis Meadows, Jorgen Randers. *Limits to Growth: The 30-Year Global Update.* White River Junction: White River Junction, 2004.

Monbiot, George. *Heat: How to Stop the Planet From Burning.* London: South End Press, 2007

Monbiot, George. *How Did We Get Into This Mess?: Politics, Equality, Nature.* London: Verso, 2016

Odum, Howard. *Environment, Power, and Society for the Twenty-first Century: The Hierarchy of Energy.* New York: Columbia University Press, 2007.

Oppenlander, Richard. *Food Choice and Sustainability: Why Buying Local, Eating Less Meat, and Taking Baby Steps Won't Work.* Minneapolis: Publish Green, 2013.

Piketty, Thomas. *Capital in the Twenty-First Century.* Cambridge: Belknap Press, 2017.

Pimentel, David, and Marcia Pimentel. *Food, Energy, and Society. 3rd edition.* Boca Raton: CRC Press, 2007.

Pizzigati, Sam. *The Case for a Maximum Wage.* Medford: Polity Press, 2018.

Reich, Robert. *Saving Capitalism: For the Many, Not the Few.* New York: Knopf, 2015

Ricardo, David. *On the Principles of Political Economy and Taxation.* London: John Murray, 1817.

Romm, Joseph. *Climate Change: What Everyone Needs to Know. 2nd edition.* New York: Oxford University Press, 2018

Saul, John Ralston. *The Collapse of Globalism: and the Reinvention of the World.* Toronto: Viking Canada, 2005.

Schumacher, E. F. *Small Is Beautiful: Economics as if People Mattered.* New York: Harper & Row, 1973.

Shuman, Michael. *Going Local: Creating Self-reliant Communities in a Global Age.* New York: Routledge, 2000.

Shuman, Michael. Local Dollars, *Local Sense; The Local Economy Solution: How Innovative, Self-Financing "Pollinator" Enterprises Can Grow Jobs and Prosperity.* White River Junction: Chelsea Green Publishing, 2012.

Smil, Vaclav. *Energy and Civilization: A History.* Cambridge: MIT Press, 2017.

Smil, Vaclav. *Oil: a Beginners Guide.* Oxford: Oneworld Publications, 2006.

Smith, Adam. *An Inquiry into the Nature and Causes of the Wealth of Nations.* London: W. Strahan and T. Cadell, 1776.

Stiglitz, Joseph. *Globalization and Its Discontents.* New York: W.W. Norton, 2002.

Stiglitz, Joseph. *The Price of Inequality.* New York: W.W. Norton, 2012.

Taibbi, Matt. *Divide: American Injustice in the Age of the Wealth Gap.* New York: Spiegel and Grau, 2014.

Wolin, Sheldon. *Democracy Incorporated: Managed Democracy and the Specter of Inverted Totalitarianism.* New edition. Princeton: Princeton University Press, 2017.

OTHER SOURCES

Hardoon, Deborah. *"Wealth: Having it all and Wanting More."* Oxfam, January 19, 2015. https://policy-practice.oxfam.org.uk/publications/wealth-having-it-all-and-wanting-more-338125

Heinberg, Richard. *"Searching for a Miracle: 'Net Energy' Limits & the Fate of Industrial Society."* Post Carbon Institute, November 12, 2009. https://www.postcarbon.org/publications/searching-for-a-miracle/

Hughes, David. *"Shale Reality Check: Drilling Into the U.S. Government's Rosy Projections for Shale Gas & Tight Oil Production Through 2050."* Post Carbon Institute, February 4, 2018. https://www.postcarbon.org/publications/shale-reality-check/

Hughes, David. *"2016 Tight Oil Reality Check: Revisiting the U.S. Department of Energy Play-by-Play Forecasts through 2040 from Annual Energy Outlook 2016."* Post Carbon Institute, December 12, 2016. https://www.postcarbon.org/publications/2016-tight-oil-reality-check/

IPCC, 2014: *"Climate Change 2014: Synthesis Report. Contribution of Working Groups I, II and III to the Fifth Assessment Report of the Intergovernmental Panel on Climate Change"* [Core Writing Team, R.K. Pachauri and L.A. Meyer (eds.)]. IPCC, Geneva, Switzerland, 151 pp., November, 2014. https://www.ipcc.ch/report/ar5/syr/

IPCC, 2018: *Special Report: Global Warming of 1.5 degrees C.* IPCC, Geneva, Switzerland, October, 2018. https://www.ipcc.ch/sr15/

Klein, Naomi. *"Capitalism vs. the Climate."* The Nation, November 9, 2011. https://www.thenation.com/article/capitalism-vs-climate/

McKibben, Bill. *"Global Warming's Terrifying New Math."* Rolling Stone, July 19, 2012. July 25, 2012. https://www.rollingstone.com/politics/politics-news/global-warmings-terrifying-new-math-188550/

↑   ↑

Dave   *Russ*